Media-Wise Family is a must for today's Christian family. It's well researched, well written, and timely. It's an invaluable resource for Christians concerned about the media's impact on us and our potential impact on the media.

> D. James Kennedy, Ph.D., Senior Minister
> Coral Ridge Presbyterian Church

Ted Baehr is more than the Paul Revere of the media industry, alerting us to current and future evils. He is also salt and light, working *in* and *through* the movie and television business to give Christians a choice and a *voice* in the directions of entertainment. You need to hear what he has to say!

> Pat Boone

Media-Wise Family is a must read. It is a shocking exposé of a well-conceived and orchestrated plan to corrupt the moral and spiritual standards not only of America but of the world. But there is hope. Dr. Baehr tells us how we can win this battle.

> Dr. Bill Bright, Founder and President
> Campus Crusade for Christ International

Media-Wise Family is the Ten Commandments of what every family should choose. . . . This book is well researched and informs you thoroughly regarding our culture and history. The writing is clear, vivid, passionate, and easily communicates its message.

> Al Kasha
> MTM

For Christians who want to thoughtfully integrate faith and culture, this is the book we've been waiting for. *Media-Wise Family* is impeccably researched, well reasoned, and readable too! This lover of film and father of four says thanks for a most useful resource. It's clearly "two thumbs up!"

> Dick Staub, Host
> Dick Staub Show

Our children are our most precious legacy and also our most valuable resource. Ted has so clearly pointed out how the mass media is shaping the minds of our kids. This is *must* reading for parents, grandparents, and friendly supporters of our young. Through it, we will understand how we can assist our kids to get a wholesome and Christian view of life and live it to the full.

> E. Brandt Gustavson, President
> National Religious Broadcasters

I admire and support the work of Dr. Theodore Baehr toward improving the ethical and spiritual standards of the entertainment media. From his new book, parents will learn how to give their children high ethical and moral standards.

Sir John M. Templeton

Ted Baehr challenges Christian families to make discerning choices about entertainment. TV and movies will continue to influence our lives. With the *Media-Wise Family*, parents have a powerful new tool to shape the children of today into the cultural apologists of tomorrow.

Janet Parshall, Host
Nationally syndicated talk show

No one is better prepared to resist indoctrination and manipulation than those who understand how others are trying to indoctrinate and manipulate them. Ted Baehr has given us a remarkable book we can use both as corrective and preventive medicine against many ills which are epidemic in our culture.

Morton Blackwell
The Leadership Institute

Media-Wise Family is an excellent resource, not only for families, but for CCD and schools as well. It most importantly helps parents and children to have discernment about different forms of media.

Rev. Paul Marx, OSB
Human Life International, Inc.

Ted Baehr presents provocative challenges that conscientious parents can't afford to ignore . . . . You will certainly benefit from confronting his arguments in this passionate reasoned, and eye-opening book.

Michael Medved
Author and Film Critic

The Media-Wise Family™

Ted Baehr

MEDIA · WISE PUBLISHING
A DIVISION OF GOOD NEWS COMMUNICATIONS

MEDIA-WISE PUBLISHING
Good News Communications, Inc.,
2510-G Las Posas Rd., Camarillo, CA 93010
805-383-2000 tel., 805-383-4089 fax

THE MEDIA-WISE FAMILY

Design by Bill Gray
Edited by C.C. Risenhoover

First printing, 1998
Printed in the United States of America
08 07 06 05 Year/Printing 8 9 10 11 12

Library of Congress Cataloging-in-Publication Data
Baehr, Theodore
   The media-wise family / by Ted Baehr.
     p. cm.
   Includes bibliographical references.
   ISBN 0-7814-0301-4
   ISBN 0-9753455-5-9

   1. Mass media-Religious aspects-Christianity. 2. Motion pictures-Religious aspects-Christianity. 3. Family-Biblical teaching. I. Title.

   BV653.B29 1998
   261.5'2'085-dc21   97-29005
                                                       CIP

This book is joyfully dedicated to:
Jesus,
our Lord and Savior,
Lili, my beautiful wife,
Peirce, James, Robert, and Evelyn, my wonderful children,
&
Ted "Bob 'Tex' Allen" Baehr, my loving father
May God protect our children from the lust of the eyes, the lust of the flesh, and the wiles of the adversary, and empower His people to take every thought captive in the mass media for Jesus Christ.

I especially want to thank my contributing authors: Elizabeth Chambers and Dan Smithwick; as well as Sandra Bell, Matt Kinne, Stephen Wistar, Roger Elwood, Andrew Ettinger, C.C. Risenhoover, Karl Schaller, Kathy Smith, Julie Smith, and Roger Parrott.

I want to give special thanks to Lucille Heimrich, who passed on to us the valiant work of George Heimrich at the Protestant Motion Picture Council.

Also, I want to thank the Directors, Advisers, and Friends of The Christian Film & Television Commission /Good News Communications, Inc.

In His Name,
Ted Baehr

HOLY SCRIPTURE

Do not conform any longer to the pattern of this world, but be transformed by the renewing of your mind. Then you will be able to test and approve what God's will is—his good, pleasing and perfect will.

Romans 12:2 (NIV)

Do not consider his appearance or his height, for I have rejected him. The LORD does not look at the things man looks at. Man looks at the outward appearance, but the LORD looks at the heart.

1 Samuel 16:7 (NIV)

Give therefore thy servant an understanding heart to judge thy people, that I may discern between good and bad; for who is able to judge this thy great people?

1 Kings 3:9 (KJV)

The Spirit of the LORD will rest on him—the Spirit of wisdom and of understanding, the Spirit of counsel and of power, the Spirit of knowledge and of the fear of the LORD —and he will delight in the fear of the LORD. He will not judge by what he sees with his eyes, or decide by what he hears with his ears.

Isaiah 11:2-3 (NIV)

Father in heaven,

Thank You for making us part of Your kingdom through the death and resurrection of Your Son, Jesus the Christ. Thank You for entertainment, joy, and imagination. Bless all who read this book. Grant us, as Your people, the discernment, courage, and wisdom to choose good entertainment and rebuke the bad. Help us communicate this discernment to our friends and our families. Help us to take every thought captive for Jesus Christ. Help us most of all to lift up Your holy name, Jesus, through the power of Your Holy Spirit. Thank You for the blessings You have bestowed upon us. Amen.

CONTENTS

PREFACE

1 GRACE UNDER FIRE: SETTING THE STAGE..............15

PART I: THE FOUNDATIONS OF DISCERNMENT
2 OVERCOMING THE MEDIA MINDSET 21
3 COPYCATS 56
4 IN THE LINE OF FIRE..87
5 THE AGE OF INNOCENCE...111
6 THE RATINGS GAME 147
7 TRUE LIES..173
8 BASER INSTINCT...190
9 UNFORGIVEN 227

PART II: THE KEYS TO DISCERNMENT
10 WORLDVIEW..245
11 THE LAST ACTION HERO 269
12 CHILD'S PLAY 322

CONCLUSION:
13 WINNING THE CULTURE WAR 398

APPENDIX: Action Items 411
GLOSSARY...412
REFERENCES 418

Preface

This is more than just another book about the media. It will help you turn your children's hearts away from the negative and addictive influences of the media . . . and toward God and family.

You will learn step-by-step how to teach your children to develop discernment, wisdom, knowledge, and understanding about movies, television, electronic games, and the all other media of entertainment and communication.

This will enable your children to use and enjoy the mass media of entertainment without succumbing to the vain imaginings, enchantments, and temptations of the media mindset. You will equip them with the intellectual and spiritual tools they need to deal with all the media input that confronts them.

The Media-Wise Family approach has been tested on children and parents for more than two decades, and more than 90 percent of those who have been taught this method of discernment have found it effective. For example, at the 1993 World Changers Conference for 1,000 teenagers, 98% committed to base their media decisions on the discernment tools that they learned in this course. Also, many top media executives have said that they have changed the way they view the media because of this process.

Our families, and especially our youth, are being corrupted and destroyed by the powerful transformational influences of the mass media of entertainment. Even our churches have been unable to give their members, especially their youth, help in dealing with the emotive images and idols of our entertainment culture. In fact, many churches are clueless about the extent of the problem in their congregations, while other churches have opted for anything goes. As a result, the children have suffered, and the parents are confused and often clueless as to how to deal with the problem.

Like most of the books that have addressed the problem, many leaders who are attempting to address the problem have no solution except for parents to rearrange the furniture in their living rooms, or play Scrabble® with their children rather than watch TV (these are good ideas, but they do not offer a comprehensive solution).

Part of the reason for this cluelessness is the fact that there has been a dumbing down of the country by the self-esteem, values clarification, and some other recent education fads which dispense with the fundamentals of classical education and focus on political correctness and egalitarianism. The consequence of these educational experiments can be seen clearly in the church. At the time of the American Revolution, the colonial church was praised for being highly literate with most of the churchgoing population reading and writing English, Latin, Greek, and at least one other language. Today, many experts are told to edit and adapt their communications to a fifth-grade level for church consumption.

This dumbing down has prevented many concerned Americans from developing the necessary discernment to use the media properly, rather than being used by it.

Teaching children discernment is difficult for many parents because they:

DO NOT watch the movies, hear the records, or play the games that engage their children.

DO NOT understand the cognitive, psychological, and spiritual impact of the mass media on their children.

DO NOT understand that their children view the media syntactically in terms of the visual, aural, and emotional elements of the media (such as the action and adventure in movies and rhythm and beat in music), while parents usually see the media semantically in terms of meaning, message, and moral implications (such as the sex, violence, language, and message in a movie and the obscene lyrics of a rap song), while reviewers critique it aesthetically in terms of their artistic elements, and very few of them understand the other person's perspective.

DO NOT understand how the mass media of entertainment influences their children at various different stages of cognitive development.

DO NOT comprehend the principles behind teaching discernment and media awareness other than discussing a particular television program or locking the television in a closet, and then playing board games or going for walks.

Therefore, this book will clearly set forth the practical tools you can use to teach your children discernment. Other books have presented the problem eloquently, but *The Media-Wise Family* differs in that it presents the solution in a comprehensive, intelligible way that will help your children learn how to use the media for entertainment, information, and even education without being conformed and addicted to it.

Most books in this area fail to teach how the media works and how it psychologically, emotionally, cognitively, and spiritually influences children. To equip your children with the tools to develop discernment and use the media appropriately requires:

Teaching them the visual, aural, and logical grammar of the media (which differs from the grammar of the written word).

Teaching them how to ask and answer the right questions about the communications and entertainment media that they are using.

Teaching them to compare their answers to the biblical norm and biblical principles.

In addition, this book will:

Help you understand why and how your children are affected by the mass media of entertainment.

Help you understand how adults look at films as opposed to how children do.

Help you understand how other groups, including Hollywood talent, look at movies and entertainment.

Help you teach your children the basic principles of media awareness and discernment, including the right questions to ask in order to gain a better understanding of the influences and messages in movies, television programs, or computer games.

Help you with practical, specific examples of movies that can be used to teach your children discernment.

Help you and your children understand the language and grammar of the mass media of entertainment.

To achieve these goals this book will:

Expose the nature of the problem that the mass media of entertainment presents (because understanding the problem is the first step to developing discernment).

Explain why there is a problem.

Illustrate how some of the mass media of entertainment works and how it affects all of us.

Set forth in detail all the tools and techniques of discernment.

Teach how to use the media without being used by it.

Give practical information about how to work toward redeeming the values of the mass media.

The Media-Wise Family will help you tame the media shrew so that she becomes a helpful ally in providing you with information, education, and entertainment. It will help you help your children deal with the images that have already influenced their lives in negative ways and help them to follow Jesus Christ more closely.

As one friend noted when he came to faith in Jesus Christ, "God gave me back my mind." God wants us to think clearly, and so He tells us in His Word to develop discernment, get wisdom, and acquire knowledge. This book will help you to do just that by giving you the media awareness and biblical discernment skills to overcome the powerful influences and artificial peer pressure of the mass media of entertainment.

1

GRACE UNDER FIRE: SETTING THE STAGE

INTRODUCTION

> For though we walk in the flesh, we do not war after the flesh: (for the weapons of our warfare are not carnal, but mighty through God to the pulling down of strong holds;) casting down imaginations, and every high thing that exalteth itself against the knowledge of God, and bringing into captivity every thought to the obedience of Christ.
>
> 2 Corinthians 10:3-5 (KJV)
>
> It's the movies that have really been running things in America ever since they were invented. They show you what to do, how to do it, when to do it, how to feel about it, and how to look at how you feel about it. Everybody has their own America, and then they have the pieces of a fantasy America that they think is out there but they can't see.
>
> Andy Warhol[1]
>
> To educate a man in mind and not in morals is to educate a danger to society.
>
> Theodore Roosevelt
>
> **Fact:** *The average American family spends seven hours each day watching television, making television the number one consumer of people's leisure time.*[2]

Four of every five parents think popular culture such as music, television, and movies negatively affects children.[3] Single parents, especially, say they need help shielding their children from the mass media of entertainment's emphasis on perverse sex, gruesome violence, and shrill obscenity.

Most parents are concerned about popular culture because their children are being conformed in dress, actions, and ideas to the images of Hollywood idols such as Madonna, Michael Jackson, and Beavis & Butthead, rather than to positive, moral images of virtuous men and women and, in particular, to the image of Jesus Christ.

Parents should be concerned because the mass media of entertainment are among the most influential teachers of our children. In the United States the average child sees 15,000 to 30,000 hours of television[4] by the time he or she is seventeen years old. During this same period a child spends only 11,000 to 16,000 hours in school,[5] and 2,000 hours or less of quality interaction with his or her parents.[6] Many American children spend more time with a television set before the age of six than they will spend with their fathers during their lifetime. Thus, television has the educational edge in terms of "class" time.

A primary teacher of our youth

Children learn in part by teachers presenting information and/or behavior, repeating the information and/or behavior, and rewarding the accurate feedback of the information and/or behavior. Television presents, repeats, and rewards behavior and/or information much more often than parents and teachers do, not only because it occupies more of a child's time but also because it is constructed to deliver more information per second. Also, it often presents, repeats, and rewards behavior and/or information more effectively than do parents or teachers because it is entertaining, exciting, and captivating.

To a greater or lesser degree, depending on the medium, electronic games, MTV, and the other media of entertainment have the same type of educational impact as television and sometimes even more so. For example, electronic games allow the player to interact with the game, which provides a means of cognitive growth and comprehensive education in the skills of the game.

Because the entertainment industry quotes educators who say that television does not educate, it is important to understand that even though television provides behavioral modeling and information (known as physical or "P" education), it is deficient in providing cognitive growth because cognitive growth requires interaction and reflection. Since cognitive growth is necessary in order to develop higher thinking skills (known as logico-mathematical or "LM" education), many educators do not consider television an educational tool. In fact, studies have shown that television often inhibits cognitive growth and may produce symptoms of learning deficiency in children. Therefore, many experts claim correctly that television does not educate because they are concerned about cognitive growth, even though television does educate from a layman's perspective in terms of behavior, psychological development, and emotional development—often to the detriment of the viewer. Even those educators who focus on cognitive growth agree that television can assist in educating if used properly in the classroom with other educational tools and techniques that produce cognitive growth.

To comprehend this important distinction so that you are not confused by reports on this issue, two examples may suffice. Many parents have observed that their baby may learn to say the word "daddy" (P learning) and then call every person the child sees "daddy." It is only through interaction and reflection that the baby correctly identifies his father with the word "daddy" (LM learning). Research and parents have also observed that young children will tend to hit each other while watching a violent television program (P learning), but if the researcher or parent asks the child what he is watching, the child will respond "I don't know" because he is not reflecting on what he is watching and so he is not growing cognitively.

What's it all about?

Most parents want their children to be able to discern between good and evil so they can choose the good and thus grow and mature into adults of integrity and good character. With the power of the mass media to confuse and even undermine their teaching, these parents often have difficulty teaching their children the basics of discernment. This book will help you to do just that. You'll find many of the terms we will be using in the glossary, beginning on page 412.

Hard evidence

Aside from definitions, you should note that the examples in this book have been carefully chosen because they best illustrate a point, have been the focus of the research cited, or are the most widely known examples that could be found. Some entertainment media are very fragmented. Contemporary radio, the Internet, and other mass media entertainment such as television programs are very fleeting.

Movies are most often chosen as examples because they reach a broader audience through extensive theatrical release, cable television release, video release, broadcast television release, and direct satellite release. They also attract a larger audience as a result of millions of dollars of publicity and the cumulative force of each release.

While television is a significant part of the problem (and, perhaps, the solution), television programs are fleeting. Who can remember the fall 1982 television season, especially the movies of the week or talk show topics? Most of us can, however, remember *E.T.* well enough to discuss it intelligently.

Even though movies are so much more prominent than other mass media entertainment, especially when you look at the media worldwide, it is clear that they too are fleeting when compared to great literature and art.

When I lectured to one group of students, they had no idea who Jimmy Stewart was, let alone Robert Taylor and some of the other megastars of yesteryear. Others had never heard of fairly recent movies such as *Chariots of Fire* or *Driving Miss Daisy*, though these movies were the most profitable in the years that they were released. No example is going to be timeless, except those drawn from the Bible. I must, however, rely on examples to which most readers can relate.

It should be noted that in spite of the distinctives of each medium of entertainment, there are enough elements common to all the mass media to apply many of the same research and media literacy principles to all the mass media.

Go into all the world

Now we can lay the foundation of discernment by looking at a snapshot of our cultural environment with respect to the mass media of entertainment. That snapshot will help us to develop the perspective we need to learn the tools of discernment.

Endnotes

1. Victor Bokris, *Warhol: The Education of Andy Warhol 1937-45* (1989).
2. Nielsen Media Research, *Los Angeles Times* (August 19, 1995).
3. Family Research Council, national public opinion survey (October 1995).
4. According to Nielsen Media Research, as reported in the *Los Angeles Times*, August 19, 1995, the average daily television usage in the United States of America is:

   Children 2-11: 2 hours 43 minutes per day
   Teens 12-17: 2 hours 52 minutes per day
   Men 18+: 3 hours 52 minutes per day
   Women 18+: 4 hours 28 minutes per day
   Daily home use: 6 hours 59 minutes per day

Using these statistics, which are significantly lower than the Nielsen figures from 1980, the average child will watch over 16,000 hours of television by the time he or she turns seventeen years old. Many children, especially in single family homes and impoverished environments, watch much more television. Assuming that these children are watching whenever the television is turned on, then 30,000 hours is slightly less than six hours a day, excluding two years of infancy and perfunctory days away from the television. According to *U.S. News & World Report*, 115:5 (August 2, 1993) page 64, "our children watch an astonishing 5,000 hours by the first grade and 19,000 hours by the end of high school—more time than they spend in class."

5. 11,000 hours assumes four hours per day of classroom time for eight months a year, excluding holidays, from six years old to seventeen years old. Of course, many children start in nursery school, day-care, or preschool, go to after-school programs, and spend much more than four hours per day in the classroom for more than eight months per year. For instance, 16,000 hours assumes six hours a day from age five to seventeen, excluding holidays.

6. Several studies have wired parents and their children with recorders to see their interaction and have found that parents spend five to fifteen minutes a day with their children, which would equal 1,500 hours of interaction by the time the child is seventeen.

OVERCOMING THE MEDIA MINDSET

OR

THE GOOD NEWS

IS

THAT THE BAD NEWS IS WRONG!

In all these things we are more than conquerors through him who loved us.

Romans 8:37 (NIV)

This drug dealer, who's in my book said to me, "If God invented anything better than dope, he kept it to himself." When I heard that I thought, "Yeah, that's pretty good." But then, it occurred to me—there is one thing that's more powerful than dope, and that's movies.

Richard Price[1]

There's only one thing that can kill the movies, and that's education.

Will Rogers[2]

Fact: On television, there are five times as many love scenes between unmarried couples as there are married.

W hen I started teaching discernment to concerned parents and children in the late '70s, a significant number of people did not understand the magnitude of the problem and many others did not think that there was a problem. I began my lectures with startling information about the depth, breadth, and seriousness of the problem. Most people today have become very concerned and a few are at the point of hysteria. So it has become more important to keep in mind the good news before exploring the nature of the problem and the solutions.

Fabulous fallacies

Several years ago I received a book to review titled *Fabulous Fallacies: More Than 300 Popular Beliefs That Are Not True.*[3] I have found that quizzing people about some of these fabulous fallacies is a great way to get my audience thinking, hold their attention, and point out some of the common fallacies perpetrated by the mass media and others in our society. Keep in mind that a fallacy is a popular belief that is not true. Some of the following are trick questions, but that makes them even more interesting. (The answers are found in the endnotes.)

- Nearly every film buff thinks *The Jazz Singer* was the first talking picture (1927)? Was it?[4]
- Even people who did not see Oliver Stone's *JFK* think J.F. Kennedy was the youngest president of the United States. Was he?[5]
- Millions of families saw Disney's *Pocahontas* and millions more think Pocahontas married Captain John Smith. Did she?[6]
- For those who saw *Jefferson in Paris* and other Hollywood histories about the French Revolution, it is clear that Queen Marie Antoinette thoughtlessly uttered the famous words, "Let them eat cake." Did she?[7]

These are a few of the many fallacies in our society, but one of the most pervasive and debilitating fallacies was framed without malice by Paul Klein, a former president of the NBC television network, during a lecture that he gave to my students in 1980 wherein he claimed that:

Television is the most powerful force in the world today.

Is it?

If it bleeds, it leads

Many people have fallen for the negative fallacies spewing forth from the entertainment media. As a result, they have a growing fear of crime, politics, or whatever other institution or problem the media choose as the villain of the day.

This growing fear is the result of the program content decisions of people working in the news media who think that "if it bleeds, it leads." This emphasis on bad news rather than good news presents a very distorted picture of reality. Noted movie critic Michael Medved said, "In the bizarre world of broadcast journalism, killing is always covered, while kindness is almost always ignored."[8]

The news concentrates on the horrible story of the traveler who gets shot, not the thousands of travelers who are helped along their way. The influence of these depressing negative news stories is reinforced and augmented by television talk shows that focus on deviant, perverse, rotten, and ugly behavior, and by movies and television programs that attempt to capture an audience with perverse sex and porno-violence.

Even some church, parachurch, and missions organizations have reinforced the negative by focusing on the "bad news" in their fund-raising letters, videos, books, and other materials in order to capture the attention and support of their audience. Like the Hegelian news giants that posit a problem and then introduce their editorial solution, which often involves big government, some religious organizations resort to proclaiming a theology of fear to capture the attention of donors and then present themselves as the solution.

Better news

In the midst of this fear-mongering emotionalism there appears to be a growing awareness of the truth. In a humorous and enlightened book, Ben Wattenberg, a well-known liberal journalist turned conservative, confessed that for many years during the '60s and '70s he was swept up in the emotional maelstrom of every predicted environmental disaster. He made reference to Paul Erhlich's book *The Population Bomb,* which posited that the world's population was growing so fast that everyone would starve by the year 1975 or burn up soon thereafter as a result of their combined body heat.

As the years passed and these dire predictions of imminent environmental apocalypse (which Mr. Wattenberg reported in his columns) failed to occur, he decided that *The Good News Is the Bad Was Wrong* and titled his insightful book by that perceptive name.[9]

Even better news than Mr. Wattenberg's discovery that much of the environmental hysteria is a far-fetched fallacy is the great news that neither television, movies, the Internet, or the entire mass media are the most powerful force in the world today. In fact:

God is!

Consequently, the fear of the Lord, not the fear of the mass media, is the beginning of all wisdom, while the knowledge of the Holy One, Who loved the world so much that He gave His only begotten Son to pay the penalty for our transgressions and free us from the fallacies of our age, is true understanding.

> For where your treasure is, there your heart will be also.
> Matthew 6:21 (NIV)

Many people recognize that God is the real sovereign. Therefore, contrary to dire predictions of its demise and consistently negative images in the mass media, the church is alive and well in the United States of America.

The disparity between the strength of the church in America and the strength of the entertainment media, which many financial analysts call our leading industry and our leading export, is astounding. Despite film director Ingmar Bergman's claim that movies are the church of the twentieth century, the church in the U.S. is doing much better than its upstart rival.

A 1995 American Bible Society survey reported in *USA Today* found that going to church is the most popular leisure activity of Americans (55% say that it is their favorite activity), much more popular than going out to eat (53%), playing sports (11%), and going to movies (a mere 9% choose movies as their favorite leisure time activity).

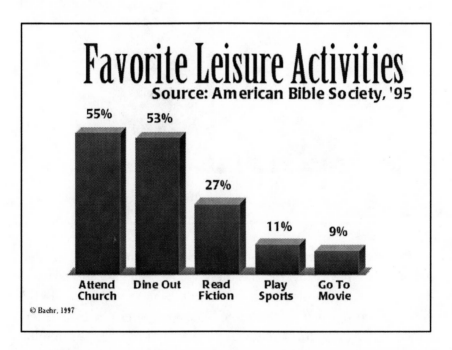

In 1995, Americans went to church five times more often (5.3 billion times) than they went to movies (1.26 billion tickets sold), and individual Americans gave twenty-one times more to church and charity ($116 billion) than they spent at the box office ($5.51 billion). Even including videos, total consumer spending on movies and videos ($31 million)[10] in 1995 was 237% less than total individual giving to church and charity. Furthermore, unlike entertainment, which has been suffering box office cycles every three to four years, total individual giving to churches and charities has increased dramatically every year since 1984.

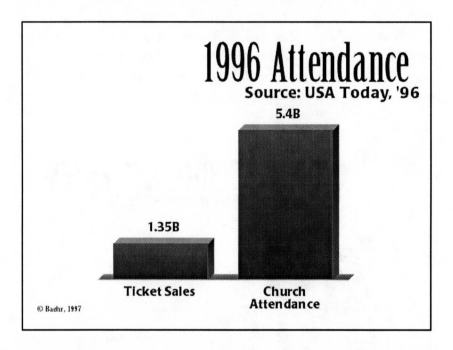

With regard to another area of entertainment—sports, in 1992, Americans gave fourteen times more to charity ($56.7 billion) than they spent on all professional sports combined (which was $4 billion), according to 1992 Associated Press research. In 1993, attendance at religious functions was fifty-four times greater (5.6 billion) than attendance at professional football, baseball and basketball games (103 million people), according to the Gallup Organization.

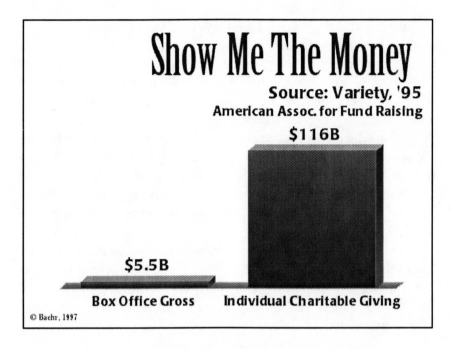

Show Me The Money

Source: Variety, '95
American Assoc. for Fund Raising

$116B

$5.5B

Box Office Gross   Individual Charitable Giving

© Baehr, 1997

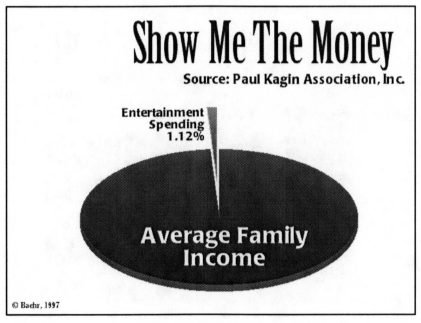

Show Me The Money

Source: Paul Kagin Association, Inc.

Entertainment
Spending
1.12%

**Average Family
Income**

© Baehr, 1997

Good will triumph when evil overplays its hand

The healthy state of the church in the U.S. is somewhat surprising considering almost thirty years of pointed media attacks on Christianity on television and in movies, attacks so blatant that for many years the last acceptable villains in Hollywood movies and television programs appeared to be Christians. In spite of these well-documented attacks, the church is not only attracting the vast majority of Americans, but the faith of America may be in the first stage of revival according to the National and International Religion Report and the Gallup Organization. These signs of revival are so pronounced they have even been noticed by the mainstream press.

A large 1994 Times Mirror study for the *Los Angeles Times* found that eight out of ten adults describe themselves as God-fearing churchgoers who pray. A *U.S. News & World Report* poll found that 62% of Americans say the influence of religion in their own lives is increasing.

Religion In America

Source: Princeton Religious Research Center, '96

96% 84% 80% 80%

Believe In God · Believe In Jesus Christ · Believe In Judgement Day · Believe In A Personal Relationship With God

© Baehr, 1997

The 1996 Report of the Princeton Religion Research Center on "Religion in America" found that among adults in the United States:

96% believe in God

95% say their prayers have been answered

84% believe Jesus Christ is God or the Son of God

80% expect to be called before God at Judgment Day to answer for their sins

80% of believers say they have a personal relationship with God

79% believe in miracles

69% claim membership in a church, synagogue, or other religious body

© Baehr, 1997

58% are Protestant by preference

25% are Roman Catholic

41% of adults describe themselves as born-again or evangelical Christians

2% of adults are Jews

Less than 1%, each, of adults state Islam, Hinduism or Buddhism as a preference

According to the October/November 1995 issue of *The Public Perspective*, nearly 500,000 churches dot the American landscape, representing about 2,000 denominations and countless independent churches and faith communities. *The Public Perspective* contends that the way to reach the American people is through their houses of worship since 60% of the populace can be found attending them in a given month.

You don't have to be a weatherman

Not only are people becoming more religious, but also, in record numbers, moral people are becoming concerned about the influence of popular culture.

After years of denying the power of the mass media, more and more people are aware of and opposed to the ungodly enchantments of it. In several 1995 polls, Americans told the entertainment industry they are very concerned about sex, violence, and profanity on television, in movies, and in music lyrics.

A *USA Today*/CNN/Gallup poll dealt with broader entertainment industry issues. This survey of 65,142 viewers found:

96% are very concerned or somewhat concerned about sex on TV.

97% are very or somewhat concerned about vulgar language on TV.

97% are very or somewhat concerned about violence on TV.

83% said the entertainment industry should make a serious effort to reduce sex and violence in movies and music and TV.

68% believe that reducing the amount of sex and violence in movies and music and on TV would significantly improve the moral climate of the U.S.

65% felt the entertainment industry is seriously out of touch with the values of the American people. Almost one-half of those believe the entertainment industry is to blame for exposing children under age twelve and children thirteen to seventeen to sex and violence in movies and music and on TV. And one-half of those who hold the entertainment industry responsible say the mass media share responsibility with parents.

63% felt the federal government should become involved in restricting sex and violence presented by the entertainment industry. [11]

Americans object not only to perverse sex and violence on television and in movies, but also cursing, according to the *USA Weekend* survey of 65,142 television viewers released on June 2, 1995. The study showed 97% of viewers are very concerned about cursing on television.[12]

Hollywood writers, talent, and executives do not realize that very few Americans curse with any regularity unless they are characters in the entertainment media or one of the denizens of the provincial nomenclature in Hollywood or New York. Professor Timothy Jay, called the "preeminent scholar of profanity" by the *Wall Street Journal*, conducted an intensive, comprehensive study titled "Cursing in America"[13] and found that only 7% of Americans curse on the job and only 12% curse in their leisure time.

A primary concern of millions of Americans is the conflict between the values being portrayed in the mass media as opposed to their own personal values. Values are a by-product of one's religion. For Christians and Jews, who hold to a theocentric or God-centered faith, values such as "Thou shalt not kill" are prescribed by God and must be observed or there are divine consequences. For those who believe that there is no higher, benevolent "other," or who believe they are the measure of all things, anything goes. They are, of course, hard pressed to explain what makes their own values better than Adolf Hitler's, Stalin's, or other famous megalomaniacs.

Another *USA Today* poll found that more than 80% of the American people think the biggest problem facing society today is the breakdown of morality. A vast majority of people think the mass media are responsible for this breakdown.

Many people are taking this perceived cultural war so seriously that they are turning off broadcast and cable television and relying on videotapes for entertainment. An insiders poll for the television industry showed the reason network viewership has declined so precipitously in the last few years is not the competition from other networks, video, and cable, but from extreme dissatisfaction with the lack of theocentric religion and moral values revealed by God represented on the networks. This poll showed that Americans think prime time, fiction television contributes to the destruction of the family and that teenagers have no place else to go for entertainment. Of those interviewed, 45% indicated they wanted programs that reflect explicitly Christian values and 70% said that a family equals mother, father, and children. This poll has confused those in the entertainment industry who are out of touch with the vast majority of the Americans.

You don't have to be a weatherman to realize that significant changes are occurring in the attitudes of the American people and that these attitudes are impacting the entertainment media.

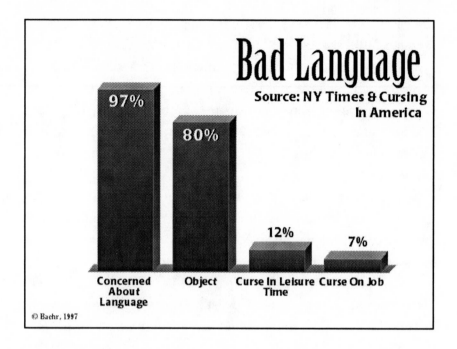

Bad Language

Source: NY Times & Cursing
in America

97% Concerned About Language
80% Object
12% Curse In Leisure Time
7% Curse On Job

© Baehr, 1997

Children now

For many years children and teenagers claimed that movies and television programs did not affect them, but according to recent surveys children no longer want to be abandoned to the television set and subject to the ritual worship of sex and violence on television and in movies. A 1992 MTV poll found that 92% of MTV's audience wanted less sex and violence in the mass media of entertainment. A 1994 Children Now poll of children ten to sixteen showed 80% saying there is too much sex in the mass media of entertainment and 62% thinking the media, especially television, influence their behavior.

The children and youth who attend my lectures are well aware of the influence of the entertainment media and want help to break the spell of the media enchantments on their lives. Most children and teenagers no longer want to be manipulated by or babysat by the television set. This change in attitude has made it much easier teach them discernment.

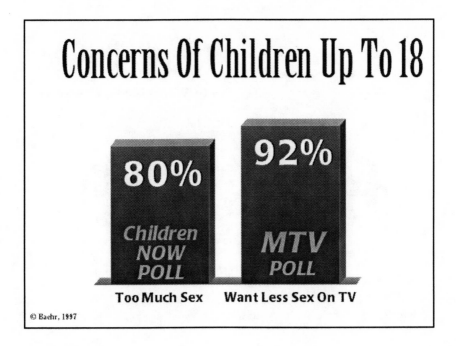

Concerns Of Children Up To 18

80%
Children
NOW
POLL

92%
MTV
POLL

Too Much Sex   **Want Less Sex On TV**

© Baehr, 1997

Awakening

Even entertainment industry leaders have changed their attitudes about the mass media. A UCLA Center for Communication Policy/*U.S. News & World Report* survey mailed to 6,300 decision-makers in the entertainment industry, receiving a 13.76% response, indicates a major turnaround. Normal response rates for surveys of this type run about 5%.

The survey found:

87% think violence in the mass media contributes to violence in society.

76% say they have prevented or discouraged their children from watching a violent show.

72% say the amount of violent programming on TV has increased over the past ten years.

63% say the industry glorifies violence.

UCLA Poll 1994
3,000 Top Media Executives

87%

Think Violence In Media Contributes To
Violence In Society

© Baehr, 1997

59% say violence in the entertainment media is a serious problem.

58% avoid movies because of violence.

51% say the problem of TV violence should be addressed by the TV industry, while 36% say parents should address it.

When asked to rank various violent incidents as always constituting an inappropriate level of violence, the entertainment leaders rated cartoon violence resulting in serious injury above other programs with depictions of rape, child abuse, stalking a woman, death by shooting, death by stabbing, and gunfire.

60% of the Hollywood elite say sexually explicit material is not a serious problem and only 15% think it is serious.

Cultural elite?

The most articulate presentation of this change in the attitudes of the media executives came from former Walt Disney Studios chairman Jeffrey Katzenberg when he spoke to 4,000 at the Video Software Dealer's Association's annual convention in 1992, on the subject of responsibility. Katzenberg said that it was ironic that Hollywood executives are called the "cultural elite," since:

> Most of our films lack culture and could hardly be termed elite. Responsibility is the issue. We should not be distracted by talk of censorship, the First Amendment, or some cultural elite. Each of us in Hollywood has the opportunity to assume individual responsibility to create films that educate rather than denigrate, that shed light rather than dwell in darkness, to aim for the highest common denominator rather than the lowest.

> To be sure, we have good excuses for not doing better more often. When our critics charge that we show violence that is too graphic, depict sex that is too gratuitous, or feature lyrics that are too inflammatory, we're all too quick to offer the defense that it's only a movie, or piously invoke the First Amendment. The sad result is that more and more movies get made that are uninspiring, or formulaic movies that are seemingly driven to offer nothing more than a cheap thrill.

Katzenberg credited Disney's success in the home video market to "high technical, artistic and moral" standards. The *Hollywood Reporter* wrote that Katzenberg's remarks were *"somewhat bold in that films exploiting sex and violence are a mainstay of the video business."*

Katzenberg's speech shows a powerful sea change in the entertainment industry at the very highest levels. Hollywood has always jealously guarded its right to make a profit off of prurient sexual content and violence, so Katzenberg's speech in effect relinquishes a prime market for entertainment profits and is a breath of fresh air in an industry too often polluted by its own product.

It is clear that the vast majority of people, including some media executives, are concerned about the influence of the media on our society, and especially on our children.

Prayer and politics

The entertainment industry should be concerned that many Americans want the federal government to intervene to change the values presented on television and in the mass media. The networks need to listen to their audiences before the government intervenes.

This concern of moral Americans is reflected in the political pronouncements of politicians, both liberal and conservative. According to Senator Joseph Lieberman, seizing the media and values issue has propelled his popularity at the polls because research shows that 95% of the public finds TV too vulgar, violent, and racy. He notes that this is the first issue upon which almost all his constituents agree. Most politicians agree with Senator Lieberman and now believe that the government must act to clean up television because television is insulated from ordinary market mechanisms by broadcast spectrum scarcity and the fact of government licensing, which restricts entry into the marketplace.

Don't throw me in that briar patch!

The clash between the libertine values of some of the leaders of the entertainment industry and the biblical values of the vast majority of Christian Americans has inclined some of these media leaders toward attacking Christians by portraying them negatively in movies, television programs, and song. This tendency to vilify Christians has been hastened by the fact that religious, racial, and sexual groups that were once vilified in the mass media have set up advocacy offices in Hollywood to express their displeasure with such negative media. Too often it seems as if Christians are the last acceptable villains in Hollywood entertainment, and so we find Christians or characters with Christian attributes as the villains in movies like *Cape Fear, The Scarlet Letter,* and *Seven.*

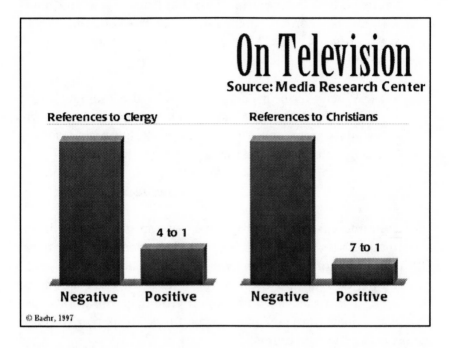

The Media Research Center found that negative references to clergy outnumbered positive ones four to one in a study of 1,000 hours of programming in the 1993 television season. The study found portrayals of lay believers even worse, with 68% of church-goers on television depicted negatively and only 18% presented positively. While the portrayal of clergy and churchgoers on TV improved slightly in 1994, the amount of anti-Christian bigotry in prime time, fiction television continued to be shocking; with 31% of the clergy and 35% of the Christian laity portrayed negatively. If the same proportion of any other religious group were portrayed negatively in prime time television, such bigotry would not be tolerated—though there are bad apples in every religion.

Even so, after all these years of Christian bashing by the mass media of entertainment, the American people have not caved in to anti-Christian bigotry. The People for the American Way, the liberal advocacy group founded by Norman Lear, commissioned Democratic pollster Peter Hart in 1994 to conduct a scientific study of U.S. public opinion on "the challenge of the Religious Right." Two of the answers of the 1,000 registered voters interviewed are quite revealing:

> When you hear people criticizing the Religious Right, do you think they are mainly raising legitimate concerns about this movement, or do you think they are just raising exaggerated fears and bias against religious people?
> Legitimate concerns.............................21%
> Exaggerated and biased fears 61%

Furthermore, with this growing attack on Christianity in the mass media, a revival of faith and activism seems to be at hand. Throughout history, persecution of the Christian faith has led to tremendous revival and growth of the church. Persecutions by Nero, Stalin, and Mao led to amazing growth in the numbers of Christian believers. The fastest way to produce Christians, it seems, is to persecute them.

As satirist Jonathan Swift said, "I never saw, heard, nor read, that the clergy were beloved in any nation where Christianity was the religion of the country. Nothing can render them popular, but some degree of persecution."[14]

Even intellectual persecution has prompted conversion. The renowned writer and intellectual G. K. Chesterton said he came to a saving faith in Jesus Christ because of the intense dislike and even fear of Jesus Christ and Christians in the academic community.

The magnitude of the current revival has been recognized by the mass media in reports on:
> The growth of the Christian right.
> The growth of megachurches.
> The growth of nondenominational churches.

The widespread occurrence of college students throughout the United States repenting, confessing, and turning to Jesus Christ.

This revival has even impacted the entertainment industry. In fact, there has been a tremendous growth in the number of Christians taking the top production positions in the entertainment industry. For example, the number-one-rated television program and the biggest box office hit of 1994 were produced by evangelical Christians. The biggest box office hit of the summer of 1995 was also written by evangelical Christians. Of the more than forty-five executive producers of the sixty prime time entertainment television programs, twenty-one of them were professing Christians in 1994, up from one professing evangelical Christian twelve years earlier.

This growth of the Christian faith in the midst of the culture wars has already had an impact on politics and will impact the mass media. This revival will, obviously, present new problems for those who labor in the mass media, especially if they are bigoted toward Christianity and intolerant of the revealed faith of the Bible.

Married with children

How do these signs of revival impact the box office? The financial impact is clear for those who understand the values of moral Americans. For many years, family movies have made much more money at the box office than R-rated fare. For instance, in 1996, family-friendly movies grossed on average 300% better than movies aimed at the adult marketplace. In 1995, G-rated movies grossed 250% more than R-rated movies. PG-rated movies grossed 168% more than R-rated movies. PG-13 movies grossed 213% more.

Long-term studies of the box office have shown that R-rated movies have a maximum earnings ceiling that is at most 50% of the earnings ceiling for G-rated and PG-rated movies.

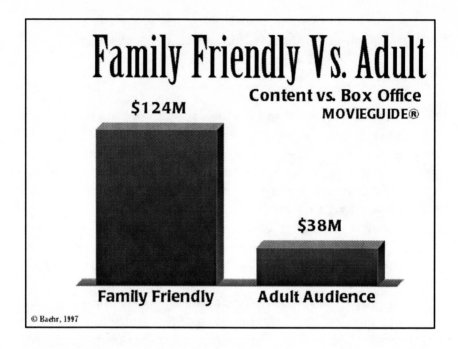

Family Friendly Vs. Adult

Content vs. Box Office
MOVIEGUIDE®

$124M

$38M

Family Friendly   Adult Audience

© Baehr, 1997

Good news sells

The spiritual sea change in America is influencing the box office in some startling ways. Movies with strong Christian content are becoming extremely profitable at the box office. In 1996, movies with strong Christian content, such as *Dead Man Walking*, and not just movies with wedding or funeral homilies, **earned $37.5 million on average** at the box office, which was:

> 2,678% better than movies with revisionist history ($1 million on average);
>
> 1,630% better than strongly humanist movies ($2.3 million on average);
>
> 340% better than movies with other religious content ($11 million on average);
>
> 300% better than movies with strong occult content ($12.5 million on average);
>
> 270% better at the box office than extremely anti-biblical movies ($14 million on average);

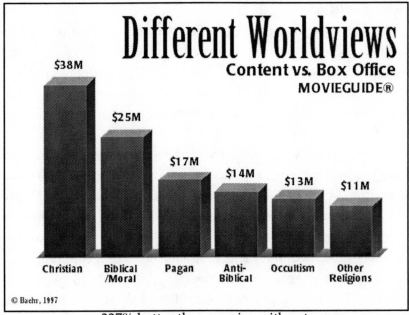

Different Worldviews
Content vs. Box Office
MOVIEGUIDE®

$38M — Christian
$25M — Biblical /Moral
$17M — Pagan
$14M — Anti-Biblical
$13M — Occultism
$11M — Other Religions

© Baehr, 1997

227% better than movies with extreme pagan content ($16.5 million on average); and,

208% better than movies with extreme sexual content ($18 million on average).

Another interesting indication of the revival that is at hand is the number of movies from unexpected sources that lift up Jesus Christ and Christianity. One of the most evangelistic movies of all time was the 1995 movie *Dead Man Walking*, which presented the Gospel of Jesus Christ with great care and passion. There are a number of 1996 and 1995 movies, such as *The Preacher's Wife*, *The Hunchback of Notre Dame*, *The Spitfire Grill*, *Independence Day*, *Richard III*, *Braveheart*, *Sense and Sensibility*, *The Feast of July*, *Persuasion*, *First Knight*, and *Cry the Beloved Country* that presented the Gospel, extolled Jesus Christ, commended the Bible, and commended church. This is a significant change from years past and bodes well for the future of the entertainment industry.

More profitable

Movies with Christian or biblical themes and elements are consistently more profitable. For instance, in 1996, 60% of the most-profitable movies in 1996 had Christian or biblical themes and elements and earned a total of $2.3 billion (for an average of $227 million) with total budgets of $265 million (for and average of $26 million) for an earning ratio of nine to one.

Morally acceptable movies were also more profitable in 1996. Sixty percent of the most-profitable movies in 1996 were deemed acceptable by MOVIEGUIDE® and earned $2.8 billion ($232 million on average) for total budgets of $345 million ($29 million on average) for an earning ratio of eight to one. Fifty-five percent of the most-profitable movies in 1996 were aimed at children, families, and/or teenagers and earned $2.7 billion ($248 million on average) for total budgets of $337 million ($31 million on average) for an earning ratio of eight to one.

On the other hand, none of the least profitable movies in 1996 received a positive acceptability rating from MOVIEGUIDE®. Sixty percent of these least-profitable movies were R-rated and earned $88 million at the box office ($7 million on average) while they cost a total of $272 million to produce ($23 million on average) for an earning ratio of thirty two to one. Eighty percent of these least-profitable movies had pagan, new age, humanist, or antibiblical themes or/and earned $149 million at the box office ($9 million on average) and cost a total of $423 million to produce ($26 million on average) for an earning ratio of thirty five to one.

The failure of immorality

The shift in values and attitudes has left movies with excessive sexual content and violence in the dust. Therefore, much to the dismay of Hollywood executives, many big-budget, porno-violent films have flopped at the box office.

"It's scary," one top studio executive said.

Another commented, "I don't know what the lessons are here, except we're making a lot of movies that people don't want to see."

Two expensive flops in 1995, *Assassins* and *Showgirls*, raised questions about the salaries of some studio executives and, more important, about the appeal of several stars, among them Sylvester Stallone, Demi Moore, and David Caruso.

The rapid failure of *Jade* was a setback for David Caruso, who left the television show "*NYPD Blue*" to become a movie star. His next film, *Kiss of Death*, also collapsed at the box office. Hollywood executives now say Caruso should narrow his sights to playing character roles rather than leads.

The stars are probably not the cause of the failure of these films, but rather the change in the attitudes of Americans who no longer want to be fed an entertainment diet of perverse sex and porno-violence.

Blame for these failures should be laid at the feet of writers and executives who tried to pander to the lowest common denominator. The failure of *Jade* was one more blow to Joe Eszterhas, the highly paid screenwriter whose NC-17–rated *Showgirls* was crushed by the critics and emerged as a major disaster.

It should be noted that the average studio movie costs more than $40 million to make and market, so a movie can now gross $50 million at the box office and be considered a failure.

While homosexuals claim movies about homosexuals do well at the box office, wholesome, heterosexual movies earned 2,400% more than overtly homosexual movies.

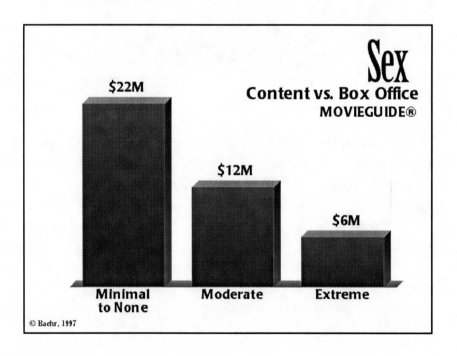

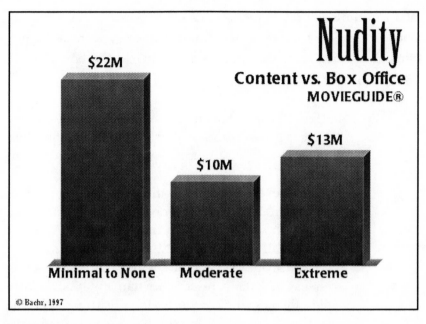

Puff the disappearing market

Even though it is evident from the box office reports that most movies with extreme sex and violence are failing in the U.S. market,

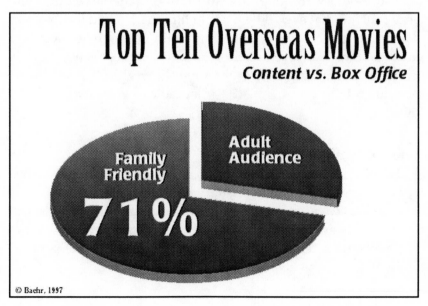

media pundits retort that movies loaded with extreme sex and violence are made for the overseas market, but even overseas, family films and broad audience movies did better at the box office in 1996. For instance:

> Seventy-one percent of the movies in the top ten overseas were movies marketed to families, teenagers, and/or children (earning $1.3 billion overseas);
>
> Fifty-seven percent of the top-grossing movies overseas in 1996 were deemed acceptable or acceptable with a slight caution for children by MOVIEGUIDE® (earning $1.2 billion overseas).
>
> Fifty-seven percent of the top-grossing movies overseas in 1996 featured Christian and biblical principles, themes, and/or worldviews (earning $1 billion overseas).

Surely there's a market

Those who want an excuse to produce extreme sex and violence contend that even if the feature film market and the overseas market are pro–broad-audience and family films, there must be a video market. However, even the video market favors morally acceptable fare. Thus, 60% of the top-selling videos in 1996 were recommended or deemed acceptable with caution by MOVIEGUIDE®.

Who's the audience?

Despite evidence to the contrary, secular entertainment industry observers often claim that family films are not doing well at the box office. The reason some family films do extraordinarily well at the box office and others flop can be attributed to several factors.

One factor is entertainment value. Too many of the summer family films are mediocre at best.

Top Video Sales
Source: Billboard, '96
MOVIEGUIDE®

Acceptable w/caution 60%

Not Acceptable

© Baehr, 1997

However, families will put up with mediocre fare if the world-view, ontology, and values of the movie agree with their values. Although many people don't know the term "ontology," it is one of the leading indicators of the potential box office value of a movie. Ontology refers to the nature of being or reality. Christians and Jews have a real ontology and believe that we live in a real world, with real problems, and we need a real Savior. New agers and many Eastern religions believe that we live in a nominalistic, imaginary world where mind can manipulate imaginary matter.

In India, a Hindu holy man, who holds to ontological nominalism, will pass a suffering child on the street and claim that the child's suffering is just an illusion. Whereas, Mother Teresa will pick the child up and take him to her hospice for treatment.

Some of the better family movies fail because they include ontological nominalism or new age elements that Christian Americans abhor. *A Little Princess* falls into that category. Although it was a fine movie that taught valuable moral lessons, many parents did not take their children because of the magical thinking and Hindu elements in the movie. *The Indian in the Cupboard* is another film audiences avoided because of its politically correct, nominalistic elements.

The fact that the box office receipts for *Pocahontas* were a third less than *The Lion King* can be attributed to the New Age and revisionist historical elements in the movie—elements that many parents called MOVIEGUIDE® to condemn.

In the nonfamily film category *The Scarlet Letter* failed miserably because of its revisionist history, anti-Christian and antinomian (denying the authority of moral law) elements.

Filmmakers who want to reach an audience need to understand that Americans are very savvy about their beliefs (though they may not be able to express those beliefs in theological terms) and do not want movies that attack or depreciate those beliefs.

Be of good cheer

Signs of revival and the changes in the attitudes of the American people are encouraging. Knowing this good news should help you and others take a stand for righteousness. By taking a stand for the good, the true, and the beautiful, you will be making a difference by influencing Hollywood decision-makers to produce more good entertainment and less immoral and amoral entertainment.

Part of the reason for the breakdown of morality in America is that the church retreated from being salt and light in the culture. Just as Edmond Burke predicted, "The only thing necessary for the triumph of evil is for good men to do nothing."[15]

In the past few years the church has started to again stand for righteousness, so the tide is turning. Remember that we are more than conquerors in Christ.[16]

We often forget that by God's grace we have tremendous power to make a difference when we take a stand for righteousness. Christian historian Kenneth Scott Latourette tells us about a saint who took such a stand:

The gladiatorial games persisted in Rome until, in the fifth century, a monk, Telemachus, leaped into the arena to stop the combatants and the mob, presumably nominally Christian, stoned him to death for interfering with their pleasure. Thereupon the Emperor [Constantine] ordered that the spectacles be stopped and Telemachus enrolled among the martyrs.[17]

The key to taking a stand is to think clearly in the midst of the babble of the mass media that so easily distracts us and tempts us to be manipulated and changed by things. The Bible tells us, "The eye never has enough of seeing, nor the ear its fill of hearing" Ecclesiastes 1:8 (NIV). The modern media work upon those senses that are most susceptible to distraction.

Take every thought captive

Extensive research indicates most Christians have the same media diet as non-Christians, though many Christians complain about the entertainment media.[18] The same percentage of Christian teenagers as non-Christian watch R-rated movies with the same frequency. There is, however, a significant minority of Christians who avoid the entertainment media, especially movies.

With the advent of videotape, cable television, computers, the Internet, and the other modern methods of transmitting and delivering entertainment, avoiding the movie theater does not always protect the individual from the vile or good images of our age, or diminish the income of the entertainment conglomerates. The media giants are now involved in many other areas of commerce, services, and industry, including Christian media.

The holding company that owns Fox TV also owns Zondervan, one of the largest Christian book and Bible publishers. It is becoming much more difficult to target these giants when they deliver products that the Christian community routinely buys.

Christ and culture

Aside from the pervasive scope of the entertainment media, it is important to understand that the church historically has always had five different perspectives toward culture. Each of these perspectives can be proof-texted with the appropriate Bible verses that support a particular position, but none of them can be shown to be the "correct" reading to the exclusion of the others. So none of them is creedal or a measure of orthodoxy.

Yale theologian H. Richard Niebuhr first distinguished between the five approaches Christians have historically taken with regard to their world in his book *Christ and Culture*.[19] His distinctions have been modified and clarified for the purposes of this book.

The first position could be called "retreat from culture," though Niebuhr calls it "Christ Against Culture." He cites the Mennonite and Amish communities as the obvious examples of this tradition, though he could have also referred to the monastic tradition in the church. While there are rich traditions of service within these groups, the world is viewed as a place from which to escape into communities of "separated brethren." The Schleitheim Confession of the Anabaptists (1527) argued, "Since all who do not walk in the obedience of faith are a great abomination before God, it is not possible for anything to grow or issue from them except abominable things. God further admonishes us to withdraw from Babylon and the earthly Egypt that we may not be partakers of the pain and suffering which the Lord will bring upon them."

The second perspective, which Niebuhr calls "The Christ of Culture," tends to equate creation and redemption and can be seen in those groups that identify Christ with utopian socialism as well as those who identify Christ with American culture. Those who follow this tradition hail Jesus as the Messiah of their society, the fulfiller of its hopes and aspirations, the perfecter of its true faith, the source of its holiest spirit. For these people there is hardly any difference between Christ and the culture. These adherents view Christ as the moral example Who points us to a perfect society.

The third approach, which Niebuhr calls "Christ Above Culture," is occupied by the centrists who live within the world though they are not of the world. These centrists refuse to take either the position of the anticultural radicals or of the accomodators of Christ to culture.

The fourth tradition is "Christ and Culture in Paradox," which refuses either to reject culture or to confuse culture with Christianity. They see these as two different realms, not two antagonistic realms. In creation God gives us work, service, pleasure, government, and family. In redemption He gives us the church, the Word, and the sacraments. These are two different realms—not two antagonistic realms, nor two identical realms. The Christian who follows the "Christ and Culture in Paradox" tradition participates in culture, but not as a means of grace. It is, rather, an aspect of being human, not merely of being a Christian.

The final category is "Christ the Transformer of Culture," which emphasizes God's lordship over all of creation and all aspects of life. Niebuhr appeals to John's Gospel as an example of this approach. Here Christ is "the Word made flesh"—not only the priest of redemption, but the king of creation. This tradition, which is represented by Augustine and Calvin, takes the world seriously and contends that Christians have the potential not only to exercise leadership in the culture but to present the Gospel as well. God loves the world, not just individuals in it (Romans 8:20-23). Those of the "Christ Transforming Culture" tradition would view culture as a distinct, though related, part of Christ's universal reign. While creating a movie, building a house, or raising a family may not be the redemptive activities of the kingdom of God, they are important activities to which Christians realize a call, because they are commanded by the universal Lord in the "cultural mandate" of the early chapters of Genesis. Though human activity can never bring salvation, the activity of Christian men and women does bring a certain transforming element as they live out their callings in distinction and honor, serving both to attract non-Christians to the Gospel and also bringing civil righteousness, justice, and compassion to bear on human relationships.

The church has historically moved through a cycle from one point of view to the other. During the middle of the twentieth century the church retreated from culture. Then the church took up the battle cry of cultural warfare to resist the moral decay in our society. Now the church is beginning to move out as ambassadors for Jesus Christ to redeem the culture.

Whatever cultural position you, your local church, or your denomination adopts, we are called to develop the discernment to know right from wrong, the wisdom to choose the right, the knowledge to pursue the right, and the understanding to persevere.

> For God hath not given us the spirit of fear; but of power, and of love, and of a sound mind.
>
> 2 Timothy 1:7 (KJV)

Endnotes

1. Richard Price, *Movieline* (October 1992).
2. Will Rogers, *The Autobiography of Will Rogers*, (New York: AMS Press, 1979), ch. 6.
3. Tad Tuleja, *Fabulous Fallacies: More Than 300 Popular Beliefs That Are Not True* (New York: Harmony Books, 1982).
4. No, the first full-length talking picture was *The Lights of New York*. Sound technologies had been around for nearly twenty years. The French inventor Eugene Augustin Lauste had demonstrated a practical system as early as 1910. *The Lights of New York* played in 1928, but was soon forgotten, and so it was *The Jazz Singer* that got audiences hooked on sound. Even though *The Jazz Singer* had only a minimum of dialogue it demonstrated that sound technology could be successfully employed in a full-length dramatic movie. *Fabulous*, 10.
5. No. J.F. Kennedy was forty-three when he was elected president, while Theodore Roosevelt was forty-two when he took the oath of office after the assassination of William McKinley. *Fabulous*, 33.
6. No, she was never married to Captain John Smith. She was only twelve years old when she rescued Captain Smith. However, she was married twice: once to Kocoum, and then to John Rolfe after she was baptized. She died at the age of twenty-two in England. The descendants of Rolfe and Pocahontas are rumored to have included the Jeffersons and the Lees. *Fabulous*, 46.

7. No. The famous quote exemplifying royal callousness to the hunger of her people came from the mouth of a character in Jean Jacques Rousseau's *Confessions*, "and the incident referred to happened around 1740—fifteen years before Marie was born." *Fabulous*, 150.

8. Michael Medved, "Protecting Our Children From a Wave of Pessimism," *Imprimus* 24:12 (December 1995).

9. Ben Wattenberg, *The Good News Is the Bad News Is Wrong* (New York: Simon & Schuster, 1984).

10. Paul Kagan Associates, Inc., 1996.

11. *USA Weekend* (June 2-4, 1995).

12. *Ibid*.

13. Timothy Jay, *Cursing in America* (Philadelphia: John Benjamins Publishing Company, 1992).

14. Jonathan Swift, "Thoughts on Religion" (published in *Works*, vol. 15, 1765).

15. This may be a paraphrase of an Edmond Burke statement in his *Thoughts on the Cause of Present Discontents*.

16. Romans 8:37.

17. Kenneth Scott Latourette, *A History of Christianity*, (New York: Harper & Row, 1975) 245.

18. 1996 Special Report: Christians in America (San Antonio: Soma Research, Inc.)

19. H. Richard Niebuhr, *Christ and Culture.*

COPYCATS

> **What causes fights and quarrels among you? Don't they come from your desires that battle within you?**
> James 4:1 (NIV)
>
> Commercial jazz, soap opera, pulp fiction, comic strips, the movies set the images, mannerisms, standards, and aims of the urban masses. In one way or another, everyone is equal before these cultural machines; like technology itself, the mass media are nearly universal in their incidence and appeal. They are a kind of common denominator, a kind of scheme for pre-scheduled, mass emotions.
> C. Wright Mills[1]
>
> Those who corrupt the public mind are just as evil as those who steal from the public purse.
> Adlai Stevenson[2]
>
> *Fact: Crime occurs ten times more often on television than in real life.* [3]

Contrary to common sense and the weight of evidence, for many years people in the audience accepted the fallacy that the media did not influence their behavior. These people failed to make wise choices in their media consumption and, consequently, contributed to the support of degrading, unwholesome, and often immoral media.

Of course, many of them wanted to believe the media myth because they lusted after the illicit, the emotive, and the evocative much like media-addicted children who argue the media don't influence them while begging and whining for the latest trendy, media-hyped product or article of clothing.

Most people no longer believe the false disclaimers of the media spokespersons and now think the biggest problem facing our society is a breakdown of morality, which they attribute to the negative influence of the mass media.

After years of denial, even 87% of the top media executives now admit that the violence in the mass media contributes to the violence in society.[4] And children, too, are aware of the ability of the entertainment media to influence their behavior.

People throughout the world have a particular distrust and disdain for the negative influence of the explicit entertainment being produced by Hollywood.

While such awareness is important, awareness alone is not the answer to the problem. It is, of course, the first step toward the answer.

The print media, more than any other, have consistently contributed to these exposés of the failings of the newer media. The print media have been aided and abetted by politicians who have jumped on the "blame-the-media" bandwagon. This carping has often created a climate of fear, anger, and reaction. Some communications about the problem have been so argumentative and biased that they have contributed to the problem rather the solution.

The answer is to go beyond complaining. People must be

helped to develop the media awareness and discernment skills to use the entertainment media without being abused by it.

A short cut is the longest distance

The next step toward a solution is to become informed about the influence the entertainment media have on our society, particularly with regard to violence, sexual activity, and values, and to develop discernment and biblical critical thinking skills regarding such influence. Children, in particular, are motivated to change their media habits by an awareness of the influence of the entertainment media on these areas of their lives.

Once children understand the potential power of the mass media to negatively influence them, they will become your ally in the culture wars. They will want to develop media awareness, discernment, and the critical thinking skills necessary to choose the good, reject the bad, and overcome the negative images of the mass media of entertainment.

Why should we be concerned?

Throughout history people have understood the power of communication, art, and entertainment to change lives and shape society. Leaders have called people to action, philosophers have intoned ideas that shaped civilizations, and prophets have proclaimed truths that transformed history. From Moses' demand of the pharaoh to "Let my people go!" to the phrase "Liberty! Equality! Fraternity!" that ignited the flames of the French Revolution, communications have stirred people to action, to great sacrifice, and even to great cruelty.

Christians, in particular, have understood the power of the word:

> In the beginning was the Word, and the Word was with God, and the Word was God. He was with God in the beginning. Through him all things were made; without him nothing was made that has been made.
>
> John 1:1-3 (NIV)

As his desire to lead, influence, and inspire has grown, man has searched for new media to transmit his creations and communications to others—from cave drawings to hieroglyphics to the printing press to the Internet. Every new medium of communications has brought hope and engendered fears.

Many in authority, such as Henry VIII, condemned the printing press as a tool of the Devil, fearing that the words that it was used to print would topple their regimes—which, quite often, it did. Critics of the new media have only to cite anarchist pamphleteers like Bakunin who used the media effectively to cause great harm.

Just as history is replete with stories about the adverse effect of the older media, shocking stories abound about the negative impact of the newer media. Despite the self-interested protests of media mavens who dismiss these stories as anecdotal evidence of the power of the mass media to influence individuals, recalling examples of the impact of the mass media is an excellent way of grasping the magnitude of the problem.

Expose the fruitless deeds of darkness

First, God calls us to expose "the fruitless deeds of darkness" (Ephesians 5:11 NIV) so the light of truth can help us clean out those areas of life that are infested by these deeds. The Bible is full of examples of God exposing the fruitless deeds of darkness in uncompromising terms that, when considered apart from the rest of the Bible, would shock many concerned Christians.

Second, when I speak there is usually some concerned mother, and sometimes even a concerned father, who tells me afterwards that his or her spouse is taking their children to see inappropriate movies or allowing them to watch inappropriate television programs. We need to manifest a sense of shame by helping to open the eyes of such men and women to the truth. Sanitized language doesn't normally penetrate their tough desensitized behavior. They will usually say that they didn't notice a lot of foul language in a movie until you point out that there were hundreds of obscenities and profanities. Many of them, especially fathers, will discount the ruthless nature of the violence in a movie until it is clearly pointed out to them.

Third, after many years we have found the people do not act on the content section of MOVIEGUIDE® unless it is clear and precise. For example, a woman wrote MOVIEGUIDE® that she had rented a movie that we had reviewed and was shocked by some of the sexual content. She noted that we had listed in the content section *sexual activity and innuendo,* but this did not deter her from renting the movie (we had also given it an *extreme caution* rating). However, when we list *fornication, copulation,* or another precise term instead of *sexual activity,* people understand clearly why they should avoid a movie.

Fourth, lawyers win trials by presenting the evidence or facts. If a lawyer doesn't have the facts, he can try using the law or argumentation, but these devices are never as successful as presenting the facts. Teenagers, in particular, should be confronted with the facts. If a parent simply says to a teenager, "I don't think this is a movie you should see," the response might be, "Why? All my friends have seen it and think it's okay." Without the facts, a parent is usually at a loss as to how he or she should respond.

MOVIEGUIDE® arms parents with the facts so that they can say to their teenagers, "MOVIEGUIDE® lists knifings, slashing, fornication, and forty-four obscenities in this movie." If a teenager understands how the mass media can influence his or her behavior, he or she will be swayed by the evidence.

Selling Murder

To illustrate the power of media, consider the work of Dr. Joseph Goebbels, who was the National Socialist (Nazi) propaganda minister from 1933 to 1945. He exploited radio, press, cinema, and theater in Germany to destroy the Jews, evangelical Christians, handicapped Germans, and other groups. In 1994, the Discovery Channel aired *Selling Murder,* an important documentary investigating how Goebbels used mass media to influence the

German people to accept the mass murder of human beings.

The documentary shows that at a time when a majority of German people rejected mercy killings (an euphemism for murder), Goebbels produced a movie called *I Accuse*, an emotive feature film about a beautiful, intelligent woman who is dying of an incurable disease and begs to be allowed to commit suicide. After the movie was released, a majority of German people said they had changed their minds and now supported mercy killings. After a few more of Goebbels' films about invalids and handicapped people, the German people became strong believers in the efficacy of mass mercy killings.

While the attempted annihilation of Jews by the National Socialists is well documented, the atrocities did not stop with the Jewish race. The main focus of *Selling Murder* is a group that has been somewhat overlooked: the mentally and physically ill of Germany. In 1939, Hitler ordered the killing of the mentally and physically disabled, labeling them as "life unworthy of life." His reasoning was that the cost of keeping them alive in asylums and hospitals was too great. The real reason, however, stemmed from the government's determination to eliminate any threat to its idea of producing a superior race.

As an insight into the power of the mass media, historian Paul Johnson writes in his book *Modern Times*, "Hitler appears always to have approached politics in terms of visual images. Like Lenin and still more like Stalin, he was an outstanding practitioner of the century's most radical vice: social engineering—the notion that human beings can be shoveled around like concrete. But in Hitler's case, there was always an artistic dimension to these Satanic schemes. Hitler's artistic approach was absolutely central to his success. [Historians all agree] the Germans were the best-educated nation in the world. To conquer their minds was very difficult. Their hearts, their sensibilities, were easy targets."[5]

Indoctrination, with specific use of newsreel and films, was vital to Hitler's control of the new generation. Gerhard Rempel, in his book *Hitler's Children: The Hitler Youth and the SS*, wrote: "Each day began with a newsreel, followed by the various types of training. On Sunday mornings, an ideological program was substituted for church services, and Sunday nights were set aside for motion pictures."[6]

Selling Murder is must viewing for every moral person concerned about the use of the mass media of entertainment to influence societal behavior. Similarities between the National Socialist use of film and contemporary television programs about Dr. Kevorkian, abortion, and euthanasia are frightening. Two weeks before this documentary ran on the Discovery Channel, a network television program examined the current practice of killing patients by doctors in the Netherlands. The rationalization for these wholesale murders of patients in the Netherlands were all too similar to the Nazi propaganda in *Selling Murder*.

Incite to riot

There are also numerous examples of media-induced mass hysteria and violence that can be gleaned from newspapers and in television news reports. Following the destructive looting and rioting in Los Angeles and around the country after the four policemen involved in the Rodney King case were first acquitted, a few media professionals admitted that their coverage of the Rodney King affair may have been partly responsible for inciting the riots.

For instance, Ed Turner, vice president of CNN (no relation to his boss, Ted Turner), admitted that TV as a whole played the most violent excerpts of the King beating too often. Another broadcaster equated TV's preoccupation with the violence to snuff films (films of people actually being killed), which precipitated a wave of copycat crimes.

Glorifying gangs

Closely related to the riots are gang movies that have left a trail of tears and death. Police have called some of these films irresponsible and exploitive. Several people have been killed and wounded at the openings of films that exploit gang violence.

At the opening of filmmaker John Singleton's movie *Boyz N the Hood*, thirty-three people were injured and two people died from gunshot wounds. When *Boyz N the Hood* was shown in one California prison, fourteen people died in one night of race rioting in the prison.

When *New Jack City* opened, riots broke out in Los Angeles, New York, Chicago, and Houston. More than 1,500 teenagers rampaged through Westwood, Los Angeles. A teenager was killed in Brooklyn, where rival gangs fired more than 100 shots.

Violence broke out in at least eight states after the premiere of *Juice*. A girl caught in the cross fire of two rival street gangs died. A man coming out of a theater showing the film was paralyzed from the neck down after he was shot. At one theater, two rival gangs had a shooting match in the lobby.

Some time later, copying a murder scene from *Juice*, a teenager named Hicks, who killed a man for his tires, pleaded guilty to malice and armed robbery in what a prosecutor called a totally pointless murder.

"One of the co-defendants [Mr. Clegg] said he and Mr. Hicks [the killer] had seen the movie *Juice* the weekend before this particular incident, and there was a sequence in it where a totally pointless murder was committed," Clegg said. "I'm told the words Mr. Hicks spoke at the time he fired the shot came from that movie: 'Oh, by the way, BAM!'"[7]

Bizarre behavior

The impact of the mass media on gang violence and gunplay has been discounted because, after all, the people involved in gangs have a predisposition toward violence. However, there are more peculiar and particular manifestations of the influence of the mass media that seem to point only to the media event itself as the source of the behavior in question.

For example, when the movie *The Program* was first released, several teenagers mimicked the stupid stunt pulled by the main characters in the movie by lying down in the middle of the road.

These copycat incidents resulted in two severe injuries and two deaths. Touchstone Pictures, a division of The Disney Company, quickly edited out the offensive scene.

On the other hand

On the positive side of the influence of the entertainment media equation: the epic television program *Jesus of Nazareth* introduced millions of people throughout the world to Jesus Christ; *A Man Called Peter*, about the preacher Peter Marshall, brought a flood of many young men into the pulpit; and *Chariots of Fire* brought many to Jesus and gave many more a sense of God's purpose in their life.

Child's play?

It is clear to any parent with a baby that children learn to a large degree by mimicking the behavior of the adults around them, including those on television and in movies.[8]

One of the most famous examples was the connection that a judge in Liverpool, England, made between the horror movie *Child's Play 3* and the murder of two-year-old James Bulger by two eleven-year-old boys, Robert Thompson and Jon Venables.[9] According to the judge, the horror movie *Child's Play 3* presents some horrifying parallels to the actual murder of little James Bulger, and the movie was viewed repeatedly by one of the killers just before the murder took place. The judge noted:

> The horror movie depicts a baby doll who comes to life and gets blue paint splashed in its face. There was blue paint on the dead child's face.

> The movie depicts a kidnapping. James was abducted by the two older boys before they killed him.

> The climax of the movie comes as two young boys murder the doll on a train, mutilating the doll's face. James was first mutilated and bludgeoned by the two older boys and then left on a railroad track to be run over.

This story was widely publicized around the world, but the link to *Child's Play 3* seldom made the news. Why were these facts overlooked or withheld by the mainstream media? Why not ask your local paper or TV news department? The answers could prove enlightening.

Beavis & Butt-Head

Television also influences young minds negatively. MTV's series *Beavis & Butt-Head*[10] was blamed for giving a five-year-old Austin Messner the idea to set a fire in his own home that killed his two-year-old sister, Jessica. In western Ohio, three young girls set another fire while imitating a trick from the show.[11] In Sydney, Australia, three teenage girls set fire to a apartment complex after viewing the animated program.[12]

The cartoon comedy *Beavis & Butt-Head* features two teenagers who comment on rock videos and spend time burning and destroying things. The show also advocates disobedience, disrespect for all adults (especially parents), and promotes such fun ideas as "fire is cool." The program is totally offensive in nature and content, with no redeeming value whatsoever.

In response to the uproar, one insider made the following cynical comments:

> I wouldn't be able to ignore the millions of dollars in sales . . . controversy sells.
>
> > Glenn Hendricks, vice president
> > of licensing for OSP Publishing,
> > producers of *Beavis & Butt-Head*
> > T-shirts, posters, and buttons.[13]

Slasher Movies and Stephen King novels

In 1993, thirteen-year-old Eric Smith lured four-year-old Derrick Robie into the woods, bludgeoned his head with rocks, and sodomized the body. According to press reports about the crime, Eric loved reading Stephen King novels and watching gruesome slasher movies—the more pornographic the better. Jurors found Eric Smith guilty of second-degree murder.

In Houston, Texas, Scott Edward May, a seventeen year old obsessed with slasher movies, the occult, and heavy-metal music, attacked a girl during their first date, stabbing her when she closed her eyes for a good-night kiss. They had just seen the movie *The Cutting Edge*. May told police he had urges to kill since childhood. "I love knives," May's statement reads. "I like to go to the movies a lot. A lot of people get stabbed in the movies. I really liked the *Texas Chainsaw Massacre*. A lot of people got stabbed in that."[14]

Natural born killers?

The Oliver Stone movie *Natural Born Killers* has produced a slew of copycat murders.

Nathan K. Martinez, an unhappy seventeen year old obsessed with the movie *Natural Born Killers*, murdered his stepmother and his half-sister in their suburban home fifteen miles southwest of Salt Lake City.

In Georgia, Jason Lewis, a fifteen year old, murdered his parents, firing multiple shotgun blasts into their heads. Letters found in his room indicated he worshipped Satan and, along with three friends, had formulated a plan to kill all their parents and to copy the cross-country swing of violence portrayed in *Natural Born Killers*.

Christopher Smith, an eighteen year old, shouted at television cameras, "I'm a natural born killer!" echoing the words of actor Woody Harrelson in the movie *Natural Born Killers* following his arrest for shooting to death an eighty-two year old man.

In Toombs County, Georgia, four people in their twenties were charged with abducting and killing a man, stealing his truck, and fleeing in it after watching the movie *Natural Born Killers* nineteen times.

One gruesome incident prompted novelist John Grisham to suggest that the survivors of these killing sprees should sue Stone.[15]

The incident that incensed Grisham occurred in March of 1995 when two teenagers saw *Natural Born Killers* in Oklahoma, then drove to Mississippi and killed Bill Savage in the same randomly violent way the movie's protagonists do. They then went to Louisiana and nearly killed a women in a convenience store (she is now a quadriplegic). One of the two said the movie led directly to their actions.

Grisham lived near Savage and wrote a passionate four-page letter about the murder to a literary magazine. He concluded his blistering attack on Stone's movie and on Hollywood's unwillingness to take responsibility for its product by suggesting:

> The last hope of imposing some sense on Hollywood will come through another great American tradition, the lawsuit. A case can be made that there exists a direct causal link between *Natural Born Killers* and the death of Bill Savage. . . . It will take only one large verdict against the likes of Oliver Stone, and then the party will be over.[16]

Hannibal the Cannibal

Over the years, there have been innumerable reports of grisly crimes that were inspired by and mimicked the fictional product of the entertainment media. It is important to take note of these stories to realize the scope of the problem and the powerful influence of movies, television programs, music, and the other mass media.

One of the most notorious movies spawning copycat murders is *The Silence of the Lambs*, a movie about a serial killer known as "Hannibal the Cannibal" who mutilates and eats his victims.

The same week that *The Silence of the Lambs* won the 1992 Academy Award for "Best Picture," a young man decapitated his handicapped mother and yelled, "I'm Hannibal the Cannibal!" as he was led away by police.[17]

In related case, Brian Allender told a psychiatrist he had a lifetime preoccupation with pornography and *The Silence of the Lambs* shortly before murdering and mutilating a Vancouver prostitute in

January of 1992.[18] Dr. Shabehram Lohrasbe interviewed Allender eight times following the murder and said he displayed no clinical signs of a major mental disorder or sexual deviancy. He concluded that Allender's conduct was caused by three factors: an unnatural relationship with his mother, a preoccupation with pornography and voyeurism, and viewing *The Silence of the Lambs* prior to picking up the prostitute.

The same effect on you and me

It is strange that our society has become so desensitized and confused that even prisoners are fed a mass media diet of movies like *The Silence of the Lambs*. As publisher of MOVIEGUIDE®, I received the following very incisive analysis of the effects of sex and violence on captive minds from an prisoner's perspective:[19]

> [I]n many (perhaps most) prisons, . . . the movies are selected by an inmate advisory council. . . . Would it surprise you to learn that the favored genres are those containing the most naked flesh engaging in fornication, the most horrific gore and the most gratuitous violence? . . .
>
> . . . It is my observation that most imprisoned men [lose themselves] in mindless television, films, printed pornography, hard rock music, etc. . . .
>
> I've observed groups of convicts watching violent films. . . . [A] gruesome bloodbath may bring forth much response—everything from increased attention to involuntary facial expression (clenched teeth, twitches) and quite often inappropriate responses (smiles, laughter, cheers, etc.). These inappropriate responses ultimately translate to joy at the suffering of others. It doesn't matter in the least whether good guys or bad guys get killed, as long as somebody gets killed.
>
> . . . I spoke with an older repeat offender . . . [who said], "Sometimes I watch a video and get real angry. Takes me

an hour or so afterward to stop being p****d off. I don't like that. I've tried very hard for a long time to get over my anger, but these videos bring it out." . . .

Drastic changes in personality can happen in the space of a ninety-minute film. After a violent martial arts movie some inmates think they are tougher than any ten men. And, woe betide the person who gives them any excuse to prove it.

. . . Men are highly aroused sexually through what they see. . . . Incarcerated men are already in a sexually frustrating situation, and arousal of sexual thoughts and feelings only aggravates the problem. . . .

Masturbation is . . . unsatisfying. This leaves the door open to experiment in deviant sexual behaviors. . . . Others let their sexual frustration turn to anger . . . even to the point of male rape. . . . Still others fall into the abyss of homosexuality and transvestitism, literally giving themselves over to a depraved mind for the degradation of their bodies.

. . . there is not a man in here . . . who can watch sex on the screen without being affected by it in a manner that is emotionally and spiritually detrimental.

. . . Allow me to be blunt: IT IS AN ABSURDITY TO BELIEVE THAT THE EFFECT OF SEX AND VIOLENCE IN MOVIES IS ANY DIFFERENT UPON YOU AND YOUR CHILDREN THAN IT IS UPON ME AND MY FELLOW INMATES. A short while ago many of us stood in the same ticket lines as you. We've sat in the same movie theaters, watching the same movies. We've rented videos from the same video stores as you. The world system touches every life, and every person is led into sin in the same ways, through the lust of the eyes, lust of the flesh, and the sinful pride of life (1 John 2:15-16).

How many minds out there are being programmed right now to do the things that could result in their joining us in prison? How many people are being desensitized, emotionally manipulated to follow harmful role models and conditioned to accept aberrant sexual behavior as normal? How many hearts are being turned to stone?

Another prisoner wrote that his institution was showing prisoners about to be released into society the violent, anti-Christian movie *Cape Fear* as part of a rehabilitation program. This ultraviolent movie is about a released prisoner who takes gruesome revenge on the lawyer who helped to convict him. Would you want your local prison to show this horrific movie to convicts as part of their socialization before they go out and live in your neighborhood?

After supplying this prisoner with MOVIEGUIDE® and significant research and information, he was able to encourage the legislature of the state where his prison was located to ban some offensive movies from correctional facilities.

Why do critics love these repellent movies?

In response to the critical acclaim movies like *Natural Born Killers* and *The Silence of the Lambs* have received, the March 17, 1991, Sunday *Los Angeles Times* Calendar section asked, "Why Do Critics Love These Repellent Movies?" Stephen Farber responded that moviegoers looking for guidance are becoming alienated by the reviewers' penchant for grotesque violence. He said it has become chic to praise a movie for being nihilistic, macabre, unsentimental. He concludes that "in contemporary . . . criticism, there's no perspective, no sense of what is truly valuable, that critical discourse has sunk to a new low."[20]

Lethal weapons

With TV sets turned on in the inner city for eleven hours a day and multiplying satellite, cable, and broadcast channels, television "has become the closest and most constant companion for American children," according to Mortimer B. Zuckerman writing in *U.S. News & World Report.* In fact, Zuckerman continues:

> It has become the nation's mom and pop, storyteller, baby sitter, preacher, and teacher. Our children watch an astonishing 5,000 hours by the first grade and 19,000 hours by the end of high school—more time than they spend in class. The question more and more concerning parents, psychologists and public officials is this: What is all this viewing doing to them?[21]

A 1992 report from the American Psychological Association states, "Television can cause aggressive behavior and can cultivate values favoring the use of aggression."[22]

According to Dr. Victor Strasburger, chief of The American Academy of Pediatrics' section on adolescents, "We are basically saying the controversy is over. There is clearly a relationship between media violence and violence in society."[23]

A report on four decades of entertainment TV from the media research team of Robert Lichter, Linda Lichter, Stanley Rothman, and Daniel Amundson found about fifty crimes, including a dozen murders, in every hour of prime time television. This indicates that our children may see from 800,000 to 1.5 million acts of violence and witness 192,000 to 360,000 murders on television by the time they are seventeen years old.[24]

This contrasts radically with the generations of men and women who grew up *without* this flood of violent images from the entertainment media. Lichter and his fellow authors wrote, "Since 1955 TV characters have been murdered at a rate 1,000 times higher than real-world victims."[25] Michael Medved said if the same murder rate was applied to the general population, everyone in the United States would be killed in just 50 days.[26]

Surveys show that 60% of the children in our society watch TV without any supervision and 40% have a TV set in their room. However, television is just a part of their entertainment diet.

Radio, CDs, videos, video games, computer games, magazines, comics, the Internet, and much more constitute the rich media diet of most American children.

If you are over forty, you probably watch only six movies a year in theaters, most of which are family films. Teenagers average watching fifty, 80% of which are R-rated or PG-13. They watch another fifty movies a year on video.[27]

Cigarette companies are no longer allowed to advertise on television because of the threat to human life and health that such advertisements pose. Yet, television and movies advertise sex and violence day after day to the detriment of thousands of people who are maimed, raped, or robbed by the deluded Ted Bundys of this world.

Jungle fever

In Sandusky, Ohio, in 1992 a thirteen-year-old boy raped his eight-year-old female cousin after watching *Jungle Fever*, an R-rated tale of explicit fornication. The children told police they watched the movie prior to the incident.[28]

Such incidents involving youngsters are no longer unusual. Juvenile sex offenses increased 380% within the last five years in the county where the incident occurred. Between 60% to 80% of all juvenile sex offenders are between twelve and sixteen years old. Research shows that for every sex offense a juvenile commits, he or she is likely to commit fifty-five sex offenses as an adult if not stopped.[29]

Fatal attraction

In his book *The Home Invaders*, the Rev. Donald E. Wildmon provides other pertinent examples:

> In St. Petersburg, Florida, a seven-year-old boy testified that he and his nine-year-old brother were imitating actions they had seen in their mother's pornographic magazines when they assaulted an eight-month-old girl who

died in the attack. The infant was found on the floor in the bedroom where the two young boys were sleeping.[30]

For two years, starting at the age of four, a child watched cableporn in his own living room before he was caught. He got up late at night and turned on the cable without sound so he would not be heard. Wanting to imitate what he saw, he started undressing his sister who was two years younger than he and still in diapers. He would pull her diapers off, take his clothes off and lie on top of her. Later he started playing with her body parts. As she grew older, she watched the movies and played with him. The children were six and four when they coaxed a neighborhood boy into their bedroom and asked him to expose himself and participate in a touch and feel game. The boy was scared and fled but returned later in the day to hit his former friend with a baseball bat. When confronted, the child who had watched the cable movies said, "Big people do it. I just wanted to be big."[31]

It should be self-evident that it is very traumatic for young children to be introduced to sexual activity through explicit magazines, movies, and videos, especially X-rated videos. The consequence of this easy access to explicit sexual material may be reflected in the fact that from 1950 to 1979 serious sexual crimes committed by children increased by 11,000.[32]

Prosecutors and investigators throughout the United States have confirmed that pornography is the link and catalyst in the chain of child sexual abuse.[33] One judge who prosecuted close to 1,000 child sexual abuse cases found that only four did not involve some type of pornography. He concluded that pornography fueled and assisted the seduction process that led to molestation.[34]

Many child molesters have confirmed that "without pornography, the molestation would not have occurred or been possible to accomplish."[35] Several studies have shown that there is a significant link between juvenile prostitution and child pornography. An extensive Canadian study revealed that 60% of both male and female juvenile prostitutes had participated in the making of pornography.[36] An American study found that 75% of male teenage prostitutes had participated in pornography.[37]

When Dr. James Dobson served on The Attorney General's Commission on Pornography, he described the state of pornography at that time as follows:

> X-rated movies and magazines today feature oral, anal, and genital sex between women, monkeys and donkeys, . . . and dozens of other animals. In a single sex shop in New York City there are forty-six films and videos available which featured bestiality of every type. Other offerings focused on so-called "bathroom sports" including urination, defecation, mutilation of every type. . . .
>
> Simulated child pornography depicts females who . . . appear to be young [young teenagers]. . . . Their "fathers" are often pictured with them in consummate, incestuous settings.
>
> The magazines in sex shops are organized on shelves according to topics, such as Gay Violence, Vomiting, Rape, Enemas, [Bondage and Domination (B and D) Torture], and topics that I cannot describe even in a frank discussion of this nature.[38]

Pretty women

Callused members of the legal community contend that prostitution is a victimless crime. The reason some consider this degradation of human beings as victimless is because Hollywood continually shows us prostitutes who are beautiful, intelligent, strong, and often rescued by some knight in shining armor. The quickest way for a beautiful actress in Hollywood to be considered for an Academy Award is to play a prostitute. Of course, the prostitute whom this star will play will have nothing in common with the wasted, abused, disease-ridden hookers you find on the streets of the nation's major cities.

I will never forget the sad face of the tearful father who told me about his thirteen-year-old daughter, who saw the film *Pretty Woman* with a girlfriend. The movie, about a prostitute who meets her wealthy Prince Charming and marries him, glamorizes prostitution. The thirteen year old and her friend got so emotionally and psychologically aroused that they decided to try it.

The movie, which seduced her into this lifestyle, did not prepare her for the psychological and physical diseases that followed. She didn't find a man who wanted to marry her, but many who wanted to degrade and hurt her.

There were, obviously, other factors involved in this young girl's decision. She was extremely bright (bright children are more susceptible), sensitive, and physically advanced. She felt as if she didn't fit with her classmates at school. She was already dating and had seen several erotic movies with her friend, who wasn't from a Christian home.

Like most children, she was vulnerable to peer pressure, teenage anxieties, and media pressure. *Pretty Woman* was simply the stimulant that persuaded her to pursue a jaded dream of finding Prince Charming in the sordid world of prostitution.

Her parents did not find her for several weeks. Like many parents, they were unaware of movies she was watching with her friend.

Movies like *Pretty Woman* convey the message that prostitutes lead fun-filled, exciting lives and that men give them expensive clothes and gifts. Young people who have not been taught discernment can easily conclude that being a prostitute is a desirable lifestyle.

Voyeurs

That young actors are particularly vulnerable was brought home to me when I read an article in the *New York Times* commending Barbra Streisand for her direction of the movie *Prince of*

Tides. This article noted how difficult it was to film the scene where the escaped convict rapes the young boy.

Evidently, the boy didn't have the right expression so Streisand roughed him up, applying physical pain to make him appear to be experiencing the pain of sodomy. The praise of the *New York Times* for Streisand's technique is a heinous example of political correctness and insensitivity, especially in light of that newspaper's vociferous editorials against parents who abuse their children.

My wife knows the mother of the young actor in the movie. The mother said the incident really happened as described and that she was horrified and upset and didn't know what to do about it.

Just say no?

While the Centers for Disease Control (CDC) and other authorities tell teenagers "just say no to sex, delay the initiation of sex, be monogamous," Dr. Sevgi Aral says teenagers either do not hear the message or simply do not act on it. Statistics from the CDC show that more than half the young women between the ages of fifteen and nineteen years of age have had premarital sex.

The question that must be asked is: Why aren't teens heeding the warnings of the CDC and other authorities? The answer is simple. Teenagers are responding to the message coming across in movies and TV shows. "Sexuality is all-important, and it's very glamorous," said Aral.[39]

With all the pressure that the federal government has put on television executives to clean up the violence on TV, sex has replaced violence as television's number-one obsession. A study of prime time television conducted by *U.S. News & World Report* found that out of fifty-eight programs monitored, almost half contained sexual acts or references to sex. The magazine reported that a sexual act or reference occurred every four minutes on average in prime time programs.[40]

Perverse sex and violence are two of television's most effective lures for capturing an audience. Traditionally, conservatives have complained about excessive or perverse sex on television, while liberals have complained about violence. Now both camps have joined in the battle to clean up both excessive sex and violence, though perverse sex is still a matter of debate.

Using the *U.S. News & World Report* findings, the average child who watches broadcast television sees 240,000 to 480,000 sexual acts or references to sex, including everything from touching to kissing to intercourse,[41] by the time he or she is seventeen. Since MTV averages 1,500 sex acts per hour,[42] if we add some MTV and cable television to their mass media diet, children may see millions of sexual acts or references to sex by the time they are seventeen. This does not include the sexual acts or references to sex they will see or hear in the other entertainment media.

Carnal knowledge

Television is an "important sex educator" that teaches children to "go for it," according to the National Institute for Mental Health.[43] On TV, "it's absolutely taken for granted that you date somebody a couple of times and sleep with them," said Michael Josephson, president of the Josephson Institute of Ethics.[44] Contrary to real life, premarital fornication on TV outnumbers sex within marriage by eight to one, according to the Media Research Center.[45]

What boggles the mind is that neither movie nor television characters are ever shown to reap the consequences of their actions. The heroine rarely gets pregnant. If she does, she conveniently obtains an abortion. Nor do the involved parties come down with genital warts, herpes, gonorrhea, syphilis, or AIDS.

The mass media must reverse its trend of portraying immoral sex as glamorous and desirable when, in fact, promiscuous sexual activity can be psychologically and physically ruinous and can even lead to death. It is time to promote a ruthless new honesty in the media with their all-powerful influence on our culture, especially on our young.

The Roman Colosseum

David Puttnam, former president of Columbia Pictures and the producer of *Chariots of Fire*, in an interview with Bill Moyers on PBS, explained that once people are exposed to the spectacle of blood and sex, they want more and more as they become hardened to the titillation of the last violent or sexual act they see. Just as a drug addict who becomes less and less responsive to a drug keeps looking for the initial "ideal" rush, so those who are addicted to the sex and violence in films seek increasing doses of sex and violence to appease their lust. Since the days of the bloody sports in the Roman Colosseum people have demanded increasing decadence with each voyeuristic exposure to the violation of moral taboos.

What compounds the horror of this excess of violence is the grotesque gags that go hand in hand with bloody gore. This blend of humor and violence is lethal in undermining the moral restraints inhibiting a susceptible individual from getting his way through violence. In fact, this noxious blend will no doubt serve to inflame the violent tendencies in susceptible youth.

Guns and roses

Researchers say MTV, the marriage between television and music, is especially destructive. The book *Dancing in the Dark* calls MTV "one of the most powerful forms of contemporary propaganda."[46]

Child psychologist Dr. David Elkind writes in *The Hurried Child*, "Music can influence young people as much as any visual media."[47] Dr. Joseph Steussey, professor of music history at the University of Texas, told the U.S. Senate Commerce Committee, "Music affects behavior. . . . It affects our moods, our attitudes, our emotions, and our behavior."[48]

The average teenager listens to rock music four to six hours each day.[49] The Parents Music Resource Center reports that teenagers listen to an estimated 10,500 hours of rock music between the seventh and twelfth grades.[50]

Like movies and television programs, the recent history of popular music is not without its many anecdotal examples of copycat crimes, such as:

John McCullum's parents brought a suit against Ozzy Osborne after their son committed suicide while listening to his song "Suicide Solution."[51]

A devil-worshipping cult called The Knights of the Black Circle gathered at a park in North Point, New York, and performed rituals that killed Gary Lauwers, seventeen, stabbing him while forcing him to say "I love Satan." They later gouged out his eyes. They left the names of their favorite rock stars, Black Sabbath and Ozzy Osborne, who sings of satanic possession and once bit off a dove's head during a performance.[52]

Two fifteen-year-old girls left suicide notes that quoted lyrics from Pink Floyd's 1979 album, *The Wall*. They wrote, "Good-bye cruel world, I'm leaving you now."[53]

In their book *Don't Touch That Dial: The Impact of Media on Children and the Family*, Barbara Hattemer and Robert Showers enumerate the influence of heavy metal music and MTV:

Aggressive rebellion

Abuse of drugs and alcohol

Graphic violence and suicide

Fascination with the occult

Sexuality that is graphic and explicit[54]

Pulp fiction and revolting rhymes

In an interview in *Time* magazine, fifteen-year-old Christopher Zahedi spoke for many teenagers when he expressed his opinion on the movie *Pulp Fiction*: "I liked the part in *Pulp Fiction* where the guy points a gun and says a prayer from the Bible and then kills everybody. You hear the gun go *brrrr*. It's cool."[55]

Given the impact of violence and erotica on our youth, it is extremely regrettable that children are seeking and gaining access to more and more porno-violence, which they can easily find in video stores, theaters, and even on their computers. Video rentals and sales are almost three times bigger than the theatrical box office in dollars, with video and computer games almost 50% more than the theatrical box office.[56]

The Bravo cable service has aired an animated special called *Revolting Rhymes* aimed at six to twelve year olds. The animated program lived up to its title by depicting the characters of classic fairy tales as unlikable, cruel weirdos. Cinderella's Prince Charming is actually a spoiled brat who likes to chop off people's heads. Little Red Riding Hood skins the Big Bad Wolf and wears him as a coat. Other stories that get gory revisions are *Goldilocks and the Three Bears*, *The Three Little Pigs*, and *Snow White*.

Eclipse Enterprises of Forestville, California, offers several lines of children's trading cards that range from the cynical to the repulsive. "Coup d'Etat: The Assassination of John F. Kennedy" features Lee Harvey Oswald, Marilyn Monroe, and others allegedly involved in JFK's life and death. "Savings and Loan Scandal" features Michael Milken and the Keating Five. "Bush League" is an offshoot of the successful Iran-Contra scandal series. By far, the most popular and repugnant of the sets is the "True Crime" set that features the likes of Jeffrey Dahmer, Ted Bundy, Al Capone, David Berkowitz, and the Zodiac Killer.

Eclipse defends the cards as "educational" and claims the "True Crime" series covers both organized crime and sociopathic crime in one informative 110[57] The cards have been banned in Canada, but in the U.S. only Nassau County, New York, has banned sale of the cards to minors.

Faces of death

A teenage cult following is developing for the *Faces of Death* series on videotape. These non-rated documentary-style films contain vicious, graphic violence depicting numerous deaths by various grotesque means and feature close-up shots of gory decapitations, shootings, and animal attacks.

In addition, hard-core pornography and violence is easily accessible to children over computer services such as the Internet and computer bulletin boards.

Computer and video games are of concern because they not only display extreme sex and violence, but also have the child who is playing the game participate in the violence. Thus, the children who play these games are learning how to commit violent acts. Sorcery, magic, and Satanism are often part of these games, teaching children occult and demonic techniques as well as the methods of murder and rape.

Cyber-smut

Lisa Palac, editor of *Future Sex* magazine and a self-proclaimed "sex-positive feminist," claims that "computer science is changing the way we think about sex." Cybersex is "just you alone with your fantasies, some space-age gadgetry and the discretionary income to run up very large electrical bills." The cover of one issue proclaims; "Strap in, tweak out, turn on."[58]

Computer technology is not "changing the way we think about sex." It is simply providing a new and tragic medium for lonely people with money to become enslaved in perversion.

Beyond the fringe

Regrettably, there is also far too much anti-Christian bigotry in the mass media. This anti-Christian bigotry is hypocritical in a nation where the media, the courts, educators, social scientists, and our official minorities keep preaching that we need to be more tolerant and more sensitive to the effects of odious phrases and names—from stereotyped descriptions to demeaning racial references, sects, and non-Christian religions. This anti-Christian bigotry is rampant in newspaper editorials and articles calling Christians opposed to immorality, perversion, and killing babies right-wing fanatics.

This name calling is an immature approach to disagreeing with Christians over values. Regrettably, it has spread from the media to the government and the schools.

In Nazi Germany, the pillory of one religious group led to persecution. In America, it may lead to a backlash.

The reel world

Many aspects of Hollywood's virtual reality skewer our children's attitudes and prompt them to imitate self-destructive or uncivil behavior. Confusing the *reel* world with the *real* world can create fears and anxieties that are abnormal.

The entertainment media, including entertainment television and movies, do not portray reality or real life but a particular and intentionally emotive perspective on reality. Even reality programs and television news programs concentrate on the exploitable and the emotive.

Hollywood often becomes boringly repetitious, recycling the same plots, ideas, and characters to the point of nausea. In an analytical examination of the messages of the *reel* world, Dr. Robert Kubey pinpointed the primary messages of the media:

Materialism.

For everything there is a quick fix.

Young is better.

Open and unfilled time is not desirable; in fact it cannot be tolerated.

Violence is acceptable.

Religion is unacceptable.

Sex is only good outside of marriage.[59]

Is this the way we want our children to view the world? Is this the way we want the rest of the world to view us? These messages are destructive of the civilization. Like cancer, they eat away at the fabric of our civilization.

No place to hide

We cannot hide from the mass media. The mass media form an integral part of the fabric of contemporary society. They reflect and shape our culture and our vision. The larger-than-life images of movies, the emotive beat of pop music, the seductive reality of television, the virtual reality of the Internet call us to appreciate our talents and take a stand for biblical principles or seduce us into perversion and senseless violence.[60]

Movies and television have more influence on our society than all the preachers and ministries combined. Every time excessive sex or violence is watched by someone in the community it has an effect on the community, even if you were not watching. According to studies by the Annenberg School of Communications, substantiated by the National Institute of Mental Health, television programs and films:

> Directly affect a small percentage of the viewers who are susceptible to the message of the movie and will emulate that message in their own lives by copying the sexual, violent, or immoral act modeled in the movie;

> adversely affect a larger proportion of the audience, causing them to fear the act in question; and

> have no apparent affect on the largest portion of the audience, although there may be long-term consequences of watching antisocial material.[61]

Excessive sex and violence in music, television, and film affects the community by affecting members of the community who go out and copy the immoral acts they hear and witness and by implanting fear in the community.

The point of this litany of problems with respect to different media and arts is simply to point out that there is no place to hide. The media and the arts are pervasive in our society. Americans are in the midst of entertaining themselves to death. Either denial or license will only allow the problems to continue to grow out of control.

Endnotes

1. C. Wright Mills, *White Collar*, (New York: Oxford University Press, 1956) ch. 15, sct. 3.
2. *Reader's Digest* (August 1994): 29.
3. "Trivia for TV Addicts: 29 Amazing Facts." For the free twenty-page booklet *TV Tips for Parents* on how to make television a tool for learning, created by the Corporation for Public Broadcasting, send a self-addressed, business-sized envelope with 39 cents postage to the Corporation for Public Broadcasting, Dept. P, P.O. Box 33039, Washington, DC 20033.
4. According to a 1994 UCLA Center for Communication Policy/*U.S. News & World Report* survey mailed to 6,300 decision-makers in the entertainment industry, receiving a 13.76% response.
5. Paul Johnson, *Modern Times: The World from the Twenties to the Nineties.* Revised edition (New York: Harper Perennial, 1992), 130.
6. Paul Rempel, *Hitler's Children: The Hitler Youth and the SS* (Chapel Hill and London: The University of North Carolina Press, 1989), 76.
7. Associated Press, (July 7, 1992).
8. Several studies have been done in this regard, which we will cite in Chapter 4.
9. *New York Guardian*, (December 1993).
10. Susan Spillman, "Film Scene to Be Cut after Fatal Imitation," *USA Today*, Final edition, (October 20, 1993): NEWS 01A.
11. Jim DeBross, "Did Show Cost Girl's Life?: Fatal Fire Is Blamed on *Beavis & Butt-Head*," *Dayton Daily News*, City edition, (October 31, 1993): NEWS 1A.
12. *Ibid.* and Drew Jubera, "Viewer Caution Advised TV Industry Warned to Clean up Violence in Programming or Face a Crackdown Through Legislation," *Atlanta Journal*, (October 21, 1993).
13. *The Hollywood Reporter*, (October 25, 1993).
14. MOVIEGUIDE® VII:10: 920522
15. John Grisham, "Unnatural Killers," MOVIEGUIDE® XI:18: 960826.
16. *Ibid.*
17. Associated Press, (March 26, 1993).
18. *Vancouver Sun*, (September 29, 1993).

19. Mark Yerkes, "The Effects of Sex and Violence on Captive Minds: An Insider's Perspective," MOVIEGUIDE® VII:21: 921102.

20. Stephen Farber, "Why Do Critics Love These Repellent Movies?" *Los Angeles Times*, (March 17, 1991): Calendar section

21. Mortimer B. Zuckerman, *U.S. News & World Report.*

22. American Psychological Association, 1992 Report: "Big World, Small Screen: the role of television in American society" (Lincoln: University of Nebraska Press, 1992) quoted by Chicago Associated Press, (June 9-11, 1995).

23. *Ibid.*

24. Jim Impoco, "TV's Frisky Family Values," *U.S. News & World Report*, (April 15, 1996): 58-62.

25. *Ibid.*

26. Michael Medved, "Hollywood's Three Big Lies," MOVIEGUIDE® XI:01 (January A): 960101, reprinted from *Reader's Digest*, October, 1995.

27. Teenage Research Institute, Wheaton, IL, as reported in MOVIEGUIDE® IX:3&4: 940207

28. *Sandusky Register*, (April 8, 1992).

29. *Ibid.*

30. Donald E. Wildmon, *The Home Invaders* (Wheaton, IL: SP Publications, Inc., 1985) 85.

31. B. Hattemer & R. Showers, *Don't Touch That Dial: The Impact of Media on Children & the Family* (Huntington House Publishers: 1993), 74

32. John Whitehead, *Stealing of America* (1983), 68.

33. William Marshal, *Report on the Use of Pornography by Sexual Offenders*, Report to the Federal Department of Justice, Ottawa Canada, 1983.

34. Hattemer & Showers, *Don't Touch That Dial*, 66.

35. *Ibid.*

36. Badgley Report, p. 1198, quoted in Hattemer & Showers, *Don't Touch That Dial,* 71.

37. Scanlon and Price, "Youth Prostitution in Child Sex Rings," 139, quoted in Hattemer & Showers, *Don't Touch That Dial*, 71.

38. *The Attorney General's Commission on Pornography, Final Report,* July 1986, (Washington DC: US Department of Justice), 73-76; Minnery, *Pornography: A Human Tragedy* (1986), 34-35; Dietz & Sears, "Pornography and Obscenity Sold in Adult Bookstores," *Journal of Law Reform* (1988), 21, quoted in Hattemer & Showers *Don't Touch That Dial*, 44.

39. MOVIEGUIDE® VI:24: 911206 & VI:23: 911122. See also "Research Issues in Human Behavior and Sexually Transmitted Diseases in the AIDS Era," editors: Judith N. Wasserheit, Sevgi O. Aral, and King K. Holmes, (American Society for Microbiology Press, 1991).

40. Impoco, Jim, "TV's Frisky Family Values," *U.S. News & World Report*, (April 15, 1996): 58-62, quoting, in part, a study by the media research team of Robert Lichter, Linda Lichter, Stanley Rothman, and Daniel Amundson. The *U.S. News* poll of the general public was of 1,000 American adults conducted by Celinda Lake of Lake Research and Ed Goeas of the Tarrance Group, March 16-18, 1996. The margin of error for the study was plus or minus 3.1. The poll of the Hollywood leaders was a mailed survey that went to 6,059 persons and for which there were 570 responses. Among those who helped at the UCLA Center for Communication Policy on the Hollywood poll are Jeffrey Cole, Michael Suman, Phoebe Schramm, Marde Gregory, James Reynolds, Scott David, and Jeff Shore.

Percentages listed in each of the surveys may not add up to 100 because some respondents answered "Don't Know."

41. *NYPD Blue* was famous for its premier episode on September 23, 1993, containing a bedroom scene with partially covered intercourse and then full nudity after the act.

42. *U.S. News & World Report*, supra.

43. *Ibid.*

44. *Ibid.*

45. *Ibid.*

46. Robert L Maginnis, "Parents Want Help Fighting the Pop Culture's Adverse Influence," MOVIEGUIDE® XI:01: 960101, quoting from Schultze, Quentin J., *Dancing in the Dark: Youth, Popular Culture, and the Electronic Media* (Grand Rapids, Mich.: W.B. Eerdmans Pub. Co., 1991).

47. Maginnis, "Parents Want Help Fighting the Pop Culture's Adverse Influence," quoting from Elkind, David, *The Hurried Child: Growing Up Too Fast Too Soon* (Reading, Mass.: Addison-Wesley, 1988).

48. Maginnis, "Parents Want Help Fighting the Pop Culture's Adverse Influence."

49. *Ibid.*

50. *Ibid.*

51. Hayton, "The Effects of Indecent Broadcast Programming on Children," (Paper delivered to the National Family Foundation Media Workshop, Pittsburgh, PA, November, 1990), quoted in Hattemer & Showers, *Don't Touch That Dial*, 145.

52. The *Washington Post* (July 9, 1984) A1, 14, quoted in Hattemer & Showers, *Don't Touch That Dial*, 145.

53. Schlafly, Phyllis, "Rock Music and Teenage Suicide," *Union Leader* (Manchester, NH, July 18, 1985), quoted in Hattemer & Showers, *Don't Touch That Dial*, 145.

54. Hattemer & Showers, *Don't Touch That Dial*, p. 45

55. Lacayo, Richard, "Violent Reaction: Violence and Sex in Popular Music, Television and Films," *Time* 145:24 (June 12, 1995): 24

56. Theatrical box office is approximately $5.7 billion per year, while video rentals and sales are approximately $15.8 billion per year, and video and computer games are about $9 billion per year.

57. *Insight Magazine*, (July 13, 1992).

58. *San Francisco Chronicle* (November 29, 1992).

59. Kubey, Robert, "Media Use and Its Implications for the Quality of Family Life" (Paper delivered at the NFF Media Workshop. November, 1990).

60. John Hinckley claimed that *Taxi Driver* caused him to shoot President Ronald Reagan.

61. Annenberg School of Communications.

IN THE LINE OF FIRE

Do not be misled: Bad company corrupts good character.

1 Corinthians 15:33 (NIV)

You know that everything we're exposed to influences us. . . . Those [violent] films influence us, and the TV programs we see influence us. The weaker your family is, the more they influence you. . . . The problems with families in our cities are catastrophic—but when you put violent programs [before] people who haven't had a lot of love in their lives, who are angry anyway, it's like pouring gasoline on the fire.

Ted Turner[1]

People sometimes say that the way things happen in the movies is unreal, but actually it's the way things happen to you in life that's unreal. The movies make emotions look so strong and real, whereas when things really do happen to you, it's like watching television—you don't feel anything."

Andy Warhol[2]

Fact: 97% of all American households own at least one television set—which is more than those possessing indoor plumbing or refrigerators.

M ost parents intuitively know what the scientific and educational communities have confirmed over the past seventy-five years: the messages of popular culture are very persuasive in affecting behavior. Parents also realize children are designed to mimic adults, that they learn by copying adults, and that the most exciting and the most frequent adult behavior they see and hear is displayed in the entertainment media.

So that you can make informed media decisions and help others to do the same, let us look at some of the facts and research in this important area.

Irrefutable

There have been over 3,000 psychiatric, psychological, sociological, pediatric, and medical studies researching the effects of the mass media on behavior, including laboratory experiments, field experiments, correlational studies, and longitudinal studies.[3] So much research has been conducted in this area that Senator Paul Simon has stated that the influence of the mass media on violent behavior is now irrefutable.

Most people are unaware of this research because we get so much of our information from television, and television and other media executives have a self-interest in not emphasizing their influence on human behavior, except to exploit it through commercials.

Scientific research has focused both on the quality and quantity of violence on television. Most research has focused on the quantitative content analyses, especially whether the amount of violence on television was increasing or decreasing. Some of the early research that counted acts of violence did not examine the context of television violence. Qualitative analysis required exact definitions of violence to determine whether the act was counted or not. It was necessary to decide if verbal violence should be counted or whether comic violence such as cartoons would be registered.

Consider a cartoon in which a character is hit by a hammer, the character shakes his head, and continues on his way. Many researchers consider this "happy violence" the worst type of entertainment violence because it is unrealistic. Such cartoon violence might encourage children to imitate it because it shows no consequences. Others think children understand that cartoons are make-believe. Scholars usually have included cartoon violence in their research.

Many movies aimed at children have contained excessive violence. The partly animated *Who Framed Roger Rabbit?*, has fifty-two acts of violence. The children's fantasy movie *Ninja Turtles* contains 194 acts of violence, many committed by the heroes, including kicking, concussion-dealing blows, and characters delighting in inflicting violence.

The problem of what kind of violence to include and exclude in a study also pertains to slapstick humor and violent sports such as football, which may make violence an acceptable or even desirable part of American life.

It is helpful to look at violence within the framework of the context in which the violence occurs. Looking at the context focuses the research on distinguishing between violence that raises issues of concern and that which does not. It is also helpful to use a broad definition of violence, such as violence is anything that involves physical harm of any sort, intentional or unintentional, self-inflicted or inflicted by someone or something else. Verbal violence is of secondary importance.

If violence was removed from all movies, television programs and other mass media there would never be a documentary series such as *The Civil War* or important movies such as *Schindler's List*. Portrayals of violence are necessary to tell stories that send anti-violence messages. The issue is not the mere presence of violence and other offensive elements, but the nature of these elements and the context in which they occur. Context is an important key to the determination of whether or not the use of certain otherwise questionable elements is appropriate.

Mass media violence is that violence portrayed by any of the methods of mass communication, including television, movies, video games, toys that are mass produced, comic books, the Internet, CDs, CD-ROMs, DVDs, and computers. Most of the research has to do with television, movies, and pornographic materials.

A broad definition might yield a high violence count on a given television program or in a given medium. This is not important since the focus is on whether the violence raises concerns within the context of the show. For example, it is possible that a situation comedy might yield several scenes of violence, but the context in which it occurs might lead to the conclusion that none of these scenes is inappropriate.

All violence is not created equal. It is important to distinguish between uses of violence that raise concern and those acts which, because of their nature and the context in which they occur, do not.

It is important to examine the full range of portrayals of violence in the media, including the type of violence your child has been exposed to if your family is at all typical of families in general.

Elementary, my dear Watson

Research into this area can be divided into deductive reasoning from prior principles and inductive reasoning from a set of specific observations. Using deductive reasoning, researchers posit the basic principles of human learning and then see if any of them predict a causal relationship. Using inductive reasoning, researchers study the real-life behavior of a person after that person has been exposed to a measurable degree of excessive violence, pornography, or other media influence.

There are several principles of learning from which experts deduce the influence of entertainment.

One is the principle of modeling. Research shows that children imitate, even from the moment of birth. Children follow the examples that are set for them, not only in real life, but also in literature. Parables are examples of teaching tales people have used to help children learn how to live. Research shows that the entertainment media provide "scripts" for a child's future behavior.

Studies have looked at the real-life behavior of children and have counted their episodes of imitation of the violent or nonviolent behavior. In general, these laboratory studies demonstrate that when you present to children a filmed model of someone's doing something, children are more likely to do that something after having seen the film. Experiments have shown that withdrawn children can even learn to socialize better if they are shown a video of a child gradually starting to make friends.

A second basic principle of learning is that the more one practices a behavior, the more ingrained it becomes. Even practice in imagination, or fantasy rehearsal, is an effective way of ingraining a pattern. For young children, dramatic play is the prototypical fantasy rehearsal method.

The third is the principle of reinforcement, which holds that behavior that gets rewarded, gets repeated. Vicarious reinforcement also works. Characters in action and adventure movies are rewarded for their proficiency in violence. Often the reward for a male is the admiration of a sexy woman.

The power of modeling, practice, and reinforcement in human learning predict that media violence increases the likelihood of real-life violence.[4]

The California Medical Association study found that 22% of all crimes committed by juveniles is directly copied after what is seen on television programs right down to the minute gory details.[5] A study published in the *Journal of the American Medical Association* shows one-third of the young male prisoners convicted of violent crimes say they were consciously imitating techniques they learned from television.[6]

Special effects

Research into the influence of violence in the mass media on behavior has focused on several effects:

aggression that results in increased violence toward others;

a victim effect that manifests itself in increased fearfulness;

desensitization that results in increased callousness; and

self-socialization demonstrated by willfully exposing oneself to further risk.[7]

Some of the research in this area has been conducted by Ron Slaby, Ph.D., a senior scientist at the Education Development Center in Newton, Massachusetts, who has studied the media's effect on children for twenty-five years. He documented these four previously mentioned effects on children as a result of viewing TV and film violence:

The "aggressor effect" is often demonstrated by boys who identify with violent male heroes and therefore are more likely to behave aggressively. The "victim effect" is usually evident in girls who identify with females they see being victimized and are accordingly more fearful, mistrustful and self-protective. The "bystander effect" produces an increased callousness, behavioral apathy, and emotional desensitization toward violence. Finally, the "appetite effect," exhibited by some children who've viewed a great deal of glorified violence, is the heightened desire to view more violence and engage in violence-related activities, such as joining a gang or carrying a weapon.[8]

One of the most important "natural experiment" studies in this area was conducted by Brandon Centerwall, M.D., of the University of Washington. He found that there was a doubling of the murder rate some ten to fifteen years after television was introduced into several countries. The time lag occurred because children are most influenced by television violence during early life, but most prone to commit murder in adolescence and young adulthood. The conclusion of Centerwall's research is that of the approximately 20,000 murders that take place in the U.S. each year, some 10,000 of them would not occur without the influence of television!

A study of a town in Canada that had had no television because of being in a "geographical blind spot," nicknamed Notel, found that aggression increased dramatically in the children in the town after they received television for the first time. Also, the reading ability of the children decreased because the children were spending hours watching television instead of reading, having a conversation, or doing something that would increase their verbal ability more than sitting passively.

Other research involving thousands of subjects, of both sexes, ranging in age from young children to older teenagers, from a wide range of socioeconomic and ethnic backgrounds, and from several countries has shown that children who watch more violent television tend to be more aggressive. The relation between viewing television and aggressiveness is thus extremely well documented.

Another group of researchers decided they would try to convince a bunch of children that television violence was not good to imitate. If violent TV has nothing to do with behavior, you wouldn't expect this intervention to do much. On the other hand, if the violence on TV is connected with real-life behavior, you would expect the result that occurred: the children who underwent this intervention experienced positive effects on their own aggressiveness.

The catharsis theory of anger has been extensively studied. The notion that you get aggression *out* by performing aggressive acts either in real life or in symbolic activities is an interesting idea; however, we do not have this notion about other emotions. Do we get our friendliness *out* by acting friendly to people, or do we rehearse acting friendly? The studies show that watching people do or say hostile things makes the child more likely to be aggressive, not less likely.[9]

In 1979, Professor Mary Magee of Hunter College of City University of New York correlated some of the valuable research on the effect of television:[10]

Among heavy users of television, the feeling is strong that certain material goods are "necessities" whereas light users of television usually consider the same material goods "luxuries."

Literacy is markedly lower among heavy users of television than among light users.

Anxiety and anger among heavy users of television are measurably higher than anxiety and anger among light users of television.

Among heavy users of television, the incidence of alcohol and drug addiction and abuse is significantly higher than such incidence among light users.

Wife abuse and child abuse are highest among men who (a) watch a lot of television and/or (b) watch predominantly action-adventure television fare.

Anxiety-related crimes, automobile accidents, and illnesses (mental and physical) occur most frequently among people who watch a lot of television.

These heavy-viewing groups are those in which the largest increase in violent crime has occurred over the past few decades.

The forest and the trees

Scientific evidence strongly indicates a connection between television violence and violence in the real world. The cumulative effect of all these studies indicates a statistically significant connection between watching violence on television and behaving aggressively. These studies have prompted the American Medical Association, the American Psychiatric Association, the American

Academy of Pediatrics, the National Association for the Education of Young Children, and many other organizations to issue policy statements condemning violence in the media.

The tide turns

Research that did more than any other to turn the tide of opinion, especially in the press, was the aforementioned thirty-year study of Dr. Brandon Centerwall. A *New York Times* editorial reporting on this study concluded that "much of TV violence may serve the needs of the entertainment industry, [therefore] it fully warrants treatment as an issue for public health and social policy, and a special challenge for parents."[11]

Almost immediately after this *New York Times* editorial, which in effect told the intellectual community that it was okay to criticize television and movie violence, many entertainment industry decision makers decided to produce movies and television programs that would reach a broader audience by toning down or even removing the perverse violence in them. Several Hollywood CEOs gave our Christian Film & Television Commission scripts to review and made clear to us their commitment to family films.

Politicizing pornography

Under morally conservative President Ronald Reagan, pornography replaced violence as the hot political issue.

In 1987, the Attorney General's Commission on Pornography found that adolescents reported the most frequent exposure to pornography—not mature adults![12] Researchers at the University of California projected that "depictions of pornography and violence . . . have the greatest impact on persons already predisposed to favorable attitudes about sexual violence, or who have very poorly formed attitudes, such as adolescents or school-age children."[13] An FBI study of thirty-six sexual murderers (sadomasochists) reveals that 82% of them reported "daydreaming and compulsive masturbation" in childhood and adolescence.[14] These behaviors are obviously encouraged by pornography, which was their highest sexual interest.

A 1988 report revealed that:

91% of male and 82% of female teenagers under eighteen years old have seen extreme, X-rated, hard-core, pornographic sex-and-violence.

66% of the males and 40% of the females wanted to copy what they see.

More than 25% of the males and 15% of the females admitted to actually copying some of the things sexually they had seen in the pornography within a few days after the exposure.[15]

This data strongly suggests the "modeling" effect or "imitative learning" effect that even nonviolent pornography has on human behavior.

Prurient interest

The word *pornography* is used in everyday speech to usually mean "graphic and explicit depictions of sexual activity." The word *obscenity* is a legal term defined by the U.S. Supreme Court in the 1973 case, *Miller v. California*. In that landmark case, the U.S. Supreme Court found that for something to be legally obscene a jury must find three things wrong with it:

(1) It must appeal to a prurient (sick, morbid, shameful, or lustful) interest in sex.

(2) It must be patently offensive (e.g. go beyond contemporary community standards with regards to depictions of sexual content or activity).

(3) Taken as a whole it must lack serious literary, artistic, political, or scientific value.[16]

The communication, speech, or entertainment in question has to fail all three tests before it can be found legally obscene and any penalties prescribed. Therefore, something can be regarded as pornographic but still not be legally obscene, such as explicit sex films used to teach students about human sexuality or even a film or book with some artistic and/or literary value that had explicit sexual content.

Essentially harmless?

While objecting to violence in the media has become politically correct, concern about pornography and obscenity in the mass media is much more pronounced among moral conservatives, particularly Christians. In response to those few people who hold to the myth that pornography is essentially harmless, Dr. Victor B. Cline has said:

> For someone to suggest that pornography cannot have an effect on you is to deny not only its unique educative impact but to deny the whole notion of the educative process itself. . . . If you say that a pornographic book can't affect you, then you also have to say that Karl Marx's *Das Kapital* or the Bible or the Koran also have had no effects on their readers. And that's nonsense. . . ."

> Or consider also the spread of sex education instruction throughout schools in the U.S. The assumption is that you can change attitudes and behavior about sex through some form of teaching and instruction. If you assume that this is so, then you have to admit to the possibility that films, magazines, and books which model rape and the dehumanization of females in sexual scenes are another powerful form of sex education. And, thus, educate too.

> Many of the educated commentators or even "experts" that I know who suggest that pornography has no effects— really don't believe what are saying or they will reluctantly admit to the possibility of harm from just "violent pornography." In many cases they are pretending "not to know" because of their concern about censorship, and loss of First Amendment rights. Thus, for some of them, the issue is really political. It also has to do with their personal

values—and much less with what the objective truth is. They fear the tyranny of a moralist minority who might take away their rights to view pornography, then, later maybe, free speech and expression."[17]

Strip tease

As a clinical psychologist who treated over 240 sex offenders or individuals (95% male) with sexual illnesses, Dr. Victor Cline has found that there is a *universal four-factor syndrome* common to nearly all sex offenders, with almost no exceptions:

First was an addiction effect. Once involved in obscene materials they kept coming back for more and still more. The material provided a powerful sexual stimulant followed by sexual release, most often through masturbation. The pornography provided exciting fantasies which they recalled in their fantasies.

Secondly, there was an escalation effect. With the passage of time, they required more explicit, rougher, more deviant sexual material to get their highs. It was reminiscent of those individuals afflicted with drug addictions.

Third was desensitization. Materials that were originally perceived as shocking, taboo breaking, repulsive, or immoral became acceptable and commonplace. The sexual activity they witnessed (no matter how gross or deviant) in time became legitimized.

Fourth was an increasing tendency to ACT OUT SEXU-ALLY the behaviors viewed in the pornography they viewed and read—including compulsive promiscuity, exhibitionism, group sex, voyeurism, having sex with children, rape, and inflicting pain on themselves or partner during sex. This behavior quickly grew into a sexual addiction which they found themselves hooked on and unable to change or reverse—no matter what the consequences in their life.[18]

Bound

It is very important for families to understand that destructive sexual content is not found just in sleazy sex shops. Research has shown that the exposure of randomly selected male college students to sexually suggestive R-rated theatrical movies increases their aggressive behavior towards women and decreases both male and female sensitivity to rape and the plight of the victim. Both males and females after viewing this type of material judge a female rape victim to be less injured, less worthy, and more responsible for her own plight.[19]

Extensive research has been conducted on the aggressive pornography to be found in R-rated films. These movies are easily accessible to teenagers. Many of these movies are broadcast on cable TV. The typical film shows nude females in sexually arousing situations being raped, tortured, etc. The research shows that male viewers can be conditioned by watching these movies into associating sexual arousal with inflicting injury, rape, humiliation, or torture on females. As Dr. Cline has noted, "Where these films are available on videotapes (which most are), these can be repeatedly viewed in the privacy of one's residence and masturbated to with the associated risks of negative or antisocial conditioning noted above."[20]

Research indicates that violence against women in sexually nonexplicit (R-rated) contexts are capable of producing the same antisocial effects as are violent pornographic depictions. Content analyses of videocassettes suggest that the viewer is more likely to encounter harmful depictions in R-rated than in X-rated materials. R-rated films more often contain a higher percentage of aggressive scenes and more graphic forms of violence than X-rated videos. R-rated videos also contain more scenes of sexual violence in which a partner did not engage in sex freely.

Devil in a blue dress

Some observers and behavioral scientists have contended that if we would just eliminate the violence, the sex would be okay. Not so, for it is very clear that there are several types of non-violent pornography which almost no one would regard as healthy models of sexual behavior, such as: (1) child pornography; (2) incest pornography (e.g. mother seducing son, daughter seducing father, older brother seducing young sister, etc.), (3) sex with animals, (4) group sex; (5) sex which humiliates and denigrates women without overt violence, (6) pornography involving the eager girl teenagers having two-on or, (7) obscene films which present a massive amount of misinformation about human sexuality.[21]

In 1965, McGuire's investigations found that exposure to special sexual experiences, including pornography, combined with masturbating could lead to participation in deviant sexual acts.[22]

In 1968, Dr. Stanley Rachman demonstrated in his conditioning laboratory that sexual deviations could be created in individuals through the use of highly erotic pictures. He noted that he was on the verge of conditioning 100% of his male subjects into sex deviancy through repeated exposure to pornography.[23]

The 1970 Presidential Commission on Obscenity and Pornography financed a study of seven different populations of subjects. That study analyzed the relationship between exposure to pornography and moral character, deviance in the home and neighborhood, and statistical treatment. It concluded that "exposure to pornography is the strongest predictor of sexual deviance among the early age of exposure subjects."[24] The research also indicated a: "positive relationship between sexual deviance and exposure to pornography at all ages of exposure levels: In the early age of exposure (to pornography) subgroup, the amount of exposure was significantly correlated with a willingness to engage in group sexual relations, frequency of homosexual intercourse, and 'serious' sexual deviance; and, there were trends for the number of both high school heterosexual partners and total homosexual partners to be positively related to (pornographic) exposure."[25] Because this study took into account and isolated as much as possible the contribution of other key variables, the possibility of harm as a result of exposure to pornography was highly probable.

From the research, Dr. Cline has concluded that:

> The best evidence to date suggests that all sexual devi-
> ations are learned. None are inherited. As . . . a man repeat-
> edly masturbates to a vivid sexual fantasy, . . . the pleasur-
> able experiences endow the deviant fantasy (rape, molest-
> ing children, injuring one's partner while having sex, etc.)
> with increasing erotic value. The orgasm experienced then
> provides the critical reinforcing event for the conditioning
> of the fantasy preceding or accompanying the act.[26]

Boy toys

Dr. Judith A. Reisman has found that when teenage boys view
pornography it leads them to a pattern of same-sex experience—
sex with themselves, conditioning them physiologically to male
sexual touch.[27] Dr. Reisman notes that most pornography teaches
the viewer that women enjoy engaging in what were once understood to be deviant homosexual practices.

A study by Mills College sociologist Diana Russell found that
the depiction and dissemination of the "rape myth" in pornography reduced inhibitions to the use of violence, habituating both
males and females to the idea of rape and also accepting sexual
aberrance as "normal" behavior. She also discovered that "once
the seeds of deviant behavior were planted in the male fantasy, the
men she studied were inclined to act out their fantasies."[28] She
concluded that the acted out fantasies and the fantasies themselves
led to considerable conflict and suffering on the part of both males
and females particularly in their sexual relationships with intimate
partners.[29]

In her published paper, "Pornography, a Feminist
Perspective," Russell states:

> Pornography is vicious, anti-woman propaganda. It
> tells lies about us. It degrades women. Pornography is not
> made to educate but to sell, and for the most part, what it
> sells is a bunch of lies about sex and women. Women are

portrayed as enjoying being raped, spanked or beaten, tied up, mutilated, enslaved, or they accept it as their lot as women to be victims of such experiences. In the less sadistic films, women are portrayed as turned on and sexually satisfied by doing anything and everything men order them to do and what this involves is for the most part totally contrary to what we know about female sexuality i.e. it is almost totally . . . devoid of foreplay, tenderness, or caring, to say nothing of love and romance."[30]

In her book *Against Our Will*, Susan Brownmiller sees an intense hatred of women in pornography:

The gut distaste that a majority of women feel when we look at pornography comes from the gut knowledge that we and our bodies are being stripped, exposed, and contorted for the purpose of ridicule, to bolster that "masculine esteem" which gets its kicks and sense of power from viewing females as anonymous, panting playthings, adult toys, dehumanized objects to be used, abused, broken, and discarded.[31]

In a study by Dr. W. Marshall almost half of the rapists he studied used consenting sex pornography to arouse themselves preparatory to seeking out a victim to rape.[32] This research was corroborated by a study conducted by Darrell Pope with the Michigan State Police who found that out of the 38,000 cases of sexual assault in Michigan, 41% involved pornography just prior to the act of during the act.[33]

Cable guy

Many physicians who treat heavy consumers of pornography, detect evidence of arrested development in the sexual maturation of these heavy users. Psychiatrist Harold Voth, from the Karl Menninger School of Psychiatry in Topeka, Kansas, sees pornography as "typically depicting perverse sex, degradation through sex, transient meaningless sex, and violent sex—all of which is a reflection of incomplete and abnormal human development."[34]

Voth said some men become dissatisfied with their wives after viewing the exaggerated sexual prowess depicted in the typical pornographic movie. He reasons that society has the responsibility to protect itself from the elements within society which harm it, and since mature sexuality is so very essential to the heterosexual family life, steps must be taken to protect society against the many unhealthy risks associated with the consumption of pornography.[35]

Girl 6

In the '80s, society suffered a tremendous growth of the pornography industry with the widespread use of Dial-A-Porn. A 1994 U.S. Department of Justice field study conducted by Dr. Cline on the effects of Dial-A-Porn on children found:

> With Dial-A-Porn when one makes a call, it is usually answered by a very sexy seductive sounding female (actually a recording) who talks directly to the caller about how bad she wants to have sex with him now. She then with panting voice tells him all of the things she wants to do to him such as oral sex. . . . There may be a second young woman on the line, and they may talk about having sex together. . . . They may mention having a sex marathon . . . with all of the explicit details. In some cases, bondage is part of the scenario. . . . Sex with animals is also included as well as group sex . . . , lesbianism, rape, . . . and general physical abuse. . . . The messages keep changing . . . in order to encourage call backs.

> Any youngster of any age can tap into these porno lines and get these messages from any place in the country. All they need is a phone number to call. And these numbers are very easy to come by (on the playground of nearly

every school in America). If parents put a "block" on their phone to prevent these calls—the children merely use another phone.

With every one of the children we studied we found an "addiction effect." In every case without exception the children (girls as well as boys) became hooked on this sex by phone and kept going back for more and still more. They did not cease until found out. . . . Disclosure usually occurred when the parents received an enormous phone bill. . . . There was always a major confrontation. . . .

In the case of one one-parent family, the young son still continues to make Dial-A-Porn calls and the distraught mother has found no way to get him to stop. Threats, physical abuse, nothing works.

I found that nearly all of the children had clear memories of . . . the calls they heard. I also found that almost without exception, the children felt guilty, embarrassed, and ashamed about their involvement with Dial-A-Porn. . . . Some children . . . as a result of their hearing these kinds of Dial-A-Porn messages . . . engaged in sexual assaults on other children. One twelve-year-old boy in Hayward, California, listened to Dial-A-Porn for nearly two hours between church meetings one Sunday. . . . Some time later he sexually assaulted a four-year-old girl in his mother's day care center. He had never been exposed to pornography before, was sexually chaste, and not a behavior problem in the home. He had never hear or knew of oral sex before listening to Dial-A-Porn. And this was how he assaulted the girl, forcing oral sex on her in direct imitation of what he had heard on the phone. I later interviewed a number of children in Michigan where similar sexual assaults occurred, males in their early teens "raping" younger females as a result of listening to Dial-A-Porn. All of these children might be considered victims.[36]

The effects of combinations of sex and violence

Empirical research on the impact of sexual violence found in slasher films has revealed antisocial effects on both male and female college-age viewers. In one study, males were exposed to five full-length slasher films over a period of two weeks. Following exposure, the men evaluated a videotaped trial involving a female victim of sexual assault as part of an ostensibly unrelated study. Subjects also perceived less violence in the films and evaluated the films as less degrading to women over time. Most important, subjects exposed to the filmed violence against women expressed less sympathy for the victim portrayed in the rape trial than did control groups who had not been exposed to such films.

Teenagers are heavy consumers of sex and violence. The National Coalition on Television Violence reports that 40% of the audience of violent, R-rated, horror films with strong sexual content is made up of young teenagers under the age of seventeen, which is supposedly the minimum age for R-rated movies.[37]

Research shows that 80% of teenagers under seventeen in the United States have gotten into R-rated films with no trouble at all.

Pretty baby

Experts are concerned with the corruption of youths watching pornography, movies, and television programs containing sexual content and suggest these programs contribute to rising rates of unwed, teenage motherhood. Research also indicates that adult men are highly susceptible to sexually explicit material and are the key to the problem of teenage motherhood.

Neither officials nor the media have publicized what decades of U.S. and California birth records show: 70% of the partners in teenage births are over age twenty. Worse, when it comes to rape and sexual abuse, the male offenders who victimize children average about thirty years old. Recent studies have found that two-thirds of all teenage mothers were victimized by rape or sexual abuse by men averaging twenty-seven years of age.

Similar statistics show adults account for large majorities of sexually transmitted diseases and nearly all AIDS cases. Assuming TV and other entertainment media sex influences behavior, this research indicates that we should be just as concerned about adults viewing sexually oriented programs and movies as we are about teenagers and children. Perhaps the question is not whether children should see these movies, but whether anyone of any age should see them.

Susceptible

The key word in many studies is *susceptible*, though there is a growing body of research suggesting that everyone is susceptible. It appears that most people viewing a violent or sexual television program or film seem to be unaffected or desensitized by what they see. A minority of those viewing the same television program or film become paranoid, depressed, and see themselves as the victim. Some want more programs of the same nature to satisfy their emotional appetites. A few want to go out and replicate or mimic the actions of the protagonist in the program.

This breakdown into three groups seems to hold true whether the program in question is an advertisement selling beer, a religious program seeking conversions, or a violent program depicting rape. Most who view it will be unaffected, but a significant percentage will want a beer if they are susceptible to beer. Often, these categories overlap and sometimes they are mutually exclusive.

Radical violence

Using computer modeling, James Fox, dean of the criminology department at Northwestern University, is looking into the future. What he sees is murder.

"This is the lull before the crime storm," he said. "There is a tremendous crime wave coming in the next ten years and not by hardened criminals but by the young and the ruthless, young people who are turning murderous."[38]

The number of teenagers age fourteen to seventeen will peak in the year 2005. This age group is committing far more murders than previously, up 165% between 1983 and 1993 alone and, according to Fox, the nation's overall murder rate will follow suit.

"We have seen a radical change in the nature of violence," Fox said. "Murderers are getting younger and younger."[39]

Fox said teenagers are much more threatening than adults:

> Because . . . murder is just not the taboo that it once was. A lot of that is television. Now, kids have become desensitized. They'll rent movies and play their favorite scenes—often the most violent—over and over. What do you think the effect on a young kid is when his first exposure to sex is a brutal rape scene? That is a very powerful image.

> Kids are the least deterrable. They don't consider the consequences of their actions and many of them don't expect to live to be twenty-one years old. Why would they worry about prison? You can try a fourteen year old as an adult, but a fourteen year old is not an adult.

> There has been a pervasive disinvestment in American youth over the last thirty years—negative forces such as drugs, guns, gangs, television, and movies have grown more powerful as the positive forces of family, school, church, and community have grown weaker. Too many kids are unsocialized and unsupervised.[40]

A heinous plan

The adversary, of course, wants susceptible individuals addicted to films and television programs that mainline their lusts and desires. By hooking them on sex, violence, or horror presented by the entertainment media, he turns susceptible individuals into his pawns to mimic the heinous acts that arouse them when they watch movies and television programs. Just watching these programs and movies is a form of Satan worship because they extol evil and denigrate good.

Sexually violent movies, television programs, and other media attract teenagers and young adults by appealing to their curiosity. As one producer pointed out, this audience is interested in peeking at the forbidden taboos of our society such as lesbianism, necrophilia, and sadomasochism. The more teens are exposed to these taboos, the more desensitized they become. So new taboos have to be violated to arouse the teenager's curiosity.

Even so the mass media's role in contributing to violence in society should be kept in perspective. Many other factors contribute to violence, delinquency, and immorality, not the least of which is the sinful condition of man especially in a society that has turned away from the Ten Commandments and the salvation from sin that is available only through Jesus Christ. It will take more than cleaning the TV screen to begin to deal with the problem of violence in America—it will take revival. We must pray that God's truth will be spread throughout the world so that His salvation will deliver us from the false gods of the mass media.

Endnotes

1. Ted Turner, *Los Angeles Times*, (April 3, 1994): Calendar section
2. Andy Warhol, *From A to B and Back Again* (New York: Harcourt Brace, 1975) ch. 6.
3. Stephen F. Rohde & Roger L. Kohn, editors, "Report of the Beverly Hills Bar Association Ad Hoc Committee on Violence and the Media," *Beverly Hills Bar Association Journal*, (Spring, 1996) 4.
4. Joseph Strayhorn, M.D., "Information on Media Violence and Its Effects on Children," National Conference on Ratings and Ratings Boards (November 16, 1990).
5. B. Hattemer & R. Showers, *Don't Touch That Dial*, 128.
6. *Journal of the American Medical Association* (June 10, 1992): p. 3059; quoted in

MOVIEGUIDE® X:6: 950313.

7. Rohde & Kohn, "Beverly Hills Bar Association Ad Hoc Committee on Violence and the Media," 5.

8. Mary Granfield, "Who Invited Them Into Your Home?," *Family Circle* (February 22, 1994).

9. *Ibid.*

10. Mary Magee, "Notes on the Significance of Crime Statistics," *On Television* (New York, 1980). Also, please note that in 1979, the U.S. Surgeon General called for a synthesis and evaluation of the vast amount of research by the National Institute for Mental Health (NIMH). This resulted in the 1979 Surgeon General's report "Television and Behavior: Ten Years of Scientific Progress and Implications for the Eighties," an important review of the research that had been conducted prior to that time. A more recent survey of the research can be found in the "UCLA Television Violence Monitoring Report," UCLA Center for Communication Policy, (September, 1995).

11. MOVIEGUIDE® VII:6: 936308.

12. "The Attorney General's Commission on Pornography, Final Report, July 1986," (Washington D.C.: US Department of Justice), quoted in MOVIEGUIDE® VIII:16: 930802.

13. Ted Baehr, *Hollywood's Reel of Fortune*, (FL: 1991), 7.

14. *Ibid.*, 8

15. Victor B. Cline, Ph.D., *Pornography Effects: Empirical Evidence*, (1988). Dr. Cline is citing a study by Dr. Bryant of 600 American males and females of junior high age and above who were interviewed about their "out in real life involvement with pornography."

16. *Miller v. California*, (1973).

17. Cline, *Pornography Effects*

18. *Ibid.*

19. *Ibid.*

20. *Ibid.*

21. *Ibid.*

22. McGuire, "Sexual Deviations as Conditioned Behavior: A Hypothesis," *Behavior Research Therapy*, 2:185 (1965), cited by Cline, *Pornography Effects.*

23. Dr. Stanley Rachman, "Experimentally Induced 'Sexual Fetishism'A Replication and Development," *Psychological Record*, 18:25, (1968), cited by Cline, *Pornography Effects.*

24. Drs. Davis and Braucht, reported in Vol. VII of the Commission's Technical Reports, (US Govt. Printing Office, 1971), The Presidential Commission on Obscenity and Pornography Report, 1970.

25. *Ibid.*

26. Cline, *Pornography Effects.*

27. Judith A. Reisman, Ph.D, "All Pornography Is Homosexual," In "Values & Practices," MOVIEGUIDE®, XII:1: 970114

28. Diana Russell, "Pornography, a Feminist Perspective," (Berkeley, 1977), as cited by Cline, *Pornography Effects.*

29. *Ibid.*

30. *Ibid.*

31. Susan Brownmiller, *Against Our Will* (New York : Simon and Schuster, 1975) as cited by Cline, *Pornography Effects.*

32. Dr. W. Marshall, "Report on the Use of Pornography by Sexual Offenders," Federal Dept. of Justice, Ottawa, Canada, (1983), cited by Cline, *Pornography Effects*.

33. *Paducah Sun-Democrat*, "New weapon against obscenity" (June 3, 1983), cited by Cline, *Pornography Effects*.

34. Cline, *Pornography Effects*.

35. *Ibid*.

36. *Ibid*.

37. Dr. Thomas Redechi, The National Coalition on Television Violence.

38. *USA Today* (April 11, 1995).

39. *Ibid*.

THE AGE OF INNOCENCE

> **But if anyone causes one of these little ones who believe in me to sin, it would be better for him to have a large millstone hung around his neck and to be drowned in the depths of the sea.**
> Matthew 18:6 (NIV)

> Movies are one of the bad habits that corrupted our century. Of their many sins, I offer as the worst their effect on the intellectual side of the nation. It is chiefly from that viewpoint I write of them—as an eruption of trash that has lamed the American mind and retarded Americans from becoming a cultured people.
> Ben Hecht, screenwriter[1]

> The United States is unusual among the industrial democracies in the rigidity of the system of ideological control—"indoctrination," we might say—exercised through the mass media.
> Noam Chomsky[2]

> **Fact:** *Children see 20,000 TV commercials a year.*

A few years back the evening news broadcast a story about a baby-sitter in Dallas, Texas, who had molested the baby she was supposed to protect. The parents, who had become suspicious of the sitter, installed a hidden camera in their living room. The evening news showed what the parents saw—the baby-sitter starting to undress in front of the baby—and then cut away. The news anchors were horrified and wondered how the parents had failed to check this sitter's credentials. The news team closed by remarking that this type of abuse probably occurred more often than anyone knew.

They were right. There is one baby-sitter who is constantly abusing millions of our children. That baby-sitter is a television set. No one fires this baby-sitter or brings criminal charges against it, nor do many people try to rehabilitate it.

No matter how much we condemn the mass media for influencing the behavior of our children, we must admit that there are several accomplices in this tragedy. They include churches that don't teach parents how to teach their children discernment and parents who allow their children to watch television, go to movies, or surf the Internet without adequate supervision or training in the necessary discernment skills.

Seek understanding

Understanding why and how the mass media affect children and adults the way they do is an extremely important step in protecting your children and helping them to develop the necessary critical thinking skills and discernment.

Many scientists have argued that there is such a significant body of evidence on the connection between the content of the mass media (such as violence) and behavior (especially aggressive behavior) that researchers should move beyond accumulating further evidence and focus on the processes that are responsible for this relationship. Recent research has focused on developing theories that explain why and how that relationship exists.

Big

Many of the theories that have developed involve the stages of cognitive development of children. Although there are many factors that are common to all ages of development, there are also unique distinctions between each stage of child development that require different treatment with regard to exposure to and training about the mass media

Children often see the world and the media quite differently from adults. Parents generally look at television programs semantically in terms of the meaning of what is said or what is happening. Children see syntactically in terms of the action and special effects in the program. Thus with regard to music, a mother will say to her child, "Did you hear the lyrics in that awful song?" And, the child will respond, "Ah, Mom, I don't listen to the words. Did you hear the rhythm and the beat?"

This generation gap was highlighted when Mr. Rogers of *Mr. Rogers' Neighborhood* was talking to a class of little children and a little girl asked him how he got out of the television set to be with them that day. He said that he was never in the television set and carefully explained how TV worked. Then, he asked the girl if she understood him. She said "Yes, but, how are you going to get back into the TV so I can watch you this afternoon?"

Growing pains

Cognitive development is often directly impacted by the mass media, especially television. It is important to understand that cognition is not thinking; rather, thinking is part of cognition, and cognition itself is the process of knowing, which philosophers and theologians call epistemology. Cognitive development is similar to building a house step-by-step from a blueprint, or to adding colors to your mental palette, or to installing an operating system in a computer so that the computer can then do all the tasks, or thinking, that you direct it to do.

Each of these tasks must be done correctly and in the right order or the result will be a disaster. The human operating system develops over many years in a series of stages. Each stage has unique characteristics and each stage must develop properly.

For instance, once when I was teaching at an Ivy League graduate school, a women in the audience shrieked because her toddler had picked up a sharp instrument and was about to do what every toddler does with whatever he or she picks up, which is put it in his mouth. After quickly taking the sharp tool away from her toddler, the mother started to lecture him.

After the wave of concern in the room died down, I noted that toddlers are in the sensation stage of cognitive development, which merely means that they learn through their senses, and that taking the object away from her child was the right thing to do, but lecturing the toddler would have no effect because the toddler was not at that stage of development where he could understand the logic of her arguments. Thus, I noted, toddlers have to be protected by their parents and cannot be expected to make wise decisions when they are presented with dangerous situations.

When you pass from one stage of development to another, you tend to forget what the previous stage was like. Thus, when my six-year-old boy, Robby, was frightened by a thunderstorm, my eleven year old, Peirce, tried to get his younger brother to be quiet by telling him, "Shut up." When this compassionate request didn't work, my oldest told Robby that the reason for the thunderstorm was that God was angry at him. Of course, this only aggravated Robby's fears. I pointed out to Peirce that Robby was affected by the storm very differently than he was because Robby was in the imagination stage of development wherein his imagination was predominant, and he was trying to sort out the difference between fact and fiction.

I reminded Peirce about the time he had a friend stay over night when he was nine, and the friend had nightmares all night long. The next morning, I asked the young boy what was bothering him, and he said that his father had taken him to see the R-rated movie *Total Recall*, an extremely violent movie. The boy said that he didn't like the scene where Arnold Schwarzenegger shoots

Sharon Stone, who is posing as his wife, and says, "Consider that a divorce."

When I called his father to tell him of the fears expressed by his son, he replied that his son was a man and that he took his son to a lot of R-rated movies. I noted that his son was in the imagination stage of cognitive development and was incapable of dealing with the violence in many R-rated movies. I said that taking him to see these films was like putting him on the front line of psychological and spiritual warfare just like sending children into battle without adequate training and before they are big enough to carry their weapons. After three months, the father called to say that I was right and that he could see that his son was disturbed by the movies to which he had taken him.

Five seasons

To understand why children are affected by the mass media, we need first to understand cognitive development itself. In the late 1970s, building on the research of the renowned child psychologist Jean Piaget,[3] television researcher Robert Morse adapted Piaget's stages of cognitive growth so that they can be more effectively applied to research into the mass media.

Each stage represents a growing differentiation between the person and the object. At the youngest stages the child assumes that he is the center of the universe, and the child sees everything as an extension of himself. The saying "out of sight, out of mind" takes on a very concrete meaning with respect to the baby, because when something is removed from his field of vision, he will act as if that something no longer existed. As we mature, however, we begin to see that things are not projections of ourselves, but distinct and different, which means that we must act toward them differently.

Every child goes through the following stages:

The **sensation stage**[4] (approximately ages birth to two) where the child's sole means of processing reality is his or her senses. These young children think that they are the center of the universe, something exists only if they can see it, and, that everything around them serves them.

The **imagination stage**[5] (approximately ages two to seven) where the child's cognition is dedicated to the acquisition of representational skills such as language, mental imagery, drawing, and symbolic play and is limited by being serial and one dimensional. During this stage the child has a very active imagination, often confusing fact and fiction.

The **concrete operational stage** (approximately ages seven to eleven) where the child acquires the ability of simultaneous perception of two points of view, enabling him or her to master quantities, relations, and classes of objects. At this stage there is a strong correspondence between the child's thoughts and reality. He or she assumes his or her thoughts about reality are accurate and distorts the facts to fit what he or she thinks.

The **reflection or formal operations stage** (approximately ages twelve to fifteen) where abstract thought gains strength. In this stage there is still incomplete differentiation as a result of the adolescent's inability to conceptualize the thoughts of others, as exemplified by the assumption that other people are as obsessed with his or her behavior and appearance as he or she is. For example, if he has a pimple and walks into a room filled with friends, he will usually think that everyone is looking at his pimple. In this stage, the adolescent still has difficulty conceptualizing the consequences of his actions. Therefore, the adolescent will often take risks without regard to consequences.

The next stage is the **relationship stage** wherein the adolescent grows into a mature adult, and there is complete differentiation. As a result, the adult understands that others are different and accepts those differences by learning to relate to others. Furthermore, the adult is able to conceptualize the consequences of his actions and take the necessary steps to reduce his risks.

Babes in toyland

Research has confirmed these stages and shown that younger children are less able to integrate pieces of information or narration together from stories and then to draw inferences from such information.[6]

Younger children react to direct violence but not to suspense. Children in the concrete stage of cognitive development are more upset by suspense than direct violence. Thus, little children will get bored by *Jaws* which is mostly suspense, while older children may be traumatized by it.

During the imagination stage, when children have trouble distinguishing between fact and fiction, children are uniquely susceptible to what they see on television and in movies.

The program

Teenagers in the reflection stage of development often have difficulty thinking about the consequences of their actions and continue to be more vulnerable to the influence of movies and television programs than mature adults. In fact, research shows that teenagers are physiologically limited in their ability to focus on the consequences of their actions. Perhaps this is why teenagers are willing to take such great risks.

For instance, as previously noted, when the movie *The Program* was released several teenagers mimicked the main characters by lying down in the middle of the road to prove their courage. Some of these teenagers were seriously injured and some were killed.

One national radio personality said that these teenagers were really stupid. However, one of the teenagers who died was at the top of his class. What the radio personality did not understand was that these teenagers were in a stage of development when they were the most impulsive and the least able to consider the consequences of their actions. Like most adults, the radio personality didn't remember what it was like to be in a previous stage of cognitive development.

The borders between these stages depend on the child. Some children never mature beyond an early stage of cognitive development. These children and adults may be very smart in some ways while cognitively immature, like Raymond in *Rainman*. Furthermore, there may be incomplete development or advanced development. However, for the vast majority of children will fit within the norm.

From *Psycho* to *Seven*

Research shows that younger children in the imagination stage of cognitive development are more frightened by different types of stimuli and events than are older elementary school children.[7] Researchers Barbara J. Wilson, Daniel Lynn and Barbara Randall have examined the harmful effects of graphic horror on children and discovered some important distinctions:[8]

Visual versus nonvisual threat

The principle of perceptual dependence suggests that younger children are likely to be frightened by films with visually frightening creatures like witches and monsters. Older children will focus more on conceptual qualities, such as the motives of a character,[9] and are likely to be more upset by an evil, normal-looking character or by an unseen threat than by a benign but grotesque character. Therefore, *The Wizard of Oz* is more frightening for younger children than for older children, while older children are more frightened by movies such as *Poltergeist* and *Jaws*, which rely more on nonvisual threats.

Reality versus fantasy

Younger children are unable to fully distinguish between reality and fantasy.[10] Although the terms real and make-believe may be used in conversation, younger children do not understand the implications of these terms. The notion that a character or an event is not real has little impact on a younger child's emotions. Therefore, fantasy offerings involving events that could not possibly happen are more frightening to younger children, whereas fictional programs involving events that could happen were more frightening to older children.[11]

Abstract versus concrete events

A concrete threat is explicit and tangible. For example, an evil character might attack a victim. In contrast, abstract threats must be inferred from information in the plot. Examples might include movies about evil conspiracies, or disasters such as poisonous gases. Younger children have difficulty drawing inferences from entertainment and are more likely to focus on explicit rather than implicit cues in the plot,[12] and so they will be more frightened by a movie depicting a concrete threat than one involving an intangible or obscure hazard.

Threat versus victim focus

Also, cognitive stages are distinguished by the degree to which the scenes concentrate on the actual threat versus the victim's emotional reactions to the threat. Movies that require viewer involvement and focus primarily on the victims' emotional reactions are less upsetting for younger than for older children. *Jaws* is a good example because the viewer often sees only the upper bodies of the victims as they are attacked by the unseen sharks.

Children experience fear reactions to horror entertainment, and exposure to large amounts of violence can produce either desensitization or imitation. Since all human beings want to cope with the problems they face, the child may try to immerse himself in the problem (horror movie, violence, or whatever) so he can come up with a solution. This immersion in unpleasant media is a form of cognitive dissonance reduction.

More important than the sheer amount of mass media horror and violence children watch is the way in which even small amounts of violence are portrayed.[13] Therefore, "a number of contextual features of violence are critical determinants of whether such depictions will facilitate aggressive behavior."[14] According to Wilson, Lynn, and Randall, these contextual features are:

Reward versus punishment associated with violence

Violent depictions for which the aggressor is rewarded are most likely to produce imitation effects or foster attitudes supportive of aggression.[15] In fact, characters need not be explicitly rewarded for such effects to occur. As long as there is no punishment associated with a violent act, young viewers will often imitate such depictions.[16] The lack of punishment is a reward for such behavior. Much media violence is portrayed without negative consequences; neither perpetrators nor victims suffer much, and the perpetrator is often rewarded for antisocial actions.[17]

The timing of the reward or punishment has important developmental implications.[18] In many movies, the perpetrator receives material rewards immediately after performing an aggressive act. Punishment, however, is typically delivered toward the end of the movie. Since younger children are less able than older children to coherently link scenes together and to draw inferences from them,[19] younger children are more likely than older children to see the violence as acceptable and to imitate such behavior when rewards are immediate and punishment is delayed in a movie.

Degree of reality of violence

Violence perceived to be realistic is more likely to be imitated and used as a guide for behavior.[20] Older children are better able to distinguish reality from fantasy and are more emotionally responsive to programs that depict realistic events. Thus, older children are affected more by violent movies that feature events that are humanly possible. Younger children are responsive to both realistic and unrealistic violence as long as the acts are concrete and visual.

The nature of the perpetrator

Children are more likely to imitate models who are perceived as attractive or interesting.[21] Children who strongly identify with violent media characters are more likely to be aggressive themselves than are those who do not identify with such characters.[22]

Younger children are more likely to focus on the consequences of a character's behavior in determining whether the character is "good" or "bad," whereas older children focus more on the character's motives.[23] Such age differences are presumably due to the fact that motives are typically presented early in a plot so that the viewer must be able to draw inferences in order to link them to subsequent behaviors. Therefore, younger children will be more likely to emulate bad characters as long as they are rewarded, whereas older children presumably will be cognizant of the characters' motives in selecting role models.

Justified violence

Violence that is portrayed as justified is more likely to be imitated.[24] A common theme in many movies is the portrayal of a hero who is forced to be violent because his job demands it (e.g., Dirty Harry) or because he must retaliate against an enemy (e.g., Rambo). Although the message may be ultimately prosocial (e.g., "don't be a criminal"), the moral is conveyed in a violent context.

In one experiment examining "mixed messages,"[25] children viewed either a purely prosocial cartoon or a cartoon that contained a prosocial message delivered through justified violence. Kindergartners were more likely to hurt than to help a peer after watching the prosocial-aggressive cartoon. Moreover, both younger and older children showed less understanding of the moral lesson when it was conveyed in the context of violence versus no violence. Therefore, a hero who commits violence for some "good" cause is likely to be a confusing and negative role model for younger and older children.

Similarity of movie situations and characters to viewer

Viewers are more likely to imitate media violence if cues in the program are similar to those in real life.[26] Also, children are likely to imitate models who are similar to themselves.[27] Thus, movies depicting children as violent are more problematic than those involving violent adults. Preschool and early elementary school children focus on younger characters who are violent, whereas preteens and teenagers attend more to aggressive teenage characters.

Amount of violence

Although the way in which violence is portrayed is more critical than the amount of violence in facilitating aggressive behavior, the sheer amount and explicitness of the violent content is important with regard to the viewer's emotions. Excessive exposure to violence may produce a "psychological blunting" of normal emotional responses to violent events. Children who are heavy viewers of television violence show less physiological arousal to a clip of filmed violence than light viewers.

In one experiment, children who watched a violent film were subsequently less likely to seek help when the other children became disruptive and violent. Thus, exposure to media violence leads to a lack of responsiveness to real-life aggression.[28]

Dangerous minds

Television researcher Robert Morse has found that the very medium of television, apart from the content of what is being shown and communicated (such as the perverse sex and violence that is the subject of so much research), can cause severe cognitive problems when viewed in excess.[29]

Morse notes that the medium of television is effective at **converting** (e.g., from one product to another or one point-of-view to another), **motivating** (e.g., to buy a product that you may not need) and **informing** (e.g., the news).[30] The result is that many viewers can be converted from one product to another and even from one political candidate to another, as evidenced by the voter swings after the Carter/Reagan and the Bush/Clinton television debates.[31]

Many viewers are influenced to look at the world in the way television does since their information about the world is filtered through the unique nature of the television medium. Thus, Morse has found that television is very effective at transmitting emotions and concrete physical information or facts to the viewer, but he also found that it is deficient in promoting or affecting cognitive growth.[32]

Cognitive growth is that process by which we come to understand something so well that we set up the cognitive structures to use that thing we now know and the structure we have developed to think and reason.

For example, a baby can look at a door and learn to call it a door without understanding what it is. Only after the child plays with the door, opening and closing it, will the child come to know what a door is and experience cognitive growth.

Through exhaustive testing, the producers of *Sesame Street* found that the children who watched *Sesame Street* would often acquire words from the program which they could repeat but did not understand, so they were unable to use those words correctly or to use them in reasoning. Perhaps this problem arose because *Sesame Street* used a "distracter machine" with a test audience to insure that viewers' minds did not wander from the program. Researchers would watch the test audience to see when they looked away from the program at the distracter machine. At those points in the program where the test audience was distracted, the producers inserted a technical effect such as a pan, fade, camera move, or dissolve, or an action to hold the attention of the audience. Thus, the producers guaranteed that there was no time to stop, review, react, dialogue, and concentrate.

Part of the problem with television is that it is so effective at propelling powerful, emotional images into the viewer's mind in real time with no time for the viewer to reflect, react, or review the information he or she is receiving—processes that are absolutely necessary for cognitive development.

Therefore, the very act of watching is harmful to the cognitive development of children and, as a consequence, adversely influences their moral, social, emotional, and religious development. Television also "debilitates an important cognitive function in adults, the one that permits abstract reasoning—and hence related capacities for moral decision making, learning, religious growth, and psychological individualization."[33]

At the same time as television inhibits cognitive growth, research shows that children "habituate" to repetitive light-stimuli (flickering light, dot patterns, limited eye movement). When habitation occurs then the brain decides that there is nothing of interest going on—at least nothing that anything can be done about—and virtually quits processing information. In particular, the left brain "common internegative area" goes into a kind of holding pattern, and television viewing reaches the level of somnambulism, similar to being hypnotized.[34]

Therefore, excessive television watching can be harmful apart from the content.

The twilight zone

Children who are heavy users of television demonstrate decreases in the capacity for creative imagination, concentration, and delayed gratification. With regard to imagination, they are less able to form mental pictures, and they engage in less imaginative play. With regard to concentration, children become lazy readers of nonbooks with greatly decreased attention spans. (You have to exercise concentration or it atrophies.) With regard to delayed gratification, the children have less tolerance for getting into a book or other activities.

The symbolic function, perception, and abstract reasoning are damaged in a manner that resembles dyslexia. The rapid increase in reading disabilities, or dyslexia, in the United States may be, in part, attributed to heavy television viewing. Television inhibits eye movement and, thereby, the acquisition of reading skills.

With respect to adults, Morse said television saps the cognitive strength, analogous to the situation in nursing homes where inactivity leads to cognitive impairment. After an hour or two of television watching, people come away cranky, irritable, tired, and ready to explode.[35]

Dumb and dumber

By posing the right question, John Rosemond helps us to understand Morse's findings with regard to children:[36]

The next time your child watches television, look at him instead of the screen. Ask yourself, "What is he doing?" Better yet, since the chances are he won't be doing much of anything, ask yourself, "What is he not doing?"

In answer, he is not:

Scanning.

Practicing motor skills, gross or fine.

Practicing eye-hand coordination.

Using more than two senses.

Asking questions.

Exploring.

Exercising initiative or imagination.

Being challenged.

Solving problems.

Thinking analytically.

Exercising imagination.

Practicing communication skills.

Being either creative or constructive.

Also, because of television's insidious "flicker," (every four seconds, on the average, the picture changes) television does not promote long-term attention.

Lastly, because the action shifts constantly and capriciously backward, forward, and laterally in time . . . television does not promote logical sequential thinking.

So what? Well interestingly enough, the deficiencies noted above are characteristic of learning-disabled children, children who don't seem able to "get it all together" when it comes to learning how to read and write.[37]

The dumbing down of America

Students from six countries were tested on the effects of television by the Educational Testing Service of Princeton, New Jersey. The results were shocking. The more students watched television, the lower their academic performance. Thirteen year olds in the U.S. watched TV the most and ranked last in mathematics and near the bottom in science. South Korean students outperformed all others academically and by wide margins in mathematics. They watched television less and did more homework than their counterparts. Students in Canada, Spain, the United Kingdom, and Ireland watched more television than the South Korean students and less than the American students.[38]

A ten-year study of more than 1,000 children from inner-city Manchester, England, showed that infants who were exposed to too much television experienced severe speech and language difficulties.[39] These children were unable to understand their own names, the names of their family members or of simple objects. By age three, they spoke like two year olds. Dr. Sally Ward, author of the study, warned that parents who let the television baby-sit their children may be unwittingly damaging their infant's communication skills.

Especially vulnerable to excessive exposure to television was the skill of *mapping*, which is pointing at an object and following the child's focus of attention as he pronounces the word. This skill is crucial for teaching speech. Children who focus on the visual effects of television and are unable to focus on anything else. Ward cautioned that infants under one year should be exposed to no television while preschoolers should be limited to one hour a day.[40]

Dr. Spock

If you ask children if they would rather have spinach or ice cream, they will want ice cream. If you ask them if they want to go to school or stay home and play, they will want to stay home and play.

This seemed absurdly obvious until *USA Today* started a column with young adolescents reviewing movies—some unsuitable for the ages of the reviewers. When I wrote the paper about this problem, they replied that these children liked to watch these movies.

A comprehensive study found that teenagers prefer to learn by movies, music, and videos—in that order.[41] Please note that teachers didn't even rate consideration. The question is: Do we want to educate our children or pander to their entertainment choices?

Honey, I shrunk the kids

By contributing to cognitive impairment, television has a deleterious effect on a child's moral, social, emotional, and religious development.[42]

With regard to **social and emotional development**, a child needs dramatic play to develop in these areas, but dramatic play, as we have noticed, is inhibited by television. Watching social interaction on television is not enough because a child must do or act, not just be an observer or there is impairment of the social and emotional development.

In the case of **psychological maturation**, the necessary function of suppressing detrimental functions of the libido is impaired since television (and the other mass media) indulge these detrimental functions.

With regard to **religious development,** impairment of the symbolic function results in the "clogging of the filters of religious perception," so that the child's doorway to experience of the transcendent is blocked.[43] Television watching causes the viewer to see reality or the nature of being (ontology) as illusory or nominalistic. Christianity, however, is posited on a real ontology or nature of being because God created a real world in which real events occur independent of our consciousness and our imaginations. Therefore, television inhibits a Christian ontology and worldview.

Coming of age

Looking at the stages of cognitive development with respect to the major religious systems, there are some interesting analogies.

In the first **sensation period,** there is no differentiation between the child and the object. The child acts as if he or she is not only the center of the universe, but also as if nothing exists unless he or she is aware of it. This stage is very similar to monism and any of the monistic religious systems, such as some forms of Buddhism, Hinduism and New Age beliefs, where all is one and all is consciousness.

The child in this stage is a god, demanding and thinking that the world is ordered according to his or her whim. Others are merely there to serve him. Many people can recall a state of mind in which they thought that they were the universe or all was within their mind. Drugs and Eastern meditation can induce this state. (Most Eastern meditation focuses inward, whereas Christian meditation focuses outward on God and on His Word.) Also, by retarding cognitive development, television can induce this solipsistic state and inhibit the cognitive growth into a more mature stage.

In the **imagination stage** there is some differentiation though the child has difficulty distinguishing between fantasy and reality and assumes that everything is sentient and conscious. The child will often attribute anthropomorphic or human thoughts to the dog or cat, and the child will get totally caught up in fantasy when playing pretend games, even to the point of temper tantrums.

This stage recalls the polytheistic religious systems, such as animism, some forms of Hinduism, spiritism, and most of the new age beliefs that attribute consciousness to everything and assume that everything is sentient. Much of the mass media can also induce this stage of cognitive development. Many movies, television programs, and other entertainment media overtly promote polytheism. Horror movies and children's films based on magical thinking are particularly prone to polytheistic and nominalistic worldviews.

In the **concrete stage** the child acquires the ability of simultaneous perception of two points of view so that he or she can master quantities, relations, and classes of objects. At this stage there is such a strong correspondence between the child's thoughts and reality, he or she assumes his or her thoughts about reality are accurate and distorts the facts to fit what he thinks. This tends to be a more materialistic period, during which things take on value, especially money, and peer pressure is great. Children in this stage stop thinking that everyone thinks like them and start worrying that they are too different. To compensate, they form peer groups, cliques, and even gangs. This stage is similar to any of the materialistic religions or political systems, such as socialism and Marxism, where friends and even gangs protect the individual from the now-differentiated world. Since material things mean so much, power is used to get what the child wants as contrasted with his wishing for what he or she wants in the earlier, more nominalistic ages. In using power, especially in gangs, children can be very mean during this period.

In the **reflection or formal operations stage** abstract thought gains strength and the person learns to accept the fact that others are different. The child in this stage moves away from using power to get what he or she wants toward legalism. He or she will enforce rules, claim rights, and judge others to protect, promote, and establish himself or herself. This stage is similar to the legalistic theistic religions, such as Islam, where the person begins to understand the other, including the ultimate "Other" Who is God, but does not have a relationship of love and trust with the other. In the name of the "other," the child will take great risks.

In the **relationship stage** the adolescent grows into complete differentiation. The person understands that others are different, accepts those differences, and learns to relate to and even love others. Relationships gain predominance over possessions in this stage of cognitive development. Clearly, this stage is similar to the relationship with God in grace-oriented, theistic Christianity. The person in this stage learns to love God and others and begins to understand the love of God as manifest in Jesus Christ.

Clues

Observational learning theory suggests that children imitate modeled behavior.[44] Researchers have found that when a young viewer watches a violent television episode, he will store that behavior in his brain. Later in his life, when a situation arises similar to the one he watched on television, the viewer may retrieve and mimic the violent act once viewed.

Dr. Victor Cline reports that the more intelligent and imaginative the viewer is the more susceptible he or she is to mimicking and becoming addicted to the viewed behavior. Cline found the vast majority of criminals behind bars for sexual crimes are intelligent—Ted Bundy types. In the last interview before his execution, serial killer Bundy described in detail to Dr. James Dobson the stages of addiction that he experienced to become a killer, starting with an attraction to 1950s soft-core pornography, material which was much milder than what is being shown in most movies and television programs today.

Attitude change theory suggests that when some children watch a great deal of violent television these children develop a favorable attitude toward aggressive behavior and come to see violent behavior as normal and even acceptable.[45] This research also found that other children are anesthetized or desensitized by the same overloading process.

Virtual sociopaths

Another area of research on the influence of the mass media on children and adults is **false memory syndrome**, unchained memories, memory therapy, and associated psychological insights that have captured the national imagination.

One area of life that most likely contributes to the false memory syndrome is the tremendous amount of movie and television sex, violence, and occultism that has filled the minds of youth over the years. Nefarious films and other mass media have planted images in the minds of our youth that they have processed in the same manner as the daily activities in which they engage. However, unlike the many daily activities that are repetitive and dull, most of these entertaining movies and television programs are a potent and often cognitively dissonant, if not traumatic, brew of emotive visual and audile messages. These messages lodge in the nooks and crannies of the child's memory, waiting to pop into their dreams or consciousness.

Recent research indicates that the minds of our youth are so overflowing with movies and television programs that they confuse them with reality and history. Everyday examples abound, from the woman who saw the movie *Independence Day* and afterwards told a reporter that she believes the government is hiding a flying saucer, to those who saw the movie *The Wind and the Lion* and assume that this historical incident involved a beautiful woman and a dashing desert chieftain, rather than the real characters—an old Greek immigrant and a Moroccan thief.

Memory therapists have been able to induce adults to fabricate a childhood history from disjointed memories. Regrettably, some of these adults have acted upon these false memories.

Whether they are from a therapist or the mass media, these false memories interfere with cognitive development, reasoning, and common sense. The individuals who are confused by these false memories may develop psychoses and neuroses and attribute those symptoms to child abuse, or even lifelong tendencies. Regrettably, these individuals could become tomorrow's deviants, killers, rapists, or Ted Bundys.

Worse, a large portion of society could be suffering from the false memories planted by the thousands of hours of entertainment most people watch. As noted, by the time they are seventeen, most children have viewed at least 200,000 to 400,000 sexual acts from touching to kissing to fornication, 100,000 to 200,000 acts of violence and 17,000 to 33,000 murders. All this and more is lodged in their memory as part of the fabric of their daily life. How many of them confuse their memories of fact and fantasy is open to question, but almost everyone has a story of some young person whose view of recent history was not based on facts but on a television or movie revision of those facts.

Walter Reich in his article on "The Monster in the Mists" sadly points out:

> The institution of memory deserves all the respect and protection it can get. One indication of how vulnerable to manipulation it already is can be appreciated from the fact that Holocaust deniers have managed to receive, in recent years, a respectful hearing on college campuses and elsewhere, despite the existence of mountains of first-hand and traumatic memories of the Holocaust provided by many thousands of survivors—memories that don't have to be recovered because they are all too vividly, and all to persistently, remembered.[46]

Perhaps we have moved from George Santayana's insight that "Those who do not remember the past are condemned to relive it," to a more terrifying social condition: those who confuse the past with false memories are condemned to live out those false memories in reality. Perhaps our biggest problem is the false memories that are giving our society cultural Alzheimer's. In the end "a man's memory is all that stands in the way of chaos."

Rush

Watching fighting or other violence can make the mind believe that it is about to engage in life-threatening activity. The body will often respond by releasing adrenal epinephrine into the bloodstream, giving the viewer an adrenal rush without the threat of actual violence. Watching sexual activity and nudity makes the mind think that the person is about to mate so the body releases raging hormones that can often cause an addictive adrenal rush without the psychological burdens attendant to most human relationships. These **physiological phenomena** will engage and attract the viewer, often causing him or her to want more and more exposure to the stimuli that cause the artificial physical elation.

Psychologist James L. McGaugh posits that memories of experiences that occurred at times of emotional arousal get locked into the brain by the chemical epinephrine and are difficult to erase.[47] This research may partly explain pornography's addicting effects. As Dr. Victor Cline notes:

> Powerful sexually arousing memories of experiences from the past keep intruding themselves back on the mind's memory screen serving to stimulate and erotically arouse the viewer. If he masturbates to these fantasies he reinforces the linkage between sexual arousal and orgasm with the particular scene repeatedly rehearsed on his memory screen.[48]

So conditioned, the susceptible viewer may seek to aggressively act out these images in his or her own life to fulfill his or her desire to experience the release that comes with arousal.[49]

Scientists have discovered that mass media violence leads to aggressive behavior by overstimulating children. The more intense and realistic the violent scene, the more likely it is to be encoded, stored in the memory, and later retrieved as model behavior.

Another study showed that boys who watch a great deal of violent programming may exhibit less physiological arousal when shown new violent programs than do boys who regularly watch less violent fare.[50] This study seems to explain why consumers of mass media sex and violence need more and more prurient or more violent fare. Of course, all of this can add up to addiction (best summed up by the phrase *plug-in drug* as applied to television) because most of the offerings of the mass media are emotive, not intellectual pursuits.

The impact of excessive movie and television sex and violence on teenagers is aggravated by the fact that their raging hormones give them a predisposition to seek arousal. They are subject to tremendous peer and media pressure at an age when fitting in with their peers is extremely important even if that fitting in means rebelling against their parents. They have a predisposition to seek out movies and programs that arouse them. Some are so aroused they seek to replicate the emotive sexual or violent situations portrayed in the movie or television program in their own lives.

Hollywood idols

In her book *Soft Porn Plays Hardball*, Dr. Judith A. Reisman wrote that in 1948 there was an "incident of impotence of only 0.4% of the males under 25, and less than 1% of the males under 35 years of age."[51] By 1970, almost all "of the male population experienced impotence at some time, and chronic or repeated impotence probably affects about 30 to 40% of men at any given time."[52]

The research of Dr. Reisman and others demonstrates that much of this impotence is due to the increase in pornography in the mainstream mass media that makes males dependent on visualizing pornographic images in order to make love to their wives. In other words, they are engaged in autoeroticism, not in a relationship with their wives.

At a church where I was preaching, the pastor told me that his married daughter had received a Victoria's Secret catalog in the mail and had left it on her bed. When she came back to her room, she saw her five year old staring at the pictures in the catalog of seminude women. After a while, the boy looked up at his mother and exclaimed, "I want a mommy like that."

She immediately understood that her boy had been attracted to an image that was nothing like her and had replaced her as the ideal with an image. To a degree he had even transferred his love for her to an idol.

Deepest feelings and ultimate concerns

The mass media influence not only our behavior, but also our beliefs. Therefore, it is important to realize that religion is alive and well in the mass media—though it is not the predominantly Christian faith of our founding fathers. It is, instead, a cacophony of ill-conceived religions such as materialism, consumerism, eroticism, hedonism, naturalism, humanism, cynicism, stoicism, the cult of violence (that used to pay homage to the war-god Mars), and a multitude of other modern variations on pagan practices that now vie for renewed homage in the mass media.

These religions, many of which can trace their roots back to long-discredited ancient cults, have their rituals, beliefs, values, signs, metaphysics, cosmologies, ontologies, epistemologies, and ultimate meanings played out in programs, commercials and movies with ritualistic regularity. On any given night on prime time television, we may find happy Buddhist monks hawking athletic gear or Hollywood stars touting the virtues of astrology.

Of course, materialists might quibble that their beliefs exclude anything but the natural and Buddhists might intone that they are nontheistic, but as philosopher Ludwig Feuerbach reveals even "atheism . . . is the secret of religion itself; [in] that religion itself, not indeed on the surface, but fundamentally, not in intention or according to its own supposition, but in its heart, in its essence, believes in nothing else than the truth and divinity of human nature."[53] Feuerbach's contention grasps the essence of many anthropocentric (man-centered) religions.

For millions, in a manner not too dissimilar from pagan sacrifices, novelist E. L. Doctorow's words are apropos: "Murders are exciting and lift people into a heart-beating awe as religion is supposed to do, after seeing one in the street, . . . people will cross themselves and thank God for the gift of their stuporous lives, old folks will talk to each other over cups of hot water with lemon because murders are enlivened sermons to be analyzed and considered and relished, they speak to the timid of the dangers of rebellion. . . . "[54]

As theologian Paul Tillich explains, "Your god is that reality which elicits from you your deepest feelings and ultimate concerns" and "religion is the state of being grasped by an ultimate concern, a concern which qualifies all other concerns as preliminary and which itself contains the answer to the question of a meaning of our life."[55] British playwright J. M. Barrie summarizes that "one's religion is whatever he is most interested in."[56]

The Internet, computer games, prime time entertainment television, movies, and popular music have become a religion for too many, especially some of those employed in the entertainment industry.

Spiritual warfare

The cognitive/psychological and physiological influence of the mass media has a spiritual impact. The images of the mass media that tug at our desires, seduce our thoughts, and lodge in our memories are the demons of our age. They claw at our consciousness and entice us to do things we would not otherwise do, whether to buy a product we don't need or worse.

Just as the sovereign Lord uses films like *Chariots of Fire* and *Ben Hur* to bring people to Jesus Christ, the adversary is using the mass media to inflame the lust of our eyes and the lust of our flesh because he wants us to worship him, or if not him then ourselves or the creation or even the media itself—or in fact, anything other than our Creator.

As the prophet Isaiah notes with such prescience in discussing the foolishness of worshiping the idols of his age:

> No one stops to think, no one has the knowledge or understanding to say, ". . . Shall I bow down to a block of wood?" He feeds on ashes, a deluded heart misleads him; he cannot save himself, or say, "Is not this thing in my right hand a lie?"
>
> Isaiah 44:19-20 (NIV)

Of course, Isaiah is talking about the little household idols of wood the idolater is holding in his right hand, but he could be talking about the remote control for the television set or the mouse being used to peruse the Internet.

We often forget there is a war raging around us. It is a war being waged inside our minds, a spiritual war for our souls. The adversary is using every possible tactic to control our minds: materialism, secularism, humanism, and all the other *isms* that conflict with Christianity. He is using the most effective weapons to win: the power of the mass media of entertainment. With the corrupted movies and television programs of our age, the adversary is fueling our sinful propensity to lust and hooking us on our desires. Once hooked, he drags us down to hell.

Seducing spirits

In his book *Seductions Exposed*, Gary Greenwald suggests that there is a danger of what he terms the "transference of spirits."[57] Greenwald proposes that every mother instinctively knows about the influence on a person's spirit by surrounding spirits. He writes that when little Johnny associates with the rebellious, disobedient boy next door, he is likely to come home with a similar spirit. Johnny's mother also knows the good and bad influences on her son by each of the neighborhood children.

In fact, Johnny provides an example of the Apostle Paul's admonition in 2 Corinthians 15:33 (AMP): "Do not be deceived and misled! Evil companionships (communion, associations) corrupt and deprave good manners and morals and character."

If we are in Christ Jesus we can not be possessed by any spirit other than the Holy Spirit of God, but we can be oppressed, enticed, and deceived. Paul helps us to understand the oppression of being united with bad company while being inhabited by the Spirit of God:

> The body is not meant for sexual immorality, but for the
> Lord, and the Lord for the body. By his power God raised

the Lord from the dead, and he will raise us also. Do you not know that your bodies are members of Christ himself? Shall I then take the members of Christ and unite them with a prostitute? Never! Do you not know that he who unites himself with a prostitute is one with her in body? For it is said, "The two will become one flesh." But he who unites himself with the Lord is one with him in spirit.

Flee from sexual immorality. All other sins a man commits are outside his body, but he who sins sexually sins against his own body. Do you not know that your body is a temple of the Holy Spirit, who is in you, whom you have received from God? You are not your own; you were bought at a price. Therefore honor God with your body.

1 Corinthians 6:13b-20 (NIV)

Greenwald contends that some of the avenues in which transference of spirits can occur include movies, television, music, and magazines that contain violence, pornography, lust, and immorality. Thus, the adversary has enslaved millions with the spirit of this world through their eye and ear gates.

Because sin is seductive, Greenwald notes, we can be slowly affected by it without even realizing that our attitudes have changed. Thus, the sexual immorality and profanity on television and in movies that once shocked us no longer disturb once we grow accustomed to them. However, when it is too late, we find that we have been trapped.

The ultimate trial that we face if we have allowed ourselves to be seduced by the spirits of our age is that "we must all appear before the judgment seat of Christ, that each one may receive what is due him for the things done while in the body, whether good or bad" 2 Corinthians 5:10 (NIV).

Virtual abuse

Many parents play an unconscious role in this tragedy by taking children to unacceptable movies or by allowing them to watch unacceptable movies and television programs at home. These parents forget that if a child is being entertained, then his or her real needs are seldom discerned and that their children need attention not entertainment.

Those who say that children must be exposed to the "reality" of the entertainment media ignore the susceptibility of children, the ability of human beings to learn from secondary sources, and the unreal nature of the mass media. While animals learn from experiencing primary sources, humans can learn from secondary sources. An animal has to stick its foot in a trap to know what a trap is, while a human being can learn what a trap is from a another person, a book, or another secondary source. Thus, a person does not have to commit murder to know that murder is wrong, nor adultery to know that adultery is wrong. In fact, one does not have to watch a murder to know that murder is wrong. Those who say that one has to experience something to know if it is right or wrong do not understand how human beings learn and are inadvertently dumbing down our youth. If every child had to learn everything he or she learned experientially, then knowledge and civilization would never progress.

Truth or consequences

Since 1966 (the year the church abandoned Hollywood) violent crime has increased in the United States of America by 560%, illegitimate births have increased 419%, divorces rates have quadrupled, the percentage of children living in single-parent homes has tripled, the teenage suicide rate has increased more than 300%, and SAT scores have dropped almost eighty points. Rapes, murders, and gang violence have become common occurrences. While there are many factors that have contributed to our cultural decline, it is clear that the mass media have had a significant influence on behavior.[58]

A report by the Washington, D.C.–based Children's Defense Fund[59] states that every day in the United States:

2,781 teenage girls get pregnant (an increase of about 500% since 1966)

1,115 teenage girls have abortions (an increase of about 1,100% since 1966)

1,295 teenage girls give birth

2,556 children are born out of wedlock

4,219 teenagers contract a sexually transmitted disease (an increase of about 335% since 1966)

5,314 teenagers are arrested

135,000 children bring a gun to school

In 1993, researchers affiliated with the National Bureau of Economic Research and Stanford University wrote in the journal *Science* that America's children are fatter, more suicidal, more murderous, and scored lower on standardized tests in recent years than in the 1960s.[60]

More shocking is the fact that 98% of the American public was literate in 1900, while today only 60% of all Americans are functionally illiterate.

The biblical foundations of our society are cracking. Disaster looms in front of us. Yet, in spite of the clear correlation between violence in the mass media and violence on the street, very few people are yelling "Stop!" The growing American tolerance for brutal sex and violence in the mass media suggests the proverbial frog that calmly dies as it is slowly brought to a boil; whereas, the frog dropped into a boiling pot, jumps out.

Why?

The ultimate reason for the breakdown of our society is the fact that God curses those who reject and disobey Him. Russian writer Aleksandr Solzhenitsyn wrote:

> Over a half century ago, while I was still a child, I recall hearing a number of old people offer the following explanation for the great disasters that had befallen Russia:

"Men have forgotten God: that is why all this has happened."

Since then, I have spent well-nigh fifty years working on the history of our revolution. In the process, I have read hundreds of books, collected hundreds of personal testimonies and have contributed eight volumes of my own toward the effort of clearing away the rubble left by that upheaval. But, if I were asked today to formulate as concisely as possible the main cause of the ruinous revolution that swallowed up some 60 million of our people, I could not put it more accurately than to repeat: "Men have forgotten God: that is why all this has happened."[61]

The following Scriptures from Paul's letter to the Romans describe the conditions in which we find ourselves today:

And even as they did not like to retain God in their knowledge, God gave them over to a reprobate mind, to do those things which are not convenient; being filled with all unrighteousness, fornication, wickedness, covetousness, maliciousness; full of envy, murder, debate, deceit, malignity; whisperers, backbiters, haters of God, despiteful, proud, boasters, inventors of evil things, disobedient to parents, without understanding, covenant-breakers, without natural affection, implacable, unmerciful: Who knowing the judgment of God, that they which commit such things are worthy of death, not only do the same, but have pleasure in them that do them.

Romans 1:28-32 (KJV)

Deliverance

Protection from powerful negative spirits begins with the awareness of the subtle effect that other individuals, groups, and even the media often exert on us. Following such awareness, we need to recognize that God wants to and will deliver us from the demons of our age:

As for you, you were dead in your transgressions and sins, in which you used to live when you followed the ways of this world and of the ruler of the kingdom of the air, the spirit who is now at work in those who are disobedient. All of us also lived among them at one time, gratifying the cravings of our sinful nature and following its desires and thoughts. Like the rest, we were by nature objects of wrath. But because of his great love for us, God, who is rich in mercy, made us alive with Christ even when we were dead in transgressions—it is by grace you have been saved. And God raised us up with Christ and seated us with him in the heavenly realms in Christ Jesus, in order that in the coming ages he might show the incomparable riches of his grace, expressed in his kindness to us in Christ Jesus. For it is by grace you have been saved, through faith—and this not from yourselves, it is the gift of God—not by works, so that no one can boast. For we are God's workmanship, created in Christ Jesus to do good works, which God prepared in advance for us to do."

Ephesians 2:1-10 (NIV)

Once He has saved us from the spirits of our age, we need to walk in the Spirit of God and renew our minds according to the Bible. As Paul states in his letter to the Romans 12:1-2 (KJV):

I beseech you therefore, brethren, by the mercies of God, that ye present your bodies a living sacrifice, holy, acceptable unto God, which is your reasonable service. And be not conformed to this world: but be ye transformed by the renewing of your mind, that ye may prove what is that good, and acceptable, and perfect, will of God.

In addition, if we discover compromise in our lives, we need to repent, turn away from it, and seek the Lord with all our hearts. We also need to break off any associations not of God and renounce any ungodly spirits. Then, we must avoid any further spiritual oppression by staying in the Word of God daily, walking in the Spirit of God, and using the spiritual armor God has given us through Jesus Christ. Thus, we can enjoy the provision Christ has made for us to walk in Him and not give way to the evil that surrounds us for "greater is he that is in you, than he that is in the world" (1 John 4:4).

In all of this, it is important to remember that God is sovereign, we are more than conquerors in Jesus Christ, and God gives us the victory. In fact, this is the essence of the Good News that we need not despair and can rest and rejoice in Him.

> Rejoice in the Lord always. I will say it again: Rejoice! Let your gentleness be evident to all. The Lord is near. Do not be anxious about anything, but in everything, by prayer and petition, with thanksgiving, present your requests to God. And the peace of God, which transcends all understanding, will guard your hearts and your minds in Christ Jesus.
>
> Philippians 4:4-7 (NIV)

The magnificent glory of God's loving grace, which we meet in Jesus Christ, is magnified when we perceive the harsh reality of the judgment that awaits all those who reject Jesus as Lord and Savior.

Delivered from the judgment they deserve, those who know His salvation cannot keep on sinning for "No one who continues to sin has either seen him or known him" 1 John 3:6b (NIV).

Endnotes

1. Ben Hecht, *A Child of the Century*, (New York: Simon and Schuster, 1954) bk. 5.
2. Noam Chomsky, *Language and Responsibility*, (New York: Pantheon Books, 1979).
3. See Jean Piaget, *The Origins of Intelligence in Children*, Margaret Cook, translator (W.W. Norton Co., 1963), and David Elkind, *Children and Adolescents: Interpretive Essays on Jean Piaget* (Oxford University Press, 1970).
4. Which Piaget called the sensorimotor period.

5. Which Piaget called the preoperational period.

6. Barbara J. Wilson, Daniel Lynn, and Barbara Randall, "Applying Social Science Research to Film Ratings: A Shift From Offensiveness to Harmful Effects," *Journal of Broadcasting & Electronic Media* 34: 4 (Fall 1990): 443-468, citing the research of C.R. Schmidt, S.R. Schmidt, and S.M. Tomalis, "Children's Constructive Processing and Monitoring of Stories Containing Anomalous Information," *Child Development* 55 (1984): 2056-2071, and J.H. Thompson and N.A. Myers, "Inferences and Recall at Ages Four and Seven," *Child Development* 56 (1985): 1134-1144.

7. *Ibid.* citing J. Cantor and G.G. Sparks, "Children's Fear Responses to Mass Media: Testing Some Piagetian Predictions," *Journal of Communication* 34:2 (1984): 90-103; G.G. Sparks, "Developmental Differences in Children's Reports of Fear Induced by Mass Media," *Child Study Journal* 16 (1986): 55-66; J. Cantor and G.G. Sparks, Developmental Differences on Fright Responses to a Television Program Depicting a Character Transformation, *Journal of Broadcasting & Electronic Media* 30 (1986): 309-323; and B.J. Wilson and J. Cantor, "Developmental Differences in Empathy with a Television Protagonist's Fear, *Journal of Experimental Child Psychology* 39 (1985): 284-299.

8. *Ibid.*

9. *Ibid.* citing C. Hoffner and J. Cantor, "Developmental Differences in Responses to a Television Character's Appearance and Behavior," *Developmental Psychology* 21 (1985): 1065-1074.

10. *Ibid.* citing P. Morison and H. Gardner, "Dragons and Dinosaurs: The Child's Capacity to Differentiate Fantasy from Reality," *Child Development* 49 (1978): 642-648.

11. *Ibid.* citing G.G. Sparks, "Developmental Differences in Children's Reports of Fear Induced by Mass Media": 55-66.

12. *Ibid.* citing W.A. Collins, "Interpretation and Inference in Children's Television Viewing," in J. Bryant and D.R. Anderson (Eds.), *Children's Understanding of Television: Research on Attention and Comprehension* (New York: Academic Press, 1983), 125-150.

13. *Ibid.* citing G. Comstock and H.J. Paik, *Television and Children: A Review of Recent Research* (Report No. XX) (Syracuse, N.Y.: Syracuse University, 1987), (ERIC Document Reproduction Service No. (XX).

14. *Ibid.*

15. *Ibid.* citing A. Bandura, "Influence of Models' Reinforcement Contingencies on the Acquisition of Imitative Responses," *Journal of Personality and Social Psychology* 1 (1965): 589-595; A. Bandura , D. Ross and S.A. Ross, "Vicarious Reinforcement and Imitative Learning," *Journal of Abnormal and Social Psychology* 67 (1963): 601-607; M.A. Rosekrans, and W.W. Hartup, "Imitative Influences of Consistent and Inconsistent Response Consequences to a Model on Aggressive Behavior in Children," *Journal of Personality and Social Psychology* 7(1967): 429-434.

16. *Ibid.* citing A. Bandura, "Influence of Models' Reinforcement Contingencies on the Acquisition of Imitative Responses."

17. *Ibid.* citing Potter and Ware, 1987.

18. *Ibid.* citing A. Bandura, "Influence of Models' Reinforcement Contingencies on the Acquisition of Imitative Responses."

19. *Ibid.* citing citing W.A. Collins, "Interpretation and Inference in Children's

Television Viewing."

20. *Ibid.* citing C.K. Atkin, "Effects of Realistic TV Violence vs. Fictional Violence on Aggression," *Journalism Quarterly* 60 (1983): 615-621; S. Feshbach, "The Role of Fantasy in the Response to Television," *Journal of Social Issues* 32 (1976): 71-85.

21. *Ibid.* citing A. Bandura, *Social Foundations of Thought and Action: A Social Cognitive Theory* (Englewood Cliffs, NJ: Prentice-Hall, 1986).

22. *Ibid.* citing L.R. Huesmann, K. Lagerspetz, and L.D. Eron, "Intervening Variables in the TV Violence-Aggression Relation: Evidence from Two Countries," *Developmental Psychology* 20 (1984): 746-775.

23. *Ibid.* citing W.A. Collins, "Interpretation and Inference in Children's Television Viewing."

24. *Ibid.* citing L. Berkowitz, "Some Aspects of Observed Aggression," *Journal of Personality and Social Psychology* 2 (1965): 359-369; T.P. Meyer, "Effects of Viewing Justified and Unjustified Real Film Violence on Aggressive Behavior," *Journal of Personality and Social Psychology* 23 (1972): 21-29.

25. *Ibid.* citing M.A. Liss, L.C. Reinhardt, and S. Fredrickesen, "TV Heroes: The Impact of Rhetoric and Deeds," *Journal of Applied Developmental Psychology* 4 (1983): 175-187.

26. *Ibid.*

27. *Ibid.* citing A. Bandura, *Social Foundations of Thought and Action.*

28. *Ibid.*

29. Robert W. Morse, "The TV Report" (New York: The Regional Religious Educational Coordinators of the Episcopal Church, 1978).

30. *Ibid.* For an interesting insight into the power of television to perform these functions see Laurel Leff, "TV Comes to Town; Fads and New Wants Come Along With It," *Wall Street Journal* (October 2, 1979): 1.

31. The Roper Organization Inc. and other researchers have tabulated the extent of television's impact on voters. After the Carter/Reagan debates, 36% of those surveyed who voted for Reagan said that the televised debate was helpful in their deciding who was the best candidate to vote for, according to a report by The Roper Organization Inc. titled "Evolving Public Attitudes Toward Television and Other Mass Media 1959-1980," available from the Television Information Office, 745 Fifth Avenue, New York, NY 10022.

32. Morse, "The TV Report."

33. *Ibid.*

34. *Ibid.* citing the research of an Australian National University psychological research team, headed by Merrelyn and Fred Emery.

35. *Ibid.*

36. John Rosemond, "Pre-schoolers Who Watch TV Show Symptoms of Learning Disabilities," *The Atlanta Constitution* (Nov. 16, 1983), p. 12-B.

37. *Ibid.*

38. The first international assessment of educational progress, 1989, Educational Testing Service of Princeton, N.J.

39. Abbie Jones, "When the Telly Is on, Babies Aren't Learning," *Chicago Tribune* (March 10, 1996): section 13, 1.

40. *Ibid.*

41. A Youth Specialties survey, April, 1995

42. See Lawrence Kohlberg, "Stage and Sequence: The Cognitive-Developmental Approach to Socialization," *Handbook of Socialization and Research* (New York: Rand McNally, 1969), 391.

43. Morse, "The TV Report.": 107.

44. The UCLA Television Violence Monitoring Report, UCLA Center for Communication Policy, September, 1995.

45. *Ibid.*

46. Walter Reich, "The Monster in the Mists" *New York Times* Book Review: (May 15, 1994).

On May 15, 1994, the *New York Times* had at least four articles on the subject including a lengthy cover page critique of three new books on the subject of long-buried memories in the *New York Times* Book Review section entitled "The Monster in the Mists" and a report in the news section entitled "Father Wins Suit Against Memory Therapists."

The *Atlanta Journal/Constitution* followed suit with several articles as did other papers around the country.

47. James L. McGaugh, "Preserving the Presence of the Past," *American Psychologist* (February 1983): 161, cited by Cline, *Pornography Effects: Empirical Evidence*, 1988.

48. *Ibid.*

49. *Ibid.*

50. V.B. Cline, R.G. Croft, and S. Courrier, "Desensitization of Children to Television Violence," *Journal of Personality and Social Psychology* (1973), cited by The UCLA Television Violence Monitoring Report, UCLA Center for Communication Policy, September, 1995.

51. Dr. Judith A. Reisman, *Soft Porn Plays Hardball*, (Huntington House, LA: 1991), 56.

52. *Ibid.*

53. Ludwig Feuerbach, *The Essence of Christianity*, (New York: Harper, 1957), Preface.

54. E. L. Doctorow, *Billy Bathgate*, (New York: Random House, 1989), ch. 19.

55. Paul Tillich, *Christianity and the Encounter of the World Religions*, (New York: Columbia University Press, 1963), ch. 1.

56. J. M. Barrie, "Kate, in The Twelve-Pound Look" (1910).

57. Gary L Greenwald, *Seductions Exposed: The Spiritual Dynamics of Relationships* (Santa Ana, CA: Eagle's Nest Publications, 1988)

58. William J. Bennett, "Quantifying America's Decline," *Wall Street Journal* (March 15, 1993).

59. Quoted in MOVIEGUIDE® VI:10: 910524.

60. Quoted in MOVIEGUIDE® VII:3: 920214.

61. Quoted by Edward E. Ericson, Jr., "Solzhenitsyn."

THE RATINGS GAME

Blessed is the man that walketh not in the counsel of the ungodly, nor standeth in the way of sinners, nor sitteth in the seat of the scornful.
Psalm 1:1 (KJV)

V-chips and rating systems are two more attempts to avoid responsibility on everyone's part—the producers, the advertisers and the television audience.
Robert P. Lockwood[1]

The Ten Commandments are not laws. They are the law. They are not arbitrary regulations like the traffic laws or the election laws or tax laws. Rather they are like the laws of chemistry or physics—an expression of the Divine Mind of the Creator. That is why I have called them the great charter of human relations, the first four expressing man's relations with God and last six . . . expressing man's relation to man.
Cecil B. DeMille[2]

Fact: Women over thirty-five watch the most television, and the majority of all X-rated videos are purchased by women.[3]

Developing discernment requires more than realizing there is a problem, that the mass media influence behavior, or even understanding why people are influenced by the mass media. It also requires understanding in advance what the particular entertainment medium is offering and having systems in place to help you make the right choices.

Temptations

Advertising necessarily serves the self-interest of the entertainment companies and needs to be viewed critically. However, we live in a consumer society (which has brought us great benefits as well as significant problems), and most people in our society are susceptible to the temptations of advertisements.

Nearly everyone can testify to buying something he or she didn't need because of an advertisement. Most of us have been induced by an advertisement into going to a movie, buying some computer game, or watching a television program that turned out to be a waste of time or worse.

The goal of much of the mass media is to sell you products. Commercial television tries to attract the greatest number of viewers at the least cost (measured by the entertainment industry in cpm, which means "cost per thousand" viewers). The network, station, or program then sells these viewers to an advertiser who places commercials in the program that are designed to sell his or her products. The system is so successful that advertisers pay hundreds of thousands of dollars for a few seconds of time in some programs. For example, a thirty-second commercial during the Super Bowl can cost an advertiser more than a million dollars.

Programs are designed to complement the commercials or, at least not to denigrate or negate the commercials. Therefore, it is difficult for even the news programs to be completely unbiased with respect to the advertisers on their program. In fact, there have been several incidences where a news magazine program has refrained from investigating a company because the company was a major advertiser on the network producing the program. There have also been cases where a news magazine program has unfairly portrayed a company in the interest of an exposé that captures an audience by presenting shocking information that may not be entirely accurate.

As ownership of the mass media of entertainment has become more concentrated, the individual divisions of the mass media have started to function as advertisements for related divisions of these media empires. This concentration of ownership makes relying on the opinions of the critics employed by these media conglomerates even more problematic.

The critic

Concerned parents are often disappointed by the reviews that tout the banal, ignore family concerns, or promote movies, videos, and other mass media of entertainment that undermine cognitive development and morality. Secular critics are often ill-equipped and too desensitized to perform their defined task.

Many secular critics are compromised by their relationship with the entertainment company for which they work. Others have a very pronounced antibiblical, antireligious, and anti-Christian bias. The worldview of these critics and the values they are advocate will be directly opposed to Christianity.

Roger Ebert wrote the script for a pornographic movie early in his career, and much later, after he became a renowned film critic, hosted the first international pornography festival in the late Soviet Union in the early '90s. This predisposition toward salacious material is reflected in many of Ebert's reviews. If you examine the videos with Ebert's endorsement, you will note that a large proportion of them involve sexual themes and well-endowed actresses.

Seeking solid information from sources you can trust is a must if you want to use the mass media of entertainment without being abused by it. This is the reason that we publish **MOVIEGUIDE: A Family Guide to Movies and Entertainment**®— to help you know before you or your children go to a movie or rent a video if it's appropriate viewing.

The fox guarding the hen house

The primary guidance system in the United States to help you make entertainment choices is the Motion Picture Association of America (MPAA) rating system. Many people believe the MPAA is a government rating service or an independent agency set up to protect the moviegoer. It is not. The MPAA has been set up by the motion picture distributors to help market their movies. It has no regulatory status, but is one of the most powerful lobbies on Capitol Hill.

The MPAA ratings are merely a sugar pill to make parents and individuals believe impressionable youths are being protected, but ratings are never enforced because the MPAA has no enforcement power or procedures.

Films are rated by a full-time MPAA ratings board of seven Los Angeles area parents. The board examines each film in terms of theme, language, nudity, sex, drug use, and violence. Films may receive one of five ratings. For many years, the Motion Picture Association of America refused to explain what the ratings meant and how they classified the ratings. Following is a concise explanation of the MPAA ratings, which may not always agree with the way the board rates a particular movie:

G indicates that a film is for "general audiences" and that it "contains nothing in theme, language, nudity, and sex or violence that would be offensive to parents whose younger children view the film," said Jack Valenti, president of the MPAA.[4] No strong foul language is used, there is little violence, and there are no sex scenes or drug use. G-rated movies can and often do contain occultism or new age worldviews.

PG stands for "Parental Guidance Suggested." A PG rating is given to a film that contains themes parents may consider to be unsuitable for some children under seventeen. There may be some profanity, obscenity, or violence, but it is not deemed "strong" or "cumulative."[5] A PG film contains no illicit drug use or explicit sex, but there may be some display of sensuality or brief nudity. Parents are encouraged to find out more about the film before letting children see a PG movie.

PG-13 indicates that parents should be "strongly cautioned" because some material may be inappropriate for children younger than thirteen. Specific criteria for this rating category are ill-defined. In general, a PG-13 film is considered to go "beyond the boundaries of the PG rating, but does not quite fit within the R category."[6] This rating was added in 1984. Drug use and a single occurrence of certain explicit words will usually cause a film to carry a PG-13 rating. There may be nudity, but it is generally not sexually oriented.

R indicates that children under seventeen are "restricted" from such films unless accompanied by a parent, although this is rarely enforced and there is no enforcement mechanism. A movie will receive an R rating if it contains nudity, fornication, or the violence is "rough" or "persistent." For many years, two or more expletives involving sexually derived words would earn a film an R rating, though this standard seems to have been relaxed over the years. Thus, an R rating means that a movie contains "adult-type" material with respect to sexual content, violence or language.

NC-17 stands for "No children under seventeen admitted," though again there is no enforcement mechanism. This rating was changed from the old X rating in 1990. A movie will be given this rating if there is an "accumulation of sexually connected language, or explicit sex, or of excessive and sadistic violence."[7] Movies rated NC-17 might contain strong violence, sex, aberrational behavior, drug use, and other elements parents don't want their children to view.

Flaws in the system

Despite the widespread and potentially serious effects of extreme violence and graphic horror on children, the MPAA system does not explicitly consider such content as part of its criteria for rating films. Even if the potential of a movie to frighten was included, the current age categories in the MPAA rating system are not supported by the research findings. These findings indicate that children's attention to and interpretation of media depictions will differ significantly during the preteen years, yet the current MPAA scheme does not distinguish among children younger than thirteen.

False assumptions

Five incorrect assumptions underlie the current MPAA system. These assumptions are either explicitly stated by the MPAA or can be inferred from the board's application of ratings to certain films.

The first incorrect assumption is that viewers can be divided into three age groupings for determining the appropriateness of films: zero to thirteen, thirteen to seventeen, and over seventeen. This assumption is inconsistent with a multitude of developmental differences.

The second inaccurate assumption is that movies are more problematic for younger than for older children. The rating system would be more informative if it specified what types of films will be problematic for each age level corresponding to different developmental tendencies.

The third erroneous assumption is that the amount of sex and violence is the major criterion for determining a film's rating. This is inconsistent with research showing that contextual features, such as the nature of the perpetrator and whether the violence is justified, are important mediators of the effects of aggressive content.

The fourth wrong assumption is that sexual content is more problematic than violence. The studies on both violent and sexual content show that both are critical in producing negative effects on attitudes and behavior.

The fifth fallacious assumption is that the seven Los Angeles area parents who comprise the MPAA ratings board and are appointed by the lobbying arm of the movie industry have the ability to decide which movies are suitable for other people's children. Consistently, they have demonstrated that they are ill equipped to make these decisions because they consistently flout the values of the majority of the American people and God's timeless standards.

Obfuscation

The MPAA rating system can obscure the real content of the film rather than clarify. Two PG rated movies, *Ghostbusters II* and *Honey, I Shrunk the Kids*, both released in the summer of 1989, illustrate the problem people face when they try to rely on the MPAA ratings.

For most people the PG rating on both these movies would communicate an "okay to go to see." However, let us look at the facts:

> *Honey, I Shrunk the Kids* has no sex, violence, nudity, profanity, nor any other objectionable material except one use of the word *hell*. This film uses the science-fiction concept of a shrinking machine as an allegory. Where the film begins with division, it ends with reconciliation. For the discerning viewer, the film is filled with moral and even some biblical principles. Most of all, it conveys a vital message: the importance of bringing families back together!

> On the other hand, *Ghostbusters II* is filled with child sacrifice, idolatry, profanity, obscenity, blasphemy,

spiritism, occultism, and demonic activity. This movie presents the triumph of man through the use of occult powers: the essence of the new age movement and Satanism.

From a biblical perspective, one movie is good family entertainment and the other is the essence of evil.

The elements which Christians would identify as objectionable are not the ones used to classify a movie as an R, PG-13, PG, or G. Thus, some G-rated movies are worse from a Christian perspective than some R movies. *Labyrinth* and *Ferngully* are good examples because they promote magical thinking, which is an anathema to God. Furthermore, ratings have even kept people from movies which have a biblical worldview, such as *Eleni*, or are worthwhile viewing but have restrictive ratings for political, economic, or ideological motives, such as *The Killing Fields.*

Slippery slope

The standards for rating a movie have been relaxed. One *F* word, for example, used to be an automatic PG-13. The use of two was almost always grounds for an R rating. In the mid 1990s these guidelines seemed to disappear. This dilution of the ratings is occurring at the same time as language, perverse sex, and violence is increasing dramatically in R-rated movies.

The moral vacuity of the entertainment industry is illustrated by the comments of James Foley, director of *Glengarry Glen Ross*, which has 135 obscenities. Foley said he didn't even notice the curse words laced through David Mamet's script; in fact, he and Mamet never even talked about it. What he did notice, and what Mamet demanded, is that the carefully written dialogue spoken by such actors as Jack Lemmon and Al Pacino have the maximum aural power. "If [the actors] said one 'f—' more or one 'f—' less, it seemed to lose its rhythm entirely," Foley said. "I think it had to do with the actual sonics of the language."

According to this amoral and immature line of thought, anything goes as long as it contributes to the sonic rhythm of the speech.

The ratings games

On Sunday, February 18, 1996, the *New York Times* Arts & Leisure cover article examined "The Ratings Games at the Cineplex" and how R ratings attracted children as young as ten and how easily they were admitted into their local movie theater.

A few months before the *New York Times* article, the *Los Angeles Daily News* reported that of twenty-four kids, ages thirteen to sixteen, who responded to an informal survey at the Valencia Town Mall, said they regularly attend R-rated movies without the required accompanying adult. Eleven of them planned to see *Showgirls*.

According to the spokesperson for the National Association of Theater Owners, the MPAA's ratings guidelines are not enforceable by law:

> Unless a film is obscene, or if a state has a harmful-to-minors act, there is really no criminal prosecution. . . . The ratings operate on a strictly voluntary basis."[8]

For those involved in media research, this was not news. For years, research has shown that it is children who go to R-rated movies (80% of the audience for R-rated movies are youth—60% under seventeen years old), while more mature moviegoers prefer PG- and G-rated fare like *Sense and Sensibility* and *Mr. Holland's Opus*. Children are attracted to the restricted ratings because of curiosity, the forbidden fruit syndrome, and a desire to want to be mature.

Therefore, the ratings work in the exact opposite manner of which they purport to work by attracting vulnerable children to the more restrictive ratings that repulse most mature moviegoers. Furthermore, it often seems as if the entertainment industry is using the R rating to attracted susceptible teenagers to ultraviolent horror movies such as the *Nightmare on Elm Street* series or some of the sexually violent action movies which some in the entertainment industry call "horny boy" movies.

Facelift

The MPAA has diluted and stretched the envelope of each of its ratings over the past few years, renaming the dreaded X rating *NC-17* so a few Hollywood filmmakers can indulge their passion for prurient and violent movies without being stigmatized by the offensive X, which was the kiss of death at the box office. The NC-17 facelift has given movies that would have been X-rated access to multiplex theaters crowded with children and teenagers, and to mainstream newspapers and other media that would not touch X-rated fare. Since this generates revenue for all involved, except the poor person who pays hard-earned money to see this filth, the newspapers, TV stations, radio stations, and other media are overjoyed with this repackaged smut peddling and have joined the bandwagon supporting the new rating.

With one stroke of the pen, relabeling X-rated pornography as NC-17 further debased the moral fabric of American culture.

Proclaim the truth

Several lies were woven together into the grandiose NC-17 deceit, which must be addressed to expose the fallacies in the MPAA system:

> **The NC-17-rating was not established for artistic considerations.** The NC-17 rating has been established for monetary considerations. The new rating allows major movie companies to distribute X-rated films in major theater chains, which, prior to the new rating, would not screen these movies because of previously established laws and by-laws.

> **Movies are not art.** This is a generic deceit that would shock Aristotle. They are entertainment that employ artistic and communicative elements. Some movies tend toward art, while others tend toward pure entertainment. Some tend toward documentary realism. No matter what genre predominates, movies themselves are a commercial

medium of entertainment. No major movie company executive would put up for long with writers and directors who wanted to create art. The movie industry is a multibillion-dollar-a-year business that appeals to the public's visceral emotions in order to separate them from their hard-earned dollars.

Art is not above good and evil. It is subject to judgment on moral and ethical grounds. For example, the Holocaust Museum in Israel displays Nazi art that denigrates Jews and inflamed the German people against the Jews. This bigoted art is evil and deserves the censure that society has leveled against it. Society accepts art that is bigoted against Christians and their faith while condemning art that is bigoted against other ethnic and religious groups.

R-rated movies are very explicit. It is no great burden to the filmmaker to stop short of showing penetration, perverse sex, and pornographic violence. As one exhibitor said, "I don't think it [the new rating] is something that's needed. It's hard enough with an R rating, which includes everything from three-breasted women to necrophilia."[9]

NC-17 movies are not aimed at mature adults. They are aimed at the teenagers and young adults who frequent the R-rated movies. A Gallup survey showed that older audiences prefer milder G- and PG-rated movies, whereas younger audiences prefer rougher R-rated and even NC-17–rated films. Teenagers with raging hormones are more susceptible to the lust, sex, and violence in these films. Too much of that money already comes from so-called "horny boy" movies. These target the hormones of teenage boys who drag their dates along so they can be desensitized to promiscuous sex, hoping they will consent to fornicate afterwards in some secluded spot. What causes abortion? Inflamed lust that leads to fornication.

The NC-17 is a self-appointed classification of the MPAA, not a law. Unlike the X rating, which often excludes minors because of local laws, this rating merely takes X-rated films out of community enforcement and forces communities to either write new laws or go along with this new level of obscene degradation of their youth.

The MPAA is the public relations wing of the major movie studios who pay all its bills. The MPAA set up the rating system in 1968 because the church withdrew from monitoring the Motion Picture Code.

The X rating will not be reserved for pornography. It will be reserved for small distributors who do not own the MPAA. The big distributors like MCA-Universal want to continue to hobble the small distributors. By reserving the X rating for the small players, the big distributors will keep them out of the major theater chains, reserving those multiplex outlets for their own brand of filth. This is classic collusion in restraint of trade.

Media mendacity

An article written by Bryan Oberle in the Peoria *Journal Star*, on June 4, 1993, claims that NC-17-rated films are in no way pornographic, or morally offensive—they are merely not intended for children. Oberle blames "misconceptions" for the complaints from the few people who object to NC-17 films, stating that "some folks just don't understand the difference." (The difference in what, he fails to mention.) His further defense of the rating includes his statement that, "all NC-17 films are mainstream releases that have either excessive violence or sexual content. Sexual content which isn't—by any stretch of the imagination—pornographic."[10]

Unlike many newspapers, the Peoria *Journal Star*, with its newly enlightened understanding, now accepts advertising for NC-17 films. Could that have had *any* affect on the angle of Oberle's article?

The wages of sin

As an indication of the gap between Hollywood and America, in 1995 there were thirty-six movies released theatrically with extreme deviant sexual content. These movies had ratings of NC-17 and R. They earned an average of $900 thousand at the box office in an industry where it costs $54 million to produce and release the average movie. In other words, they bombed big time at the box office, much to the surprise of Hollywood executives but not to the vast majority of Americans who abhor perverse sex.

Pushing the envelope

Some filmmakers deliberately incur the dreaded NC-17-rating so they can get free publicity from fighting the rating. To the press, the filmmaker decries the "unfair" rating, the lack of artistic freedom, and the oppressive air of censorship. The filmmaker then "grudgingly" compromises with the MPAA, snipping a few precious seconds off the more extreme material if allowed to keep something else the MPAA found objectionable. The filmmaker then resubmits his film to the board and is rewarded with the R rating, which he is under contract to deliver to the studio. The theory is that all the publicity will prick the public's curiosity and the rerated picture will open to greater business than it would have ordinarily.

Can't indict film industry

Jack Valenti, president of the MPAA, has said, "What can and ought to be done? That's the issue. Who draws the line? Who is the guardian of the morality, the ideology, and the title deeds of freedom of this country? And who is going to guard those guardians? Who is so omnipotent, so wise, and so all-seeing that he can tell others, 'This is the line, and you can't step over it because we say . . . that only this will be allowed to be shown in movies.' I don't know how to do that. Nor does anyone else."[11]

None of us is omnipotent or omniscient, but God is. And God

has informed us of His standards in the Scriptures. We cannot plead ignorance as Valenti would have us do.

Public criticism

The good news is that many moral Americans realize that the Motion Picture Association of America ratings are problematic. The criticisms voiced by the general public over the years indicate that the general public feels that MPAA ratings may be at best uninformative and at worst misleading. Furthermore, the MPAA ratings do not provide specific information about the actual content of a given movie. For example, an R-rated movie could contain numerous scenes of extreme violence or it could contain no violence but several uses of obscenity. Also, the MPAA's recommended ages for viewing various films does not distinguish finely enough between children of differing levels of cognitive maturity. Finally, parental criticisms seem to reflect an increasing concern for the harmful psychological effects of a movie as well as for its offensiveness.

A 1995 *New York Times* poll found that 76% of the American people do not believe that the MPAA rating system keeps children away from inappropriate movies. Roughly the same answer emerged from questions about rating television programs, music recordings and video games.[12]

A 1996 American Medical Association study found that all ages, including children, want stronger ratings and less violence in movies and television programs. Young adults ages eighteen to twenty-four are most concerned about violence in music lyrics and computer games. The AMA study also found that:

66% of all adults, 73% of parents, 80% of women, and 52% of men had walked out of a movie or turned off a television program because of violence.

68% of parents, 70% of people over 65, and 56% of young adults want stronger movie ratings.[13]

Several times during the brief history of the rating system, the public has expressed outrage at the inaccuracies in the system. In 1984, the release of *Indiana Jones and the Temple of Doom* with a PG rating resulted in a series of complaints.[14] In that movie, there is one scene in which a man has his beating heart pulled out of his chest, and, still alive (anything can happen in the movies), he is lowered screaming into a pit of flames and burned to death while a triumphant pagan priest holds the now-flaming heart in his hands. According to Dr. Joseph Strayhorn a child was admitted as an inpatient at the psychiatric unit where Dr. Strayhorn worked after engaging in dangerous behavior in imitation of dangerous acts in this movie (fortunately not the heart-removing act). Because of the public outrage, the MPAA added the PG-13 rating to distinguish between content suitable for preteen versus teenage audiences.

Controversy has also risen over R-rated "slasher films." The Junior League has proposed that the MPAA incorporate a new R-V rating to indicate that a movie contains graphic sexual violence.[15]

The American Medical Association (AMA) wants a film ratings system that will target age groups and outline movie content. The group suggested rating shows for ages three to seven, eight to twelve, and thirteen to seventeen. It also recommended adding the designations "V" for violence, "S" for sexuality, "SV" for sexual violence, and "H" for graphic horror after determining that media violence can promote aggressive habits early in life.[16]

The answer is not ratings but standards—a proactive code of ethics that will guide television producers and others in the entertainment industry. All other professions hold to a code of ethics; so should the entertainment industry.

Pollution, even mind pollution, is best controlled at its source. Rating a toxic water supply is not the solution. It must be cleaned up. The same is true of the entertainment industry.

The video bazaar

Walking into a video store, being confronted by thousands of movie titles and overwhelmed by flashy video jackets, can even be a harrowing experience for movie critics.

A few years ago one of our reviewers went into his local video store to find something suitable for family viewing. Our reviewer went to the children's section and spotted a film titled *The Golden Seal*. The cover had a cute little seal with a fair-haired boy hugging it. It looked like a good family film, but it wasn't rated. That should have been the first red flag, but, after all, it was in the children's section.

To double check, he went to a huge video catalog he kept in his office and looked for the title. There it was, *The Golden Seal* (1983), but again, no rating. However, the synopsis sounded okay:

> Delightful nature tale about the plight of a golden seal and how it affects the humans around it. Beautiful photography in a fable the entire family will enjoy.

That night his family popped the corn, popped in the video, and, within minutes, his ears were popping. Much to his disgust obscenities and vulgarities were coming into his living room and into the ears of his six-year-old son and ten-year-old daughter.

Upset, he turned off the video and when he returned it the next day he chastised the store's owner for not placing a warning on the video cover. The store's owner eventually did. Our reviewer later noticed a little message on the box: "contains bad language; probably a PG-13 rating."

But even so

Many videos are rented in a clear plastic box with no indication of the content. Parents often find their children have rented a gruesome movie after they have watched most or all of the film. In most cases there is no way for the parent to know what the child rented until they run it. Then it may be too late.

In some states there is a requirement that videotapes be rated and that the rating be clearly displayed, but many stores disregard the requirement. If you have been troubled by the lack of information on rented videotapes, check to see if your state has a law requiring rating. If it does, you must enforce it by pointing out the requirement to your local store. Many laws are not enforced because people don't seem to care.

In most states videotapes that are sold or rented in your local store do not have to display the rating given to the movie when it was shown in theaters by the MPAA. Though MPAA ratings leave much to be desired, they are better than nothing, and nothing is what most people see when they rent a videotape.

If your state does not have a video rating law, then go to work placing one on the books and then make sure that you and your friends enforce it. For a sample model law, contact me at the address at the back of the book.

Misrepresentation

Compounding the rating problem is the fact that some movies are rerated when they are released in video. The movie *Pledge Night*, which should have had an X rating (it was released before the X was changed to NC-17), was being rented and sold nationwide with the wrong rating attached. Originally the theatrical version of *Pledge Night* received an X rating. The distributor submitted a letter to the MPAA asking that the movie be rated R because four questionable scenes had been edited out for the video version. Based on this letter the MPAA rerated the movie R.

MOVIEGUIDE® rented a video of *Pledge Night* and found the four scenes had not been edited out of the movie. Either the MPAA gave the R rating without screening the supposedly edited version, or the distributor added the scenes back into the movie after the MPAA screened it and revised the rating. Either way the scenes remain and the video should have an X or NC-17 rating. What good is a rating system if situations such as this can happen?

V-chip: protection or promotion?

The 1996 Telecommunications Act included the requirement that new television sets be equipped with the V-chip. The V-chip allows parents to:

> block out entire channels
>
> prevent reception at certain time slots
>
> block specific programs
>
> block any programs electronically coded to indicate content that may be unsuitable for certain audiences

The V-chip will probably further encourage media executives to broadcast and cablecast more sex and violence unless the number of people excluding this material through their programming of the V-chip makes it economically impractical. Since the vast majority of people have voted at the box office against extreme sex and violence, it is more than likely that they will do the same in programming their V-chips, thus diminishing the market for perverse sex and violence below the viable economic threshold.

However, initial experiments show that the forbidden fruit factor may apply—that is, teenagers and younger children may seek out the more prurient material because it has been rated "adults only."

In the final analysis, the V-chip is not the answer to gratuitous sex, violence, and vulgarity on television. Instead, what is needed is parental control, self-policing by the entertainment industry, and government enforcement of laws against obscene and indecent broadcasts.

At the same time the 1996 Telecommunications Act was being passed by Congress, a weighty academic study financed by the cable industry and conducted by four universities concluded that violence on TV is more prevalent and more pernicious than most people had imagined.[17] The study caused an outcry from network executives who claimed that they had reduced the amount of violence and added warning labels for the little that remained.[18]

Harvard child psychiatrist Dr. Robert Coles, commenting on this study, said, "The TV industry has to be socially responsible. We're now going after the tobacco companies and saying, 'Don't poison people.' It seems to me, the minds of children are being poisoned all the time by the networks. I don't think it's a false analogy."[19]

The United Kingdom doesn't need the V-chip

The V-chip puts a heavy burden on the consumer rather than on the broadcasters, where the onus has been placed by parliament in the United Kingdom. In the United Kingdom, parliament has gone to great lengths to establish regulatory authorities that are required to "do all that they can to secure . . . that nothing is included in programs which offends against good taste or decency or is likely to encourage or incite to crime or lead to disorder or to be offensive to public feeling."[20] In addition to observing these statutory requirements, the networks in the United Kingdom are conforming their producers guidelines to reflect the Broadcasting Standards Council's Code of Practice.

Because of this history of placing the burden on the broadcaster rather than the consumer, the mass media pundits in the United Kingdom have suggested that the "right, though far from easy, way forward is surely for the Broadcasting Authorities to ensure proper adherence to the appropriate Codes of Practice. The wrong way forward is to allow them to simply 'pass the buck' to the consumer by saying "use your V-chip or 'switch off' or 'switch to another channel.'"[21]

John C. Beyer, General Secretary, National Viewer's and Listener's Association, has pointed out that:

> A number of practical difficulties arise from this technology:
>
> Firstly, who is going to "classify" the programs as to their content and according to what standards? . . .

Secondly, the V-chip would not be universally applied. Satellite channels which transmit programs to the UK from abroad would not be affected unless the scheme were to be adopted globally. Since different standards apply in other countries it is difficult to envisage how any classification scheme could work effectively. Ordinarily, there would be some households where it would be used and some where it would not. Children of parents with the chip could easily go to a friend's house where the parents did not have it. This is a problem also with video recordings on which the V-chip, as I understand it, would not have any effect unless they too carried the same activating signal. Domestic video recorders have separate signal receiving capability. Is it envisaged that VCRs also be fitted with the V-chip?

Thirdly, the V-chip would give false legitimacy to objectionable material, whether it be violence, explicit sexual conduct, or swearing and blasphemy, which ought not to be transmitted in the first place, given the obligations to taste and decency. Broadcasters would argue, in view of audience fragmentation, that they were catering to the whole range of "legitimate" tastes. Those who like to see violent material and/or explicit sexual conduct would be able to see it if they so wish. Those who do not simply use the V-chip. Thus the whole long-standing rational for objective standards of taste and decency in programming and public accountability would be seriously undermined if not completely destroyed.

I have heard it suggested that legislation to introduce the V-chip is a "quick fix" solution which gets broadcasters and politicians off the hook. It is a way of seeming to take action on TV violence, and other objectionable material, while avoiding the much more difficult and critically important on-going issue of the broadcasting authorities failing to "secure" the required good standards in the public interest.[22]

TV rating system—more of the sham!

The MPAA movie rating system was the nail in the coffin of movie morality. This deceptive system will have the same effect on television programming. The TV rating system is based on the industry's idea of what is age appropriate, not a parent's knowledge of what is appropriate for his or her individual child.

The TV rating system gives a license to the entertainment industry to do as it pleases, since as long as there is a rating on it, the industry feels free of its moral responsibility, since the rating passes that responsibility on to the parent. Without adequate information, the parent will be unable to make informed judgments about what program their children should see and what programs they should avoid. Thus, the parent will be susceptible to the pressure tactics of the child who wants to see programs that are too mature for him or her.

A more ideal system would describe the specific content, such as violence, sex, nudity, and adult language and would specify the frequency of their occurrence. The age-based system dictates to parents what is appropriate for their children. A content-based system empowers parents to decide how much, if any, adult material they want their children to see.

The six-tier, age-based system is similar to the intentionally confusing system used for movies for twenty-eight years. Entertainment programs, including soap operas, cartoons, and talk shows will be rated using the following categories:

TV-Y: Suitable for children of all ages. Whether animated, or live-action, these programs are not expected to frighten younger children. Example: *Barney*.

TV-Y-7: Suitable for children seven and older. Material may be more appropriate for children able to distinguish between make-believe and reality. Program may include mild physical or comedic violence and may frighten children under seven years old. Example: *Goosebumps*.

TV-G: Suitable for all audiences. Program contains little or no violence, no strong language, and little or no sexual dialogue or situations. Example: *Touched by an Angel*.

TV-PG: Parental guidance is suggested. Program may contain infrequent coarse language, limited violence, and some suggestive sexual dialogue and situations. Example: *Friends*.

TV-14: May be inappropriate for children under fourteen. Program may contain sophisticated themes, strong language, and sexual content. Example: *The X-Files*.

TV-M: Designed to be viewed by adults and therefore may be unsuitable for children under seventeen. Program may contain profane language, graphic violence, and explicit sexual content. Example: *Bastard Out of Carolina*.

As many studies have shown, children will want to see television programs that fall into the more mature categories.

In the entertainment industry tradition of the fox guarding the hen house, TV shows will be rated by producers, networks, cable channels, syndicators, and others that originate programs.

The entertainment industry's system has been carefully designed not to tell parents whether there is violence in a program.

President Clinton applauded the TV industry's effort.

The real need is for standards such as the National Association of Broadcasters' Code of Ethics and the Motion Picture Code. These codes guaranteed that television programs were suitable for the broadest possible audience. The new Valenti system will drive down viewership, splinter the audience, and expose children to the worst programming. Thus, this new system marks that death knell of broadcast television, which will be succeeded by programs that are narrowcast at specific demographic groups.

Canada and TV violence—cooperation and consensus

In Canada, as in the rest of the world, concern about television violence is almost as old as the medium itself, but progress has traditionally foundered on ideological shoals: supporters of censorship versus partisans of free speech. The situation changed when fourteen young women students were gunned down at Montreal's Ecole Polytechnique on December 6, 1989.

As a result of the public outrage, the Canadian Radio-television and Telecommunications Commission (CRTC), commissioned two key studies on television violence. From these studies, the CRTC concluded that there was a link between TV violence and violence in society, and the chairman of the CRTC launched a year-long program to use consensus, cooperation, and persuasion as catalysts for effective action. At the same time, the volume of international research was quickly reaching critical mass with more than 3,000 studies underlining the long-term impact of TV violence.

In October 1993, the CRTC formally accepted and published the CAB code. Compliance with the code is a condition of license for all privately owned conventional television stations and networks. Key commitments in CAB code include:

An outright ban on the broadcast of gratuitous violence and programming that sanctions, promotes, or glamorizes violence.

A "watershed hour" of 9 P.M. before which violence suitable only for adults will not be aired.

Sensitivity about violence against vulnerable groups, such as women and minority groups.

The code also contains specific rule for children's programming:

Violence will not be shown as a preferred way of solving problems.

The consequences of violence will be portrayed.

Animated programming will not invite dangerous imitation, nor will violence be the central theme.[23]

The code is administered by the Canadian Broadcast Standards Council (CBSC), an independent organization established by private radio and television broadcasters. The council handles complaints from the public through direct contact with the station or network involved. Unresolved complaints are referred to a panel that includes public and industry representatives. The CRTC remains the court of last resort if a consumer is not satisfied with a council decision. The goal of this process is to make the council's procedures as simple, and consumer-friendly as possible and to make sure that industry self-regulation leads to a credible reduction in gratuitous, glamorized TV violence.

On the homefront

The Canadian approach is not perfect. It fails to include the source of all values, which is the Word of God, and the perspective His church should bring to this important issue. It is, however, light years ahead of the United States, where the government has been too intimidated by the mass media (remember, politicians need access to and favorable treatment from the mass media to get elected) and the public has been too confused.

Americans, when presented with an intelligent option, make wise decisions. An informal poll on the *National Review* computer bulletin board showed that 68% wanted a motion picture and television code. In fact, 50% wanted to return to the strict 1933 Code, while 18% wanted a more lenient modified code.[24] That means 68% would favor the Christian Film & Television Commission Motion Picture and Television Code.

Understanding the time

Understanding the MPAA rating system for movies and the

other devices that the entertainment industry has developed to deflect criticism and confuse the public is an important step toward media literacy and discernment. If you understand that movie, television, and computer game ratings do not deliver what they promise, but rather attract the vulnerable to the worst mass media, then you can seek better sources of information and be on guard against the deceits of the mass media.

Your children are extremely vulnerable to manipulation by the mass media of entertainment. Help them and yourself before they consume a modern media diet by knowing and understanding the problems that they might encounter in the process.

> There's a lot more money to be made on Wall Street. If you want real power, go to Washington. If you want sex, go into the fashion business. But, if you want the whole poison cocktail in one glass, go to Hollywood.
> Alec Baldwin in *Esquire*

Endnotes

1. Robert P. Lockwood, *Our Sunday Visitor*, (April 12, 1996).
2. Cecil B. DeMille, quoted in *Wisdom*, (October, 1956).
3. *American Demographics* in *Ministry Currents*.
4. Barbara J. Wilson, Daniel Lynn, and Barbara Randall, "Applying Social Science Research to Film Ratings: A Shift from Offensiveness to Harmful Effects," *Journal of Broadcasting & Electronic Media* 34: 4 (Fall 1990): 443-468, citing J. Valenti, "The Voluntary Movie Rating System," (New York: Motion Picture Association of America, 1987): 6.
5. *Ibid.*, citing Valenti, p. 7.
6. *Ibid.*, citing Valenti, p. 7.
7. *Ibid.*, citing Valenti, p. 8.
8. *Los Angeles Daily News*, (September 22, 1995).
9. Quoted from John Voland, "Cautious Praise for NC-17 from Exhibitors," *The Hollywood Reporter*, (September 28, 1990): 75.
10. *Peoria Journal Star*, (June 4, 1993).
11. Jack Valenti, MOVIEGUIDE® VIII:7: 930329.
12. *New York Times*, (August 20, 1995).

13. Kim Painter, "Violence Ratings Favored," *USA Today*, (September 10, 1996): Life section D, 1.

14. Barbara J. Wilson, Daniel Lynn, and Barbara Randall, "Applying Social Science Research to Film Ratings ," citing R. Zoglin, "Gremlins in the Rating System," *Time* (June 25, 1984): 78.

15. *Ibid.* citing Nordheimer, 1987.

16. "Election of Dr. Bristow as Next President; Calls for Tougher Ratings System Highlight AMA Meeting." *Jet* 86: 9 (July 4, 1994): 18.

17. Richard Zoglin, "Chips Ahoy" *Time* 147: 8 (February 19, 1996): 58.

18. *Ibid.*

19. *Ibid.*

20. John C. Beyer, "The V-Chip—Good for Viewers or a Cop-out for Broadcasters?" (April, 1996), citing the Broadcasting Act 1990 6(1) (a)0.

21. *Ibid.*

22. *Ibid.*

23. The CAB Code, October, 1993, The Canadian Radio-television and Telecommunications Commission (CRTC), Public Affairs, Ottawa, Ontario, K1A 0N2, Canada: Tel: 819-997-0313, TDD: 819-994-0423, Fax: 819-994-0218.

24. *National Review.*

TRUE LIES

Finally, brethren, whatsoever things are true, whatsoever things are honest, whatsoever things are just, whatsoever things are pure, whatsoever things are lovely, whatsoever things are of good report; if there be any virtue, and if there be any praise, think on these things.
Philippians 4:8 (KJV)

Hollywood is a place where they'll pay you $10,000 for a kiss and fifty cents for your soul.
Marilyn Monroe[1]

Jesus of Nazareth could have chosen simply to express Himself in moral precepts; but like a great poet He chose the form of the parable, wonderful short stories that entertained and clothed the moral precept in an eternal form. It is not sufficient to catch man's mind, you must also catch the imaginative faculties of his mind.
Dudley Nichols, screenwriter[2]

Fact: America is the largest exporter of "direct culture" (movies, books, TV, music, newspapers, and magazines) in the history of the world.[3]

W hile most of the church is still using sixteenth-century technology to communicate the Good News, the adversary is dropping smart bombs down the cable systems into the minds of our children.[4] It is not that sixteenth-century media such as books, plays, and storytelling are ineffective, it's just that some of the mass media are more effective than others in terms of converting, motivating, and informing an audience. Of course, the effectiveness of the mass media pales in comparison with the most effective medium of communication, which is the Word of God.

What makes the entertainment media so influential? What causes us to laugh, cry, and change our hearts and minds when we watch a movie, a television program, or a videotape? If we understand how the entertainment media influence us technically, we will be better equipped to use without being abused by the mass media.

The play's the thing

The story is at the heart of the influence of much of the entertainment media. The Bard said, "The play's the thing wherein I'll catch the conscience of the king."[5] The essence of the play, movies, television, and even computer games[6] is the story, the most powerful genre of communications.

Jesus told stories called parables to help people understand the kingdom of God. Hollywood tells stories through film, television, video, CD-ROMs, radio, and the other mass media. Although most of the mass media are used for storytelling, they can be used to transmit and disseminate other forms of art and communication. Some of the mass media can augment the power of the story with attractive images and captivating effects. Others can involve the audience with interactive play and feedback, but the engine that drives the newscast, the game, and the movie is the story.

For many years the entertainment industry was so clear on the importance of the story that didactic communications were shunned. Hollywood mogul Samuel Goldwyn said, "If you want to send a message, call Western Union."[7] Goldwyn's *bon mot* ignored the fact that all movies and television programs, whether dramatic, news, or documentary, communicate a message.

Most Hollywood producers, directors, and executives do not intend to create art. An artist can live and die (as Van Gogh did) without having an audience. Entertainment moguls and talent produce games, movies, and television programs to attract an audience so they can make money. Most movies and television programs employ art and craft elements only to attract an audience. Most filmmakers or television producers are not struggling artists, but court jesters, raconteurs, bards, and showmen who entertain people, sometimes communicating ideas of importance and sometimes communicating ideas that tear at the moral fabric of society.

Neither the media nor technology produce powerful communications. Only creative, dedicated, industrious people communicate effectively, using whatever medium is appropriate or available. Shakespeare didn't have a word processor. Yesterday, talented communicators used a pencil; today television; tomorrow holograms? Talent is the key to effective communication.

Many new technologies try to change what people do and fail. New technologies that help people to do what they like or need to do in an easier, more convenient way usually succeed.

Knowing how to use your medium of choice will not guarantee that a communicator will communicate effectively. Effective communication requires not only understanding the medium of choice but inspiration, honest ascertainment, and application of the principles that govern the genre of choice. However, in the beginning is the story.

In the beginning

A good, strong, clear premise that irrevocably leads to an upbeat ending with strong realistic characters and exciting pacing resulting from a strong sense of jeopardy makes a story technically good and appealing to a broad audience. Sex and violence are most often merely superficial decorations. Without a powerful premise, sex and violence do not, and can not, make a good film or television program.

Sex and violence may infrequently be used to develop the plot, but are usually inserted to cover up a weakness in the script or as an ornament in a lackluster story. Sex and violence will attract a few viewers, but box office blockbusters[8] must reach a broader segment of society by appealing to the audience's deepest concerns and confirming their cherished beliefs through a powerful premise that drives a redemptive, moral story.

A story is a connected narration of real, or imagined, events. There are many types of stories, including science fiction, romance, myth, fairy tale, tragedy, and adventure. The full range of story-telling is limited only by the human imagination, yet there are key principles that apply to all stories. And all stories can be classified in terms of different genres, categories, or subgenre—depending on how they are constructed.

In the most basic categorization of dramatic stories, Aristotle purportedly posited that there were only **four basic plots**:

> man against man,
>
> man against nature,
>
> man against himself, and
>
> man against the super- or subnatural.

Each of these plots can be the basis of any of the many different **genres**, which include action adventure, animation, biblical, religious and Christian, biography, juvenile, comedy, detective, docudrama, documentary, drama, fantasy, sword and sorcery and science fiction, film noir, historical, horror, kung fu or martial arts, nature and wilderness, musical, musical comedy, mystery, romance, spy, war, and the Western.

Each genre has its own rules and distinctives, yet each can utilize the various styles and categories common to all of them.

People react to different genres differently at various stages of cognitive development.

No matter what category or genre, stories have an internal logic driven by a premise acting through characters in conflict to move the plot from a beginning point of attack through one or more crises to a climax that resolves into a resolution.

The premise, a succinct, summary statement of what the communication intends to prove, is the engine that powers the story. Characters in conflict prove the premise dramatically. United with attractive images and presented with exciting effects, the dramatic power of the premise is irresistible.

In every movie, television program, and play, the premise can be found by analyzing the story. In the *Star Wars* trilogy, the Evil Empire is taking over the universe. A young man who is full of goodness, perseverance, and integrity is forced to fight the Empire. He wins. "Good triumphs over evil" is clearly the premise.

Every one of Shakespeare's plays, every good story, and even every commercial has a clear-cut premise. *King Lear* proves that blind trust leads to destruction. *The Velveteen Rabbit* tells us that love gives life to the beloved. Toothpaste commercials often claim that they give us the girl, or boy, of our dreams. The next television commercial you see, try to find and state the premise.

The **elements of a premise** are a subject, an active, transitive verb, and an object. The verb must be active (love conquers hate), present tense, not future or past tense, to give direction to the story. If the verb is intransitive (love is wonderful), the script will be a static photograph with no direction, not a dynamic movie. If the verb is past tense (he loved me), the goal of the story has been achieved and there is nothing to prove. If the verb is future tense (he will love me), then the premise is purely speculative.

Many well-produced films, television programs, or other media communications fail not because of the quality of the production, but because of an unclear premise, double premise, or another defect in the premise.

In a good script the environment or setting in which the action takes place must be defined in detail. The environment must be made real, even if it is far, far away in time and space. The environment and the laws that govern that environment create the illusion of reality in the story.

The style of the story must fit the premise, the environment, the characters, and the subgenre. The style, rhythm, and tone are as important as the plot. A satiric or low ironic style may be appropriate for a detective story, but not for a historic portrayal of Jesus' ministry, unless the author is attacking the Gospel or has chosen Judas Iscariot's point of view.

Here is a **concise guide to styles**:

In the **mythic** style, God triumphs or the hero triumphs, because of an act of God.

In the **heroic** style, the hero triumphs because he or she is superior.

In the **high ironic** style, the hero triumphs because of a quirk of fate.

In the **low ironic** style, the hero fails because of a quirk of fate.

In the **demonic** style, the hero is hopelessly overwhelmed by evil.

Within a style:

to **shock**, the script must make the incredible credible;

to create **irony**, the audience's assumptions must be contrary to the outcome;

to create a **paradox**, logic must be contradicted by fact;

to create **satire**, the normal is exaggerated;

to create **suspense**, withheld information must confront the desire to know.

In a good script the characters must be well-defined. The script may have two apostles, two tax collectors, or two thieves, but they must be different. They must contrast with each other so that they will move the story along. The contrast between them must be inherent in their character, which is revealed through their dialogue and actions. As the story progresses each character grows along his or her character arc.

Orchestration is simply creating well-defined, strong characters who are in conflict and therefore move the story along. Through this conflict the characters will grow and the story will develop, proving the premise.

To be effective and exciting, action, not contemplation, must prove the premise. Thus, the story must show that good triumphs over evil, not just put those words in a character's mouth or thoughts.

The protagonist, who is not necessarily the hero, is the driven, driving subject inherent in the premise, who forces the conflict that moves the story to its conclusion. He or she knows what he or she wants and will act to get it. Not only does the protagonist want something badly enough to act, but he or she will go after what he or she wants until he or she has obtained it or has been completely defeated in the process.

The antagonist is the person the protagonist must oppose to fulfill his or her goals. The antagonist reacts against the action of the subject. Depending on the outcome determined by the premise, he or she must change for the protagonist to reach his or her goal or the protagonist must change in the face of his or her opposition.

To capture an audience, a story must have the right point of attack. The right point of attack is that moment in time and space when the protagonist is at a critical turning point where he or she must act to achieve his or her goal, thereby initiating the action of the premise. Rather than ramble, looking for a place to begin, the story must start at the moment when the conflict starts, when the protagonist acts to achieve his or her goal. This moment occurs when circumstances and motivation force the protagonist to act. He or she acts out of necessity because something extremely important is at stake, such as love, survival, health, or honor. This point could be where the protagonist has made a decision, has reached a turning point, or where something important is suddenly at stake. Whatever precipitated this moment has already occurred when the story begins.

The story builds through rising conflict, which is a series of conflicts, each building in intensity on the previous conflict until the climax is reached and the premise is proved. Each conflict moves the story forward through action and reaction, attack and counterattack, which cause change, growth, and new conflict until the premise is proved.

In order to attract an audience, storytellers must appeal to people's needs. Needs are expressed by desires. There are several categories of needs: **physical** needs, such as the need for food, clothing, shelter, procreation, or survival (*Die Hard*); **security** needs, which are concerned with personal protection from danger, deprivation, or accidents (*Driving Miss Daisy*); **social** needs, such as the need for love, community, or home (*Forrest Gump*); **self-esteem** needs, such as the need for respect, productivity, or recognition (*Dead Poets Society*); **self-fulfillment** needs, such as the need for success or accomplishment (*Babe*); and, most of all, **spiritual** need, which can manifest itself as the desire for any or all of the above-mentioned needs, but, in fact, is a desire for communion with God—Father, Son, and Holy Spirit—for "man does not live by bread alone" Matthew 4:4 (NIV) (*Chariots of Fire* and *Dead Man Walking*).

Even so, pandering to people's needs alone will not make the story good or entertaining. All the elements of good storytelling must be in place or even the most expensive action entertainment production will fall flat on its face.

As Lajos Egri, the author of the quintessential book on dramatic writing, said:

> A play [or movie] can be judged before it reaches actual production. First, the premise must be discernible from

the beginning. We have a right to know in what direction the author is leading us. The characters, growing out of the premise, necessarily identify themselves with the aim of the play. They will prove the premise through conflict. The play must start with conflict, which rises steadily until it reaches the climax. The characters must be so well drawn that, whether or not the author has declared their individual backgrounds, we can make out accurate case histories for each of them."[9]

Telling your story

The best way to understand the emotive power of a story is to write your own story. First write the premise of your story. If your premise works, your story will work.

A good way to choose your first premise is to go to the Bible, pick out a parable, extract the premise, rephrase it in your own words, then write your own story based on that premise. For example, look at the parable of the Prodigal Son. The major premise can be stated as "the love of God the Father forgives the transgressions of His children."

The protagonist is God the Father. It is His love that solves the plot problem, which is the transgressions of His children. In the parable, God the Father is represented by a human father. This is incarnational theology, and one of many ways that this premise can be realized. Of course, the antagonists are the transgressing children, which include both the son who squanders his inheritance and the son who refuses to love his brother.

Note that our premise has the active verb *forgives*. If the premise had an intransitive verb, such as *is*, then the story would be static—a portrait and not a story. For example, if the premise was stated as "God is love," it would express something important about God, but it would not tell a story.

Now that you have extracted the premise, rephrase it and write your story. If you need more help, you may want to purchase a book on scriptwriting, such as my book *Getting the Word Out*, which guides you step-by-step in how to create powerful communications for the mass media.

Try some variations on the premise. Try different categories, genres, and types of story.

For example, make your story a commercial. The rule of thumb is that one page of script equals one minute of screen time. Most commercials run one minute or less. Since commercials bring together all the elements of dramatic writing in a concise form, they can serve as manageable exercises for learning the principles of storytelling.

This process of writing your own story is invaluable for developing a critical understanding of the stories that you find in the entertainment media.

Later, you can produce your story on videotape.

Beyond the fringe

The images in the visual media and the special effects help to capture and influence and audience. For movies and television programs success depends on premise, image, and effect.

The visual and audio work together to create an image in mass media. People remember about 60% of the visual and 40% of the audio.

In research on the relative influence of the visual and the audio, the producers of *Sesame Street* showed a test audience, made of people of all ages, an animated short about an ant and an elephant with the sound track informing the audience that the ant could not grow to the size of an elephant because the ant's external skeleton would not sustain such weight, while the animated picture showed the ant growing to the size of the elephant and then exploding. After watching the short, the test audience was asked if an ant could grow to be as big as an elephant. Over 90% of the test audience said *yes* because the growth of the ant was portrayed in the visual animation and the visual was so much more powerful than the audio.

Image includes not only the pretty people and interesting characters in the production, but also the environment in which the story is set. The environment has an immense impact on the audience. Because every communication excludes what it does not include, its omissions create powerful secondary messages in the mind of the audience.

Movies, television, and the electronic audio media are more prone to willful distortion of the real world than other media because such distortion is easy to effect, and because the tampered product appears to be the truth. Editing, close-ups, shadow shots, reverse shots, and other conscious camera techniques can distort the meaning of a scene.

The State University of New York researched the impact of television on children and found that the background environment of a television program had a tremendous impact on the worldview of the children. One little girl said she wanted to be a doctor when she grew up. When asked why, she did not answer that that she felt called to heal or help others; rather, she wanted a big house with a pool, a yacht, and to travel. Her image of doctors was conditioned by the environment in which they are placed on television, not by the reality of medical practice.

Since a camera excludes everything beyond its field of view, television journalism is technically biased in its reporting, yet the viewer will interpret what he sees as the truth. During my junior year at Dartmouth College, there was a small student takeover of the administration building. In the middle of the night, a friend woke me to say that the National Guard was evacuating the administration building. The landscape was empty except for a few observers, a handful of National Guardsmen, the thirty students who had occupied the building, and the television news. However, the next day on the news, the operation looked like a major military maneuver. Frightened alumni and parents from all over the country phoned the college. The TV news team had shot the scene so tight in the midst of the small crowd that the event looked larger and more important than it actually was. The camera had completely distorted the real environment where the protest had taken place.

Gerry Mander approaches what is the real world on television from a humorous perspective:

There is a widespread belief that some things on television are "real" and some things are not real. We believe the news is real. Fictional programs are not real.

Talk shows are real, although it is true they happen only for television, and sometimes happen some days before we see them.

Are historical programs real? Well, no, not exactly.

Our society assumes that human beings can make the distinctions between what is real and what is not real, even when the real and not real are served up in the same way, intercut with one another, sent to us from many different places and times and arriving one behind the other in our houses, shooting out of a box in our living rooms straight into our heads.[10]

How many Americans during World War II realized that much of the war footage they saw was shot in Hollywood? How many people in Great Britain in World War II realized that an actor was presenting most of Prime Minister Winston Churchill's most inspiring speeches over the radio?

To understand how the mass media influence us, it is important to understand that each medium has its advantages and disadvantages over the other media. To communicate how something looks, an oft-quoted, ancient Chinese proverb tells us that "a picture is worth a thousand words." If, however, we want to communicate the true nature of some person, event, or thing, then a few words, such as "the Word was made flesh, and dwelt among us" John 1:14 (KJV), says more than a thousand pictures.

Each medium can be seen primarily as a communications tool,[11] capable of accomplishing one or more communications functions. A tool is neither good nor bad. That is determined by how we use it. When we use a tool to perform a function for which the tool is intended, it performs well.

For instance, a screwdriver is very useful for driving screws; it is of some value in scraping paint off the side of a house; it is of very little value when used to hammer a nail; it is of no value in gripping a nut (under normal circumstances).

The screwdriver is neither good when used to repair a church artifact, nor bad when used to stab someone. Rather it is the person using the screwdriver who is responsible, and the same is true of the various media of communications.

Each communication medium has certain functions it performs well, others to a lesser degree, and many not at all. To develop media literacy you need to understand what functions each medium performs best, and how well each medium performs a particular function. Keep in mind that the ability of a medium to perform a specific function depends on:

> the nature of the medium.
>
> the nature of the genre.
>
> the nature of the audience.
>
> where the audience lives.
>
> the size of the audience.
>
> the cost of the medium in money, time, and energy, compared with its ability to accomplish the function, and compared with the cost and effectiveness of the other media.

Every medium has a specific audience, or market, it reaches under normal circumstances. Comic books, Christian television, and rock-music radio reach different audiences with some overlap. Some media reach markets and demographic groups also reached by other media. Television reaches many groups who can be targeted by other media, such as news magazines.

As author John Berger notes:

Compare the cinema with theatre. Both are dramatic arts. Theatre brings actors before a public and every night during the season they re-enact the same drama. Deep in the nature of theatre is a sense of ritual. The cinema, by contrast, transports its audience individually, singly, out of the theatre towards the unknown.[12]

The genre will affect who is reached by a particular medium. Research shows that television comedy will reach and impact teenagers more effectively than game shows or news programs. These same teenagers may be more interested in reading sports magazines or romance novels than humorous novels. Certain media are better suited to communicate certain genre. Poetry works well in print, but seldom succeeds on television.

Ascertainment questions

Our previous discussion of the cognitive development theory gives us some important questions to consider when reviewing the influence of any medium. These are known as ascertainment questions since they help us to ascertain important distinctives about each medium:

How well does the medium communicate physical "P" experience to the audience? As noted in Chapter 1, P experience is important with regard to behavioral modeling and information, but deficient in providing cognitive growth.

How well does the medium communicate logico-mathematical "LM" experience to the audience? As noted in Chapter 1, cognitive growth is necessary in order to develop higher-thinking skills or LM education.

How well does the medium capture the audience's attention?

How well does the medium enhance the audience's concentration?

How well does the medium allow internal review, reaction, and reflection on the part of the audience?

How well does the medium promote creative imagination on the part of the audience?

How well does the medium promote delayed gratification on the part of the audience?

How well does the medium influence the audience?

How well does the medium convert the audience?

How well does the medium motivate the audience?

These questions are not exhaustive and are dependent on many variables, not the least of which are your media literacy skills and your use of the medium in question. Therefore, you should undertake to understand and analyze each medium that you and your family uses or consumes by asking the right questions to discern the strengths and weaknesses of each medium and its influence on you and your family.

As you determine the effect and influence of the medium, you should determine the influence of the particular genre on you and your family. In this regard, you need to be familiar with the unique principles that constitute the "grammar and rhetoric" of each medium and genre and how that grammar and rhetoric influences and impacts you and your family.

One of the best ways to understand the influence and effectiveness of each medium and genre is to produce the story you previously wrote in various media such as video, a short story, or a live play at home. By getting hands-on experience with these media, you will develop a much deeper level of understanding, discernment, and media literacy. After learning about the medium, practical experience will help you to really know each medium and understand how that medium influences you and others.

Research on children who accept whatever they witness in the mass media shows that they will start to be critical of what they are watching or hearing once they learn how to produce effective stories for the mass media. One study showed that teenagers who were emotionally involved in movies with prurient sex learned to be objective and critical of such movies after learning the principles of storytelling through the media.

Therefore, an excellent exercise is to bring together several children and have them produce their own video commercial. Take them through each stage of the process and have them ask all the pertinent ascertainment questions to determine the influence of the video on them and their friends. There are several books on how to do just that. *Getting the Word Out,* a book that I authored, will specifically help you and your family to undertake these types of exercises.

As media maven Marshall McLuhan said:

> Media, by altering the environment, evoke in us unique ratios of sense perceptions. The extension of any one sense alters the way we think and act—the way we perceive the world.[13]

Endnotes

1. Marilyn Monroe, quoted in MOVIEGUIDE® IX:2: 940117
2. Dudley Nichols, "The Writer and the Film," *Theatre Arts* (October 1943), quoted in *The Columbia Dictionary of Quotations* (1993).
3. Ben Wattenberg, *Atlanta Journal/Constitution* (July 5, 1992).
4. David Outten, "The 21st Century Pulpit," MOVIEGUIDE® VIII: 12: 930607.
5. William Shakespeare, *Hamlet,* Act 2.
6. See Ted Baehr, "Behind the Myst: An Interview with the Creator of the Most Popular Computer Game," MOVIEGUIDE® XI: 13: 960617.
7. Samuel Goldwyn was a Hollywood film producer and one of the founders of Metro-Goldwyn-Mayer. His Western Union statement is quoted in the article "Lost in the Cosmos," *Newsweek* (December 10, 1984): 94.
8. *USA Today* listed the top grossing movies of all time after adjusting for inflation on August 19, 1996, and found that almost all of them were family movies, mostly G and PG, which had strong moral messages.

9. Lajos Egri, *The Art of Dramatic Writing* (New York, 1960), 263.

10. Mander, Gerry, *Four Arguments for Elimination of Television* (New York 1970), 250-254.

11. Also note that each medium is composed of one or more tools—from pencil and paper, which compose a note, to the sophisticated cameras, recorders, editing machines, satellites, and other hardware and software necessary to produce and broadcast a television program.

12. John Berger, "Ev'ry Time We Say Goodbye," *Expressen* (Stockholm, November 3, 1990) Reprinted in *Keeping a Rendezvous* (1992).

13. *The International Dictionary of Thoughts* (Chicago: J.G. Ferguson Co., 1969), 148.

BASER INSTINCT:
BIAS IN THE MASS MEDIA

And as it is appointed unto men once to die, but after this the judgment.
Hebrews 9:27 (KJV)

America has a real strong Puritan ethic. I don't like it. Pushing the edge of broadcast standards is something I've always done. Broadcast standards simply are whatever they'll finally let you do. That becomes the new standard.
Steven Bochco[1]

Most of the important decision makers in Hollywood are very rich middle-aged men who get kind of excited at the idea of seeing Demi Moore's breasts. They figure that if they get excited, so will the rest of America—and it will translate into big bucks at the box office. Well, they're wrong. They're clearly out of step with middle America, which is far more keen on a Tom Cruise action film or a Disney cartoon than it will ever be on seeing famous women's bodies.
Al Bowman, publicist[2]

Fact: Margaret Hamilton, so perfectly evil as the Wicked Witch of the West in The Wizard of Oz, *was once a kindergarten teacher.*[3]

Just as important as understanding the grammar, rhetoric, and technology of the mass media is understanding how the mass media works behind the scenes.

Because the entertainment media are so pervasive, most people assume that it is an extraordinarily large industry. Although the entertainment industry accounts for one-sixth of our gross national product, experts contend there are fewer than 100 people who make the final decision to green light an entertainment project for production and distribution by one of the eight major companies that control approximately 98% of the box office, television programs, and major media. In effect, the entertainment industry is much like *The Wizard of Oz*, where the people believe that the Wizard is omnipresent and omnipotent, but when Toto pulls back the curtain, we find just a little old man whom Dorothy chides for bullying and scaring everyone.

The power of these men and women can be seen in the length of time it takes to get a movie produced, which is on average nine years from conception to the theater. Many creative people, even those with producer credits on some of the top-grossing movies, cannot get their scripts produced without joining forces with one of the insiders who occupies the top echelon of the industry.

The exclusiveness of this club has been demonstrated by the fact that many successful outsiders have tried to produce movies and have lost their shirts. From Howard Hughes to the Japanese, Hollywood has taken these men's money and left them wondering what happened.

For the first time in history, entertainers—whether actors, producers, media moguls, musicians, or athletes—are at the top of the social order. In the past, Mozart survived at the whim of the monarch, and entertainers were thrown to the dogs if they didn't please their lords.

The primary reason for the social ascendancy of the entertainment industry talent is misuse of the First Amendment of the United States Constitution. The irresponsible behavior of many mass media productions frequently hides behind a specious distortion of the constitutional right to free speech—a right that has clear constitutional limits.

Those who yell the loudest about free speech often yell the loudest that Christians do not have a right to teach biblical principles in public schools or pray before a high school football game. How Christians came to accept this perverse worldview that it is all right to show women being mutilated in the name of free speech while it is forbidden to proclaim the Good News in strife-ridden schools exemplifies the cunning of the adversary and the lukewarmness of the church.

The First Amendment was intended to protect political and religious speech. For many years, the Supreme Court held that entertainment was not protected political speech and could be regulated by local censorship boards. In the 1950s, the Supreme Court started extending the protection of the First Amendment to non-political speech, which gave the entertainment industry the opportunity to prosper from pandering to prurient interests. The growing protection of the First Amendment gave the entertainment industry a privileged position it had never enjoyed before in history.

Even with the changing attitude of the Supreme Court, TV and radio were regulated by the Federal Communication Commission (FCC) because the broadcasters used the public airwaves courtesy of the federal government.

At the same time the court was protecting the entertainment industry, there was an increasing concentration of power within it due to mergers and acquisitions. Understanding the attitudes and worldviews of those behind the scenes in entertainment is important because their attitudes and ideas shape the communications that in turn shape our culture.

Private placement

A growing number of Hollywood executives and talent use the entertainment media to promote their particular agendas, attitudes, and ideas—which may be contrary to a biblical worldview.

Michael Medved, orthodox Jew, author, and movie critic, has the following humorous and troubling insight into the thinking of the decision makers in Hollywood:

> About a year ago, I was on a panel with executives of three major film studios. After I criticized the irresponsible behavior of the movie industry, one panelist, furious, replied that while Hollywood is always blamed for the bad it does, it's never given credit for its positive impact. "You don't acknowledge that a movie like *Lethal Weapon III* saved thousands of lives," he said.
>
> I couldn't recall a life-giving message in this blood-spattered thriller, so I asked what he meant.
>
> "Well," he replied, "in that movie, right before the big chase scene, there was an intense, three-second close-up showing Mel Gibson and Danny Glover fastening their seat belts."
>
> He was suggesting that people would immediately imitate what they saw for three seconds, but the rest of the movie's ultraviolent 118 minutes would have no influence at all. Isn't that contradiction illogical and absurd?[4]

Many moral Christians and Jews in the entertainment industry contend that there is a pervasive political correctness that will deter even the most stouthearted from going against the grain on issues such as abortion and perversion. The situation is further exacerbated by the fact that the entertainment industry makes money by violating taboos, toying with temptations, titillating the audience, pandering to prurient interests, pumping up the adrenaline with ultraviolence, and playing to the natural curiosity of the emotionally immature.

The powers behind the thrones

The *Los Angeles Times* estimates there are more than 1,000 groups lobbying Hollywood. In 1997, UCLA convened 300 of these advocacy groups to meet with the chairmen of the major entertainment companies.

These groups include the militant homosexual group GLAAD (Gay and Lesbian Alliance Against Defamation) and feminist and environmental groups (Michael Eisner is chairman of one of the more active environmental groups). These lobbying organizations not only push their individual agendas, but also enlist the support of the key men and women in the entertainment industry and educate these women and men in the politically correct thinking that corresponds to the positions of the group.

Although many people are unaware of the power of the entertainment media to shape lives, those who spend billions of dollars to advertise in the mass media and those who spend millions to produce movies that will earn billions collectively every year are well aware of the power of the mass media of entertainment. Not only do cults like Scientology (whose influence can be seen in the movies *Phenomena* and *Powder*) spend considerable time and money lobbying Hollywood, but powerful communicators throughout this century have understood the power of the entertainment media. Vladimir Lenin, the founder of the totalitarian communist state, said that he could control the world if he controlled Hollywood movies. Joseph Goebbels, the infamous National Socialist propagandist, made feature films like *I Accuse* to convert the German people from prolife to proeuthanasia, prodeath, and pro–gas chambers.

The celluloid closet

One group which has had exceptional success in Hollywood is the homosexual movement. In 1996 a documentary on the influence of homosexuals in Hollywood called *The Celluloid Closet* was released theatrically in the United States. This documentary is an important insight into the persistent work of the homosexual and lesbian communities to communicate their values through the entertainment media.

If this documentary had been produced by conservatives, there would have been an uproar about the bias of the work. The documentary shows the subtle manipulation of the mass media by the homosexual community throughout history and affirms the worst fears of moral Americans—that many of the most popular movies push a deviant political and cultural agenda.

On February 14, 1991, a top secret, high-level meeting took place in Hollywood between the heads of entertainment companies that produce movies and television programs and the Gay and Lesbian Alliance Against Defamation/Los Angeles, or GLAAD/LA. At the meeting studio heads were told how to portray homosexuals, what to say, and what not to say by a bevy of homosexuals and lesbians.

The representatives of GLAAD/LA had a list of "Do s and Don'ts," which are as follows:

Do take note of lesbian and gay history.

Do list the name of a lover of many years, upon request, in a lesbian or gay man's obituary. Recognize that it is unfair to defer automatically to the biological family of the deceased in these matters.

Do use the term *sexual orientation* (or *gender orientation*) instead of *sexual preference* or *sexual choice.*

Do address the special issues faced by the gay elderly in stories about the elderly, by gay runaways in stories about runaways, etc.

Do not use the terms *fag, dyke, homo,* or similar epithets.

Do not include homosexuality in a laundry list of social evils (e.g., "crime, drug abuse, and homosexuality").

Do not refer to the gay "lifestyle."

Do not confuse pedophilia with homosexuality.

Do not assume homosexuals are promiscuous.

The GLAAD/LA representatives insisted that "AIDS is not a 'gay disease'" and forbade the media to use the terms *AIDS carrier* (no one should be informed that the person carries AIDS), *AIDS victim* (which might make homosexuals look like the aggressive victimizers), *bodily fluids* (which might give the audience a clue as to how AIDS is transmitted), *general population* (which might suggest that homosexuals are a small, perverse group in contrast to the general population), *high-risk groups* (again this term singles out homosexuals and drug users as a small group), *innocent victims* (which also suggests that homosexuals are the aggressors), and *intimate sexual contact* (this term might also give people a clue about how AIDS is transmitted).

Imagine the church making similar demands, such as "Do not call all Christians fundamentalists," or "Do not call Christians right wing." There would be a tremendous uproar as cries of censorship rang out across the land.

Yet the entertainment companies quietly submitted to the GLAAD/LA demands and even invited GLAAD/LA representatives to the hallowed Monday morning production meetings to meet with the creative personnel and present their agenda.

Homosexuals have always used force, or *zaps*, as they called it. In 1974, a group of lesbians used an inside contact to occupy the well-guarded NBC headquarters in Manhattan and refused to leave until the network conceded to their demands. By the mid-1970s, homosexuals had become so institutionalized in network television that they rarely needed to use protests.

Success of homosexual tactics can be measured by the strong influence they now have in politics and in corporate America. In June 1991, AT&T recognized and promoted Gay Pride Week. The New York City government bathed the Empire State Building in lavender for the event. New York City firehouses were also decorated with pink posters inviting homosexuals to "out in government." A poster in the parade screamed their perverse agenda, "We're here, we're queer, and we're coming for your children."

Mein Kampf

In 1992, *Between the Lines* reported that a founder of the militant homosexual activist group ACT UP in the nation's capital was publicly apologizing for his role in creating the organization and saying Hitler's *Mein Kampf* helped inspire its frequently violent campaigns.[5] Eric M. Pollard wrote in the *Washington Blade*, a District of Columbia homosexual weekly, that he had regrets about his work in founding ACT UP/DC. "I have helped to create a truly fascist organization that I now believe to be among the greatest threats to our freedom and the healing of our people," he wrote.[6] The idea, Pollard wrote, was to start a group that was loud and brazen and that forced people to listen by using "subversive tactics, drawn largely from the voluminous *Mein Kampf*, which some of us studied as a working model."[7]

In their book *The Pink Swastika*, Scott Lively and Kevin Abrams show that this connection between the homosexual lobby and national socialism has it roots in the early Nazi movement in Germany, so it is not uncommon to see homosexual activists employing tactics associated with Nazism—such as mob violence, vandalism, intimidation, and censorship—even as they denounce their opponents as Nazis.[8]

Free for all

Feminists, pacifists, socialists, environmentalists, groups like the NAACP, the American Medical Association, the PTA, and many others have also been active lobbying the entertainment industry. Even witches, warlocks, and Satanists have gotten on the bandwagon to lobby the mass media, and recently celebrities have been forming their own organizations to push their own causes.[9] Many of these groups, such as People for the American Way, have a blatant anti-Christian agenda.

The reason all these groups are fighting to control the entertainment companies is because they understand that whoever controls the media controls the culture.

Revisionist history

Some of the bias of the media leaders is quite clear. Oliver Stone, for example, openly trumpets his peculiar political agenda and proclaims his desire to revise history with the production of movies such as *JFK* and *Nixon*. The politically correct agenda of the left can also be seen in the historical revisionism of animated movies such as *Pocahontas* as well as period pieces such as *The Scarlet Letter*. Although moral Americans consistently reject these blatant attempts to revise history, people overseas often learn about the United States through these movies and television programs and develop erroneous and negative views of American culture through these mass media products.

Some of Hollywood's revisions of history are just plain silly, although they are just as detrimental to the propagation of the truth since, as George Santayana affirmed, "Those who cannot remember the past are condemned to repeat it."[10]

In the popular movie *The Wind and the Lion* the aged Greek-American male, Ion Perdicaris, who was captured by the desert bandit, was turned into the ravishing Candice Bergen, while the despicable Moroccan bandit, Raisuli, became the dashing Sean Connery. Regrettably, people will view an inaccurate historical movie such as *The Wind and the Lion* and consider that to be the truth. In fact, one of the leading educators in the field of media literacy recommends *The Wind and the Lion* as an example of how to teach history through film.

A common distortion of reality that contemporary moviemakers undertake is turning the savage, who is as sinful as the rest of fallen man, into the noble savage. In a blatant revision of history, the animated Disney movie *Pocahontas* had the Indians as the good guys while the white settlers were greedy barbarians. And, the dismal *Scarlet Letter* had the Indians ride in to save the day at the end of the movie just as the cavalry would have done during the Golden Age of Hollywood.

Because there are many distortions of history and the nature of the world in the mass media, it is a must for you to discern how the world is portrayed in an entertainment product. Of course, to do so you must know the truth and use the truth to expose the fruitless works of darkness. Furthermore, moral individuals must demand historical accuracy in motion pictures.

Capture the culture

Richard Grenier in his book *Capturing the Culture: Film, Art, and Politics* reveals the depth of one particular political agenda. Grenier shows that the Italian Marxist Antonio Gramsci played a crucial role in Marxism's spread to the cultural realm and that he was "the most prescient analyst of the contemporary relationship of art and politics. . . . Culture, Gramsci felt, is not simply the superstructure of an economic base, the role assigned to it in orthodox Marxism, but it is central to society."[11]

Marching to Gramsci's famous slogan, "Capture the culture," Grenier documents how Gramsci's disciples continue their "long march through the institutions" of the cultural world. Although the collapse of socialism in the Soviet Union and Eastern Europe has totally discredited Lenin's political work, Gramsci's legacy remains with us in the form of a powerful cultural left. In his book, Grenier explores how "the modern artist's predisposition to estrangement has flung him, in America especially, straight into Gramsci's arms."[12]

As an example, Grenier cites *Reds*, the Warren Beatty film about the Russian Revolution, which demonstrates "what can be called the 'politics of intent,' as opposed to the politics of achievement. If one has noble intentions and means well toward one's fellow man and one's heart is pure and generous and filled with love, then that is what matters. If one's ideas are unworkable, bring social disruption, disaster and even tragedy on a colossal scale—one can't be expected to foresee all that, can one?"[13]

No moral absolutes?

To be discerning, it is important to realize that in the Marxist cultural universe of Gramsci and others who may not even understand the origin of their presuppositions, dialectal materialism means much more than a thesis and an antithesis becoming a synthesis. Instead, such thinking implies that the rightness or wrongness of any action or proposition (the thesis or antithesis) must be scrapped in favor of maybeness (the synthesis). In the process, truth is compromised and even effectively abandoned, while falsehood takes its place.

As John F. McManus has pointed out in his article "Absolutes Under Attack":

> What could be more subversive of good order? Bad philosophy, especially a system holding that absolutes are to be shunned or compromised, is the ultimate subverter. . . .

> While few realize it, much of today's thinking is based on the flawed systems produced by Kant, Hegel, and Marx. Those who take a firm stand for (thesis) or against (antithesis) almost anything should be prepared to have the label "extremist" hung around their necks. They should expect to be urged to adopt the middle ground (synthesis).

> Modern America is constantly being persuaded to avoid the "extreme" position and settle somewhere in the fuzzy middle. In the field of ethics, right and wrong is out, and "it depends on the situation" has taken over. The Rev. Joseph Fletcher, whose book *Situation Ethics* has infected millions, held membership in the Communist Party USA— hardly a surprise. What he was proposing was a synthesis as a substitute for "Thou shalt" and "Thou shalt not."

> . . . Recall how often politics has been defined as "the art of compromise," and you begin to see how the heirs of the philosophical subverters of the 19th century have been winning. Elected and appointed officials are repeatedly praised for arrival at the "middle ground." They have adopted the thinking of Karl Marx.

Bad philosophy cannot undergird a healthy civilization. . . . The entire world would be in far better shape if millions were persuaded to realize that right is right even if no one always says so. And so, too, wrong is always wrong. What is desperately needed is a proliferation of such thinking, the kind that makes a habit of championing absolutes."[14]

Alien

The movie *Aliens* was one of the first of a growing number of movies that established a feminist worldview, where the women are the strong, capable leaders, and the men are mere obstacles or minor characters.

In *Aliens*, the lone survivor of the original battle with the aliens is a woman. She goes back to the planet with a group of inept marines and a greedy businessman to save a human colony. When they arrive at the planet, they find that the aliens have wiped out everybody except for one little girl (no little boys survived) who managed to hide in the air ducts. The aliens are still implanting eggs inside humans, where they incubate and hatch right out of the human stomach.

Ripley, our heroine, finds out that the chief alien is an intelligent female, insect-like creature who is laying the eggs. Ripley kills the mother alien to save the little girl for whom she has motherly feelings. (Note that the little girl allows Ripley to enjoy motherhood without having to have a man in her life).

Unlike the first *Alien* in which the female symbolism was slightly hidden, in this movie the female motif so dominates that there are no memorable male characters, except the greedy Burke, who is a minor character.

Furthermore, this series established the fetus as a monster. In this frightening film, the alien bursts out from the stomach or womb of a human, symbolizing the hedonist's fear of the baby in the womb and effectively demonstrating the need to abort this potentially alien creature.

Beyond the fringe

Some of the quaint, uninformed views in Hollywood would be quite humorous if they didn't have such a strong influence on our children and the world.

In an essay accompanying Benetton ads in the November 12, 1992, issue of *Rolling Stone*, filmmaker Spike Lee contends that AIDS is an out-of-control government plot targeted at blacks, sodomites, and Hispanics:

> I'm convinced that AIDS is a government engineered disease. They got one thing wrong, they believed it could just be confined to the groups it was intended to wipe out. So, now it's a national priority. Exactly like drugs became when they escaped the urban centers into white suburbia.[15]

United Colors of Benetton, known for controversial ads, made a $50,000 donation in Lee's name to the United Negro College Fund Malcolm X Scholarship for the essay, which wrapped around eight pages of ads.

Overworked themes

As a result of the politicization of the entertainment industry, many of the themes in Hollywood entertainment have become boringly repetitious, recycling the same plots, ideas and characters to the point of nausea. Here are the silver screen's ten most overworked premises according to Marilyn Duff of *Between the Lines*:

> All businessmen have guns in their top desk drawers.

> The CIA is an international network of terrorists and drug smugglers.

> All Indians are wise and good-hearted. All white settlers were rapacious monsters.

> Nature is benign; all wolves are loving, loyal, overgrown puppies; any animal is better than any human.

All dysfunctional families are of Northern European origin, usually Anglo-Saxon, and most often Christian.

All Southerners are cretins.

Military men are tenuously repressed animals.

Drug addicts, alcoholics, the homeless, and gang members are that way because of society.

Automobiles were made to be crashed.

The U.S. government is evil . . . period.[16]

Subliminal messages

A few entertainment industry leaders have resorted to subliminal messages in their movies to titillate their audience.

The *San Antonio Express News* reported on October 16, 1995, that Paramount Pictures's movie *Jade* contained split-second images amid the film's normal sequences. Director William Friedkin dismisses the idea of placing a warning on the film, claiming that it is merely "a cinematic device."

The use of this technique opens up the possibility that the producer or director will use it to influence the audience.

No churches on Main Street

In recent years, every entertainment giant has produced and distributed product detrimental to the well-being of the family and moral individuals. However, the Walt Disney Company deserves special consideration as a case study herein because it has enjoyed special status in our culture as the standard-bearer of wholesome family entertainment.

As a result of the good will this family product engendered, the Walt Disney Company has become the largest purveyor of family-oriented entertainment in the world. Regrettably, in the process of expansion and growth, the Disney Company has produced some products that offend and alienate its primary market, the family.

As a result, Disney has come under growing attack from concerned Americans. Some of the complaints are misguided and misinformed, but all express the deeply felt concerns of millions of Americans.

Disney has never claimed to be a Christian company. Though Walt Disney was anticommunist, he was never pro-Christian and made some disparaging remarks about Christianity during his life. He refused to allow a church on Main Street or in the Disney World compound. He also stipulated there could not be a church in the subdivision he was planning to build at Disney World.

Occultism and violence permeated many of Disney's films from *Fantasia* to the present. In *Pinocchio*, when Geppetto dropped to his knees, folded his hands, and turned his eyes to heaven, he did not pray to God, but instead, he wished upon a star.

In the more than thirty animated features Disney has released since 1937, there is scarcely a mention of God, a portrayal of prayer, or the appearance of any symbol from the Christian faith shared by most Americans. The animated Disney classics rely primarily on mythic tales and images that are replete with witches and demons, sorcerers and spells, genies and goblins.

Research has shown that the occultism in the early Disney films influenced a significant number of people to adopt new age and even occult beliefs.

Surprisingly, after years of avoiding Christian themes, Disney released *The Hunchback of Notre Dame*, wherein the key problems are resolved by prayers to God—not to a fairy godmother or a star! During these prayers to God, there are clear images of Jesus. During the second prayer there is the clear image of Jesus Resurrected—the God to Whom the prayer is directed! *Hunchback* is not perfect, but the plot turns on God and His grace in contrast to previous Disney animated movies. This is a first for a Disney movie.

This spiritual focus may be attributed to the fact that the producer of *Hunchback* is a family man and a committed Christian, as were many of the animators working on the project.

Many new Disney movies more accurately reflect the values held by most Americans than some of the older films. For example, *The Preacher's Wife* proclaims the Good News of Jesus Christ and the Christmas story, and *Father of the Bride* is profather, profamily, and prolife.

Even so, the Disney image is being soiled by releasing products that are abhorrent to the vast majority of Americans. As an example, some say Disney has sexualized some of its most popular animated features. Recent heroines such as Little Mermaid, Jasmine in *Aladdin*, and Pocahontas manage to show lots of cleavage. The same complaints were made about some of the early Disney female characters, but that does not assuage the concerns of loving parents.

The historical documentary video *Hollywood Uncensored: Hollywood before the Code* shows that sexual innuendo, sometimes overt, was present in earlier Disney films. In fact, you will note that there was even female upper body nudity in some early Disney work!

However, this historical perspective does not excuse a disturbing incident in a scene in *The Little Mermaid* that seems to depict a priest becoming noticeably sexually aroused while presiding over a wedding. Disney spokespeople claim that this is a knee, but the artwork can easily be read otherwise. Also, a castle spire on the original *Little Mermaid* video jacket art resembled a phallus, though Disney corrected the jacket art as soon as it was brought to its attention.

Likewise, families have become increasingly concerned that humorous homosexual references have made it onto Disney's family films. For instance, in *Aladdin*, the genie gurgles to his young master, "I'm getting fond of you, kid—not that I want to pick out curtains or anything." Although homosexual groups have complained that these barbs are instances of antihomosexual bias and similar routines (such as cross-dressing) were included in some of the earlier Disney product, families have become more aware of the influence of the entertainment media on their children and less accepting of behavior condemned or forbidden by Scripture.

Of great concern to the vast majority of deeply religious Americans is the pagan and anti-Christian elements in some of Disney's recent family fare. The most egregious example is *Pocahontas*, Walt Disney Pictures' first animated feature film about real persons. In that movie, history's Captain John Smith becomes a believer in a godless nature religion, and the nature spirit of Pocahontas' mother returns to Europe with Smith. In reality, Pocahontas became a baptized, informed, godly Christian—the first Christian of her nation.

Also, Disney and its subsidiaries, Miramax Pictures, Touchstone Pictures, and Hollywood Pictures, continue to produce and distribute live-action, adult-rated, motion pictures. Included in this library of movies are:

> *Lie Down with Dogs*, a totally disgusting 1995 Miramax movie about perversion;

> *Pulp Fiction*, a 1994 Miramax movie focused on outrageous violence and shameless sex. This movie was trimmed back from an NC-17 rating to an R rating; and,

> *Color of Night*, a 1994 Hollywood Pictures/Disney Company release that shows costars Bruce Willis and Jan March entwined in numerous fornication scenes featuring full frontal nudity.

Sexually explicit movies usually bomb at the box office. In 1996, the average box office for sexually explicit feature films was just over $700,000—pitiful in an industry in which the average movie costs over $40 million to produce and distribute. The average gross for these sexually explicit movies would indicate that they attract no more than 200,000 people in a country of 260 million people. In contrast, movies with strong Christian content averaged over $37 million in 1996.

Disney's television efforts have added to the concerns of families. According to the American Family Association, Disney has been one of the top sponsors of prohomosexual TV programming. Furthermore, the Disney-owned ABC network has had some of the most risqué prime time television programming. The series *Relativity* aired an explicit love scene on January 11, 1996, that shocked many, but it was a lesbian *Ellen* coming out of the closet that crossed the line once and for all.

Furthermore, Disney's book publishing division, Hyperion Press, came out with several homosexual-oriented volumes, including *Growing Up Gay in America*, which is aimed at teenagers. Hyperion also published the drag queen's guide to happiness, *Lettin' It All Hang Out*, by RuPaul, a well-known transvestite entertainer who is applauded by Disney as a role model.[17]

A spokesperson for Disney countered that Hyperion also published *Father Greg and the Homeboys*, a wonderful story about a Jesuit priest and his work with gangs in East L.A.; *Lift Every Voice*, a powerful account of the Boys Choir of Harlem with the subtitle "Expecting the Most and Getting the Best from All of God's Children"; *Jesus CEO*, in which the author encourages leaders to review the divine excellence in themselves and in those they serve; and *The Path*, which takes its title from Isaiah 30:21.[18]

In terms of Disney's famous family theme parks, many people are concerned about the annual "Gay and Lesbian Day at Walt Disney World," which has been celebrated at the park for six years. Parents who have visited the park on that particular day have been upset at the lewd behavior and antifamily, immoral atmosphere. One family was even chased from the park by insulting homosexual celebrants.

John Dreyer, vice president of corporate communications for the Walt Disney Company, has responded to a letter on this issue saying:

> Walt Disney World does not and has not sponsored "Gay Day." There is an annual gay convention in Orlando. The event's organizers do designate a day on the agenda for their members to visit our parks. Those who choose to do so go to the park, buy their tickets, and have a good time

just like thousands of other people from around the world do every day. Some have suggested we turn them away. It raises the question of how you identify the people you would deny access to your theme park, your church, your grocery store, your library, your school, etc. We have a policy of non-discrimination. To do otherwise raises a specter of having pressure groups identify other subsets of society to turn away.

We have very high standards of behavior for our guests and employees. So long as our guests adhere to them, whether they claim to be straight or gay, we will host them and treat them with dignity.[19]

Regrettably, those standards are not being upheld according to many paying families who have been visiting the park during the "Gay Day" event.

Another concern of many who visit Walt Disney World is the revised, four-minute President Abraham Lincoln speech, which no longer quotes one of Mr. Lincoln's real speeches but instead now reflects the views of Professor Eric Foner, a well-known leftist radical and a longtime critic of the Lincoln speech used in the Disneyland show. According to Foner, freedom is "an arena of conflict, carrying different meanings for different groups of people," so the new speech says that "our nation has had to struggle to expand the idea of freedom to encompass more and more Americans," which sounds nothing like the real Mr. Lincoln. Regrettably, what is portrayed in the Hall of Presidents will pass for history for the millions of people (especially children) who hear the revisionist speech.

Probably the most disturbing change at Disney was the company's extension of health benefits to live-in partners of homosexual employees. Although Disney was the last Hollywood studio to grant such benefits, its family image made its policy change more significant to pro-family Americans. However, one of the insurance underwriters has noted that a large number of claims could cause Disney serious financial difficulty, and an employee in the legal services side of the personnel department notes that the number of homosexual employees has to be low enough that it does not financially burden the company. Contrary to self-serving reports in homosexual magazines, he puts the percentage of homosexual employees at Disney at under 10% and notes that they are far outnumbered by Christian employees who head up major divisions and productions such as the family film division and the animation department.

Regrettably, Disney's insensitive business decisions and tainted entertainment is forcing families to make some very hard decisions. Enough of those decisions may persuade Disney to return to a creative lineup free from material that families find offensive.

A good reputation is hard to gain and even harder to lose (and Disney has earned one of the best according to audience surveys), but more and more of the family audience are seeing Disney in a different light, and a growing number of Americans are starting to avoid Disney's family releases. It will take a long time for the majority of the American people to completely turn off; however, extensive surveys show that more and more people are disappointed and even angered by some of the product coming out of the Magic Kingdom.

The inmates take over the asylum

One of the problems faced by Disney and the other media giants is that although there has been a growing concentration of power occurring in the entertainment media, the worldviews and political positions represented in the media products of the entertainment industry may no longer represent the will of the top executives. In the good old days, the studio bosses wanted to reach as large an audience as possible so they could support themselves in the manner to which they had become accustomed, so they set down the rules for movie content. Some of those studio executives may have been immoral libertines, but their movies were morally uplifting because they did not want to alienate any segment of the

American public. Thus, they voluntarily supported the Motion Picture Code to ensure that there were no elements, such as nudity or profanity, that would keep any American from seeing their films.

After the 1948 Paramount Pictures case (in which the Supreme Court separated the studios from their theaters),[20] the distributors/studios converted their operations from monopolies, which controlled everything from the actors to the theaters, into vast financing and distribution organizations. These organizations provided producers with the capital and services to make their movies and distribute them to the theaters, which the distributors could now only control by acting as a gatekeeper for product being provided by the producers. This change meant that the producer often has to carry the entire cost of development, while the studio waits for the producer to present the right entertainment package to fund and distribute. Since the distributors want to protect their investment, they look for those elements that are bankable. Bankable elements mainly refer to the key creative talent such as the director and stars.

When these "bankable" creative people realized how important they were, they started to demand their creative right to do what they wanted without regard for the marketplace. The studio executives now have to deal with the public and the talent, and often the talent wins since a sizable portion of the public tends to accept whatever Hollywood gives them.

One top executive pointed out that some big name directors and actors no longer listen to the studio executives. This executive complained that one famous director refused to take one offensive word out of a movie so that the studio could sell the movie to television and to the airlines. The director, however, sold the rights to this movie to the BBC, agreeing to take out the word. Since the director was paid a flat fee in the United States, he had no incentive to consider the marketplace. However, since he owned the European rights, he modified his stance to ensure that he made a profit.

Thus, the prima donnas have taken over the industry. Since they are not as responsive to the marketplace, some of them are steering the industry onto the rocks of bankruptcy. (Orion is bankrupt, while MGM and a few others are teetering on the edge of the abyss.) So it goes with the spoiled brat pack who are not only making the business decisions, but also giving themselves awards for their efforts. The executives who pander to the prima donnas can only expect to alienate more and more of the world's population.

Every day more and more people are fed up with the incestuous dehumanization of Hollywood and more and more countries are putting up restrictions to Hollywood movies. Only when Hollywood starts to care about their customers and stops indulging their brats will it regain the stature it attained during the Golden Age of Hollywood.

Peep TV

With regard to the behind-the-scenes influences shaping the mass media, one of the more egregious examples is contemporary talk TV. Dr. Judith Reisman has found that:

> Currently, many network talk shows . . . serve as paid "advertorials" for the pornography industry. . . .
>
> *Playboy* appears to be the funding conduit to promote the sale of its own product as well as that of other pornographers (and thus organized crime). They even funnel funds through blinds and obscure channels. . . .
>
> These "talk" shows were fast becoming "TV Peep Shows" with . . . Geraldo, . . . Sally Jessy Raphael, etc. acting as the shills, the TV pimps and madams hustling their naked sex show exhibitors and freaks: "Come one, come all to . . . see Cindy Shimmer do her thing. She'll take it all off for you!" And, they generally find women who will say "I love it." Especially TV "talk" shows, no matter how humiliating and degrading, they always love it. [21]

Instead, the programs put women on who will say something like "I'm a happy grandma, and my life began when I first got tied up during sex," (*Donahue*); or a half-nude woman with whips and chains: "beating him with a whip is just fun" (*Donahue*); or with "censored" *Playboy* photos: "after my crippling accident, I thought I'd never be able to have sex, so I appeared nude in *Playboy*—and that made me a woman" (*Sally*); or more "censored" *Playboy* nude photos: "I was Mrs. Oklahoma and the best thing I ever did was to appear nude as a mom, in *Playboy*" (*Sally*).

These programs are aimed at the woman homemaker, and the TV hustlers are pushing the coarsest forms of exhibitionism and pornography on the most conservative of our women and youth. Their aim is to desensitize American homemakers because the homemakers are stumbling blocks to the pornographers' full control over the community, especially the vulnerable and lucrative juvenile population.

In the past, these homemakers would say that pornography violates their community standards and should be hidden from the children. However, their concerns will not stand up in court if ACLU lawyers prove that these same homemakers watch peep TV every day and if their children are thus exposed to the mainstreaming of sexual deviancy all week long.

Dr. Reisman says that we need to be concerned because:

> Voyeurism (the essence of all pornography) is a psychosexually devastating and often addictive experience—especially for youths, young moms, and other vulnerable shut-ins who are daily watching. . . .
>
> . . . Peep TV is Toxic Media, and as it norms pornography, it norms incest, rape, homo/bisexual dysfunction, prostitution, drug use, and every other form of psychosexual disorder.[22]

A new age

Another growing influence in Hollywood is the attraction of some of the top men and women to new age beliefs. This flirtation with occultism has spawned shows like *The Psychic Friends Network*, which are allowed to buy air time on cable and local stations to sell their so-called "entertainment services," and network programs like *The Other Side* (NBC), *Encounters* (Fox), *Sightings* (syndicated), *The Extraordinary* (syndicated), and even occasionally *Unsolved Mysteries* (NBC), which give psychic and paranormal phenomena unprecedented respectability.

The Other Side has sported such exciting topics as contacting dead relatives through psychics, teen witches, abductions by space aliens, miraculous healings by psychics, spirit lovers, ghost co-workers, psychics who talk with pets, real vampires, how to improve your luck, animistic forces in the possessions of dead people, and near-death experiences where people met spirit beings of light.

In a MOVIEGUIDE® article titled "The Other Side . . . Of What?" Derrick Warfel wrote:

> To be sure, some of this is merely wacky and sensational programming geared to boost ratings. However, *Time* magazine (May 15, 1995) commented that "though the producers treat these shows as mere entertainment, many viewers do not."

> As Christians, we recognize that a certain percent of psychic phenomena is undoubtedly fraud, and yet we also know that there is an "other side" that is not fraud, but demonic. Exposure to such programming is not only likely to increase belief in the paranormal but opens people up to demonic influence.[23]

It is hard to believe that network television has come to this. These are the same networks that have extensive rules about Christian organizations advertising on their networks. For instance, all three networks refused to sell ad time to a nationwide evangelical Christian outreach claiming that if they opened the door to one religious group, it would have to be opened up to all.

Yet they blatantly promote spiritism and the occult with their own programs.

Even more disturbing and shocking are the mainstream sponsors that are grabbing up advertising time to promote spiritism and the occult, including AT&T, Arm & Hammer Baking Soda, and Ballpark Franks.

Mother Earth

Since elves, gnomes, and fairies have charmed children throughout history, including them and their messages in children's movies and other media products tend to bypass rational scrutiny. As author Berit Kjos points out:

> Their power to persuade comes not from reliability but from desirability. . . . As the line between myth and reality blurs, anything becomes believable if it feels right and supports a person's views.[24]

Therefore, many children are learning to trust a pantheistic force rather than God, our Creator. The movie *Ferngully* is a good example of a new age movie since it contains all the basic beliefs of contemporary earth-centered spirituality:

Matriarchal leadership.

Secret knowledge.

A wise old tree spirit.

Lunar cycles.

Everything is connected (monism) through a divine spiritual force that flows through all parts of nature (pantheism).

Anyone can learn to manipulate this magical force.

It is time to revive ancient magical arts and psychic connections with all of nature.

The resurgence of nature religions satisfies the modern demand for an all-inclusive religion that can restore our original harmony with nature and each other. Of course, this harmony was permanently disrupted by man's sin and will only be restored when God creates a new heaven and a new earth. The key to this restoration is the forgiveness for sin and the salvation that is available only in Jesus Christ.

Regrettably, not only the entertainment media, but also classrooms across the country and trusted groups like the Girl Scouts are teaching children how to contact occult forces. Therefore, you need to teach your child how to recognize and resist their seductive bait by teaching them:

A biblical and historical perspective that shows the consequences of trusting pagan practices rather than God, the Maker of heaven and earth.

An awareness of the spiritual forces arrayed against God's people and a willingness to follow God, whose power is sovereign and omnipotent (Ephesians 6:10-18).

A living relationship with God through Jesus Christ.

A knowledge of His truth as revealed in the Bible.

Armed with truth, facts, a historical perspective, and a willingness to follow God, God will leads us in triumph over the forces of darkness (2 Corinthians 2:14)!

Deconstruction

Some of the move toward occultism in the entertainment media is even more sinister than Hollywood's infatuation with the new age. Gramsci's call to use art as a revolutionary battering ram to flatten the old values of society was initially conceptualized during the Romantic movement. The growth of aesthetic terrorism as a surrogate for political radicalism had its origins in France among the artistic radicals of the nineteenth century, whose fellowship frequently overlapped with the occult underworld.

Aesthetic terrorism derived from the occult desire for the supreme "knowledge of good and evil," which required subverting Christian symbols and values. These symbols and values must be ambushed, trampled down, eviscerated, and tossed aside by creating a universal sense of invincibility of evil. Aesthetic terrorism in many ways slices to the heart of what we mean by Satanism.

The problem of aesthetic terrorism surfaced in 1989 with the controversy concerning the funding by the National Endowment for the Arts of the photography of Andres Serrano and Robert Mapplethorpe. The flap over whether obscene artworks should be funded by public taxes obscured what Serrano and Mapplethorpe were really trying to do.

The issue revolved around the protests by Christian groups regarding an image of a crucifix in a pool of Serrano's urine bearing the title of *Piss Christ*. Christians complained that their taxes were being used to fund art that blasphemed God. Defenders countered that *Piss Christ* was nothing more than a pronouncement of disgust with commercialized religion.

The *New York Times* printed Mapplethorpe's 1982 work *Self Portrait (With Gun and Star)*. The picture shows the artist as a leather-clad terrorist cradling a machine gun with the star as backdrop. The star is clearly an inverted pentagram, the supreme symbol of Satanism. In another picture he is the Devil with horns. A review of Mapplethorpe in *Art News* called him "the prince of darkness, angel of light"—a most fitting sobriquet for Luciferian imagination.

This aesthetic terrorism does not stop at the door of the art institute. A TV network executive complained to me that witchcraft groups were altering the storyboards for his network's animated, Saturday morning cartoons. This executive said that he uncovered satanic symbols in storyboards coming back from animation houses and that even lyrics to children's songs had been adulterated. When one lyricist was confronted about her satanic inferences, she admitted that she was a witch.

Top journalists admit bias

The publication *Dispatches* reported in its February 9, 1994, issue that a panel of top journalists from three prominent newspapers revealed the ideological and religious bias in the major news media. Represented were *Newsday*, the *Washington Post* and the *New York Times*.

"You think you're getting objective news when really you're getting the same old slanted stuff," said Gabriel Rotello of *Newsday*.[25]

Washington Post New York bureau chief Malcolm Gladwell said news people represent a narrow segment of the population: "If we had real diversity, it wouldn't be an issue. But, we don't. Papers like the *Washington Post* have assembled staffs to write on pressing national issues where everybody's national perspective is a carbon copy of everybody else's. That's the problem."[26]

Gladwell's solution is for papers like the *Post* and others to hire national affairs reporters who are religious, who have considered voting for a Republican presidential candidate, and who live in neighborhoods "where not everybody has two cars out front and mows the lawn every night."[27]

These insiders were willing to admit what most concerned Americans already know: the mainstream press is out of step with the vast majority of the American public and are actively seeking to shape and manipulate the news to fit their narrow political agenda rather than truthfully report on it.

Caveat

While we recognize that Oliver Stone has a political ax to grind, which he freely admits, that does not mean his movies will always reflect that perspective even if he intends that they do so. Stone has often achieved his goal of making very entertaining propaganda films. In a sense he is noncontroversial because he is so forthright about his controversial positions.

It must be noted that the personality and opinions of filmmakers are not always reflected in their work. For example, many

Christians are enamored by the powerful movie *Chariots of Fire* and the superb television program *Jesus of Nazareth*. People claim they have come to Christ because of these media products.

Interestingly, both *Chariots of Fire* and *Jesus of Nazareth* were funded to a large degree by the same Muslim investor. Furthermore, *Chariots of Fire* was produced by a Jew, written by an atheist, and starred a homosexual who later died of AIDS. With regard to the powerful sermon in *Chariots of Fire*, the homosexual star said that they couldn't get the sermon right so he grabbed a Bible from the church where they were shooting the movie and paraphrased it.

The director of *Jesus of Nazareth* was an active bisexual who chased one of his male actors around his villa in Italy. (He later came to Christ after a serious car accident.)

Even the star of the popular *Jesus* film considers himself an agnostic.

Does the behavior, beliefs, and lack of Christian commitment of these men denigrate these works, or for that matter, any of the great art and literature throughout history?

We should be aware of the character and characteristics of the person in front of and behind the camera who can influence the entertainment product, but it is clear that God can raise up stones to testify to Him. If the Billy Graham Evangelistic Association had produced *Chariots of Fire* we could all feel more secure, but the fact is God has often used some of the top talent in Hollywood to glorify His name regardless of their own personalities or persuasions.

Some of the movies that have lifted up the name of Jesus were produced by known communists, socialists, and homosexuals. How does who they are relate to the wonderful testimony that they have brought forth?

Perhaps the problem is that biographical criticism can easily slide over into bigotry, which denies the sovereign power of God and the economy of His creation. We should use discernment with respect to each individual work and not allow our prejudices to blind us, for indeed, we all are sinners saved by grace, and these people, though fallen sinners, are all created in the image of God. As Jesus told the Pharisees:

> I tell you that, if these should hold their peace, the stones would immediately cry out.
>
> Luke 19:40 (KJV)

Good news

The good news is that a growing number of committed Christians are occupying positions of power and influence in the top echelons of the entertainment industry. When we started the redemptive work of The Christian Film and Television Commission in 1985, there was only one executive producer of the sixty prime-time television programs on the three majors networks who was outspoken about his Christianity. By 1994, at least twenty-three of the executive producers of the prime-time television programs on the three major networks were outspoken Christians.

A quick glance at some of the entertainment product being released indicates the great need for helping key entertainment leaders to understand a biblical worldview, which is the call of The Christian Film & Television Commission. However, the good news is that there is a growing number of informed, committed Christians in the entertainment industry and several ministries have been set up in the last few years to offer them fellowship and even discipling.

One of the animators for *The Simpsons* wrote me in 1992, saying:

> I thank God every day for my job and am doing all I can to witness and set an example to all. I recently redesigned the whole Springfield Church and for the first time ever, they've allowed me to put a small cross in the foyer of the church. I've also included Bible verses hanging on bulletin boards . . . (John 3:16-18, Eph. 1:20, 1 Cor. 6:9-11, Titus 3:5 . . .).

I pray to be used to change this industry and all the people I confront. I need strength, I need my fears to subside completely. . . . Jesus has not given me this opportunity to entertain people or to make a lot of money. I want to do what I can to bring people to Christ, before it's too late. I don't think we have a whole lot of time left, Dr. Baehr. I'm not setting dates sir, but something's happening. I join you in your fight against the evil in this industry. If there is anything I can do for you please call.

When we first met this animator told me that there were no outspoken Christians in his department. Now he is head of the department, and only one person in it is not a Christian.

Lest we forget

What most Christians have forgotten is that the church was the predominate influence in Hollywood from 1933 to 1966 through the Protestant Film Office and the Roman Catholic Legion of Decency (which we will examine in the next chapter). By enforcing the Motion Picture Code, the church offices ensured that movies were wholesome and uplifting, that they did not denigrate the law or religion, and that they did not lower the moral standards of the audience.

In 1966, the church closed these offices and abdicated its responsibility to be salt and light, leaving a vacuum soon filled by the special interest groups who currently influence Hollywood. Since that time, there has been a dramatic moral decline in the content of movies as other groups have filled the vacuum left by the church offices.

That is why we have established the Christian Film & Television Commission (CFTVC). The CFTVC employs a two-pronged approach to redeem the values of the entertainment industry. This approach was originally developed by the Christian leaders who wrote and monitored the Motion Picture Code. It is now used by many groups to lobby Hollywood.

One prong involves educating moral Americans through MOVIEGUIDE® so that they can make discerning choices at the box office and thereby influence the entertainment industry financially and through their correspondence.

The other prong involves helping media leaders understand the concerns of moral Americans. Like the church offices that inspired the Golden Age of Hollywood, the CFTVC reviews scripts and helps those in the media to work out creative solutions to moral questions so as to improve the dramatic and the moral qualities of the movies and programs they produce. The CFTVC also helps them portray religious people in a realistic and wholesome light.

By the grace of God, entertainment companies are submitting more and more scripts to us for review and more and more questions about Christianity and the Christian marketplace are being directed to our offices at The Christian Film & Television Commission. In fact, we have even been given the opportunity to work on some of the scripts for some of the top television programs and major movies.

Religion coverage

Even the news media are warming to Christians. As media consultant, Nancy Woodhull, has observed:

> "The baby boomers in the newsroom are thinking about their kids. They are wondering if they are going to heaven."[28]

For example, in 1995, ABC News named Peggy Wehmeyer the religious correspondent for ABC *World News Tonight*. Peggy had studied at the conservative Dallas Theological Seminary. Anchor Peter Jennings, who lobbied for a religion correspondent for two years, commented, "The role religion plays on today's society needs to be fully explored."

Behind the scenes, the Christian Film & Television Commission had been consulting with ABC about this issue for two years.

TBS pro-life spots

Just as encouraging as ABC News hiring a religion reporter was the fact that pro-adoption commercials aired on Turner Broadcasting's CNN, Headline News, TNT, and TBS while Planned Parenthood spots were rejected on the basis of content.[29]

Crying foul, Planned Parenthood claimed that Turner had unfairly taken sides. Evidently, Turner refused to run two pro-abortion spots without an extra disclaimer, in addition to the sponsor ID at front and back, stating that these views were not necessarily those of the network. Ultimately, Planned Parenthood dropped the campaign, but the prolife spots ran freely with no such disclaimer.

In one prolife ad, little plaid-skirted girls walk down the stairs of a private school while another girl, dressed as a cat for Halloween, plays in the front porch of her suburban home. "All of these children have one thing in common," says the voice-over. "All of them were unwanted pregnancies, pregnancies that could have ended in abortion. But their parents toughed it out. . . ." The tag line for both spots: "Life. What a Beautiful Choice."

Killer angels

Although there is a growing number of people of faith in Hollywood, it should be pointed out that some of the worst movies, television programs, and other media of the last few years have been produced by people who grew up in the church—not by people from some other religious heritage.

> Wes Craven, a graduate of Wheaton College, has produced some of the most abhorrent horror movies, including the infamous *People under the Stairs*. This is about a Christian couple who kidnap, torture, and cannibalize their neighbors.

> Paul Schrader, who wrote the script for the infamous *Last Temptation of Christ*, went to Calvin College.

And Martin Scorsese, who directed *Last Temptation of Christ*, went to seminary.

Theological confusion characterizes these graduates of Christian education. Schrader says his movie *Light Sleeper* was inspired by his chance encounter with a New Testament quote: "Behold, I show you a mystery: we shall not all sleep, but we shall all be changed." He said the movie establishes "a man on a spiritual quest—although he doesn't know it—and who achieves salvation and even heroism, although he consciously seeks neither."

Despite these grandiose claims, Schrader's mediocre movie is filled with occultism, drugs, explicit fornication, and murder. Hallucinatory drugs are a pathway to an alternate reality, but the "spiritual experience" is closer to witchcraft than Christianity. With no true correlation between the Scripture and the movie plot, the filmmaker's biblical inspiration is gratuitous and perverse.

Even so, Schrader proclaims his Christian faith and claims that he will be rewarded in heaven for movies like *Light Sleeper* and *The Last Temptation of Christ*. Clearly, something went awry in his Christian education.

All this makes one wonder about how much the church has conformed to the world.

Choices

Hollywood mogul H. Wayne Huizenga, the founder and former CEO of Blockbuster Entertainment, made a cogent observation about the problem of excessive sex and violence in the entertainment media in an interview with syndicated columnist Terry Mattingly:

> The church could have a powerful positive voice. I have little doubt studio executives would hear that voice. Look at the numbers. A lot of people go to church, and a lot a people care about their families. It would be in the best interests of entertainment people to hear those voices. . . .
>
> What impact is all of this entertainment going to have

on our future generations? When technology offers people more choices, they can make either more good choices or more bad choices. The 'information superhighway' may offer more movies and TV shows and information that we want our children to see.

The jury is still out. Things could get better, or worse. Of course, it would help if the church did a better job helping our people make these kinds of choices.[30]

The gauntlet

Not too long ago, a major Hollywood player clearly challenged the commitment of moral individuals. Jonathan Taplin, the producer of *Mean Streets*, announced that:

The American people have already taken sides in the culture war. The public casts its vote each time it turns on the TV, buys a record, reads a book, or sees a movie or a play.

Until now, the vast majority of people who vote for the culture that the Quayles hate never thought they were making a political decision. But, now they must.

What Marilyn Quayle fails to realize is that the counterculture she mocked so strongly at the [Republican] convention has become the mainstream. . . .

Every major artist in theater, modern art, photography, dance, and fashion stands opposed to the dominant right-wing of the GOP. . . . In film, Francis Ford Coppola, Oliver Stone, Martin Scorsese, Spike Lee, and Steven Spielberg are ready to do battle, while Bush has yet to find a director who will join his jihad.[31]

Taplin ends his article by noting that the people will vote at the polls the same anti-Christian, left-wing, humanist perspective which they choose every time they select entertainment.

Shortly, after Mr. Taplin threw down the gauntlet, Christians voted at the polls to give conservative Republicans a significant majority in Congress.

Our entertainment choices do matter. Instead of confessing our conformity to the secular humanist agenda of death and despair, we must reject the bad and choose the good on television, at the theater, and in the voting booth.

> Some people are making a lot of money out of the wreckage of civilization and we think they ought to stop.[32]
> Bill Bennett

Endnotes

1. Steven Bochco, in an interview with *TV Guide* (August 14, 1993).
2. Al Bowman, quoted in MOVIEGUIDE® XI:18: 960826.
3. Lester Gordon, *Let's Go to the Movies*, (Santa Monica: Santa Monica Press, 1992).
4. Michael Medved, "Hollywood's Three Big Lies," *Reader's Digest* (October, 1995), reprinted in MOVIEGUIDE® XI:01: 960101.
5. Eric M. Pollard, *Washington Blade*, quoted in *Between the Lines* (March 20, 1992).
6. *Ibid.*
7. *Ibid.*
8. Scott Lively and Kevin Abrams, *The Pink Swastika* (Oregon: Founders Publishing Corp., 1995).
9. Richard Bernstein, "Should Celebrities Set the Agenda for the Public," *New York Times* (March 10, 1991) Arts & Leisure, 1.
10. George Santayana, *Life of Reason*, "Reason in Common Sense" (New York: Scribner, 1954), ch. 12.
11. Richard Grenier, *Capturing the Culture: Film, Art, and Politics* (Ethics and Public Policy Center, 1991).
12. *Ibid.*
13. *Ibid.*
14. John F. McManus, "Absolutes Under Attack," MOVIEGUIDE® VII:18: 920918.
15. *Rolling Stone* (November 12, 1992).
16. Marilyn Duff, *Between the Lines* (March 20, 1992).
17. Hyperion Press Press Release on RuPaul, New York, 1995.
18. Kenneth Green, Director of Corporate Communications for the Walt Disney Company, in a letter dated October 25, 1996, to a denominational leader who had written Michael Eisner.

19. John Dreyer, Vice President of Corporate Communications for the Walt Disney Company, in a letter dated October 29, 1996, to a denominational leader who had written Michael Eisner.

20. *United States v. Paramount Pictures* (1948).

21. Dr. Judith Reisman, "Peep TV," MOVIEGUIDE® VII:12: 920626

22. *Ibid.*

23. Derrick Warfel, "The Other Side . . . Of What?" MOVIEGUIDE® X:17: 950619.

24. Berit Kjos, "*Ferngully: The Last Rainforest:* Animated Fantasy or Seductive Bait?" MOVIEGUIDE® VII:9: 920508.

25. *Dispatches* (February 9, 1994).

26. *Ibid.*

27. *Ibid.*

28. Media consultant Nancy Woodhull, explaining why religion reporting is growing in popularity in the *American Journalism Review* (December, 1995).

29. *Entertainment Weekly* (April 17, 1992).

30. Terry Mattingly, "Interview with H. Wayne Huizenga, CEO, Blockbuster Entertainment," MOVIEGUIDE® IX:15: 940718.

31. Jonathan Taplin, *Los Angeles Times* (September 20, 1992), Opinion Section, M2.

32. William J. Bennett, MOVIEGUIDE® XI:15: 960715.

9

UNFORGIVEN

Heal the sick, cleanse the lepers, raise the dead, cast out devils: freely ye have received, freely give.
Matthew 10:8 (KJV)

Can we have a changed norm and still have a norm? Can a ruler be twelve inches one day and fourteen inches the next? If so what are the consequences?
Professor Luke Timothy Johnson[1]

Generally, my characters were dignified and brave men who did their duty stoically. Today, the heroes are the anti-heroes of yesterday. They're motivated by hatred, greed and violence. They are rude, vulgar, ill educated and incapable of making an effort because they are totally selfish and devoid of morals.
Gregory Peck[2]

Fact: *According to the* New York Times *(May 3, 1992), it is getting harder and harder to distinguish TV from movies, especially where commercials are involved. The* Times *points out that "product placement" in movies makes it difficult to separate advertisements from the movie. In 1990 the Disney Company offered advertisers the opportunity to display their products in Touchstone films. The fees were reported to be around $20,000 for a product to be shown, $40,000 for the item to be mentioned, and $60,000 for one of the actors to hold or use the product. According to* Entertainment Weekly *(June, 21, 1991) the fees for the product placement ranged from $10,000 to $5 million, with most between $25,000 and $50,000.* Back to the Future II *incorporated dozens of futuristic products from such companies as Nike, Black & Decker, Pizza Hut, AT&T, CBS Records, Mattel, and Pepsi.* Home Alone *managed to work in thirty-one brand names, shown on-screen or mentioned by actors forty-two times.*

O ver the last several years, as a result of the growing concern of moral Americans, the aging of America, and the work of The Christian Film & Television Commission and others, there has been a significant increase in the number of good family films produced such as *Toy Story* and *Babe*, moral mature-audience movies, such as *Shadowlands* and *Sense and Sensibility*, and even movies with a strong Christian witness, such as *Dead Man Walking*. There is, of course, still too much bad entertainment.

A major reason for the lack of "good" entertainment today is the fact that the various Christian denominations abandoned their Hollywood film offices in the mid-1960s. Between 1933 and 1966, when representatives of the churches read every script from every major studio to make sure that it conformed to the high moral character of the Motion Picture Code, movies were better. Christians tend to forget that the church exerted a great influence on the entertainment industry from 1933 to 1966.

> Those who cannot remember the past are condemned to fulfill it.
>
> George Santayana

The code

The code essentially adapted the Ten Commandments to the motion picture industry and specifically discouraged senseless violence, sexual immorality, and antireligious values. The short form of the Motion Picture Code provided:

> The basic dignity and value of human life shall be respected and upheld. Restraint shall be exercised in portraying the taking of life.

> Evil, sin, crime, and wrong-doing shall not be justified.

> Detailed and protracted acts of brutality, cruelty, physical violence, torture, and abuse shall not be presented.

> Indecent or undue exposure of the human body shall not be presented.

Illicit sex relationships shall not be justified. Intimate sex scenes violating common standards of decency shall not be portrayed. Restraint and care shall be exercised in presentations dealing with sex aberrations.

Obscene speech, gestures, or movements shall not be presented. Undue profanity shall not be presented.

Religion shall not be demeaned

Words or symbols contemptuous of racial, religious, or national groups shall not be used so as to incite bigotry or hatred.

Excessive cruelty to animals shall not be portrayed and animals shall not be treated inhumanely.

During the period of the Motion Picture Code there was no explicit sex, violence, profanity, or blasphemy in movies. Films did not mock a minister of religion or a person's faith (the religious persecution in Germany prompted this wise counsel). For the most part movies and television programs communicated the true, the good, and the beautiful.

A higher standard

Most of the best films ever produced were made during that thirty-five-year time period, since creativity and imagination had to replace the cheap lures of sex and violence to attract an audience into the theaters. Many of older creative people in Hollywood agree that the Motion Picture Code made them more creative as they sought ways in which to express themselves that would not violate the code.

For instance, the renowned director Elia Kazan has noted that he did his best work (*Streetcar Named Desire* and *On the Waterfront*) when he had to carefully craft his movies to get across his radical ideas. Whereas his movies degenerated into flabby vehicles for his leftist views after the demise of the code because he no longer had to worry about the church film offices.

Historically, moral, and especially Christian, movies make money at the box office and are often blockbusters, while movies attacking religion are usually box-office failures. For example, the 1959 movie *Ben-Hur* saved MGM from bankruptcy just as *The Ten Commandments* had saved Paramount from bankruptcy in 1956.

In the beginning

In 1876, Thomas Alva Edison invented the phonograph, followed by the motion picture camera and projector. In 1884, penny peep shows appeared in arcades on Broadway in New York City and spread into large cities across America. Film producers were quick to find the formula: *excessive sex, crime, and violence equal box office.*[3] Christians proclaimed that these films were out-and-out pornography.

In the same year Edison, who held all the patents on cameras, projectors, and other equipment, formed a trust with a group of wealthy men to control the motion picture business. Their opposition were poor independents. From 1894 to 1914, the motion picture business in the United States was in constant conflict between the trust and independent producers, and European movies flooded the American market.

In 1905, penny arcades were replaced by kinetoscope arcades and the name was changed to nickelodeons. Some 5,000 of them rapidly spread across America.

In 1907, the city of Chicago formed the first censorship board. In 1908, the mayor of New York City closed all movie houses.

At the same time, the film producers formed the National Board of Censorship to fend off government censorship. Self-regulation was a smoke screen to make the public think something was being done when it wasn't.

In 1913, Cecil B. DeMille, carrying a gun, film equipment, and his small production crew, boarded a train and fled to Flagstaff, Arizona, and then to Hollywood in an effort to get away from strong-arm squads of the trust. The trust police followed him, harassed him, destroyed his film, and tried to shoot him. He survived, and the power of the trust was broken.

From 1913 to 1921, the growth of the motion picture industry was spectacular. Financial institutions poured millions into the industry.

In 1914, World War I erupted and the European film market collapsed. Furthermore, Supreme Court rulings killed the trust. The Supreme Court ruled that the producing of motion pictures was a business, not to be regarded as part of the press or as an organ of public opinion. Six states set up censorship boards.

A prominent Democratic member of the United States House of Representatives from Georgia, who was a Baptist, was the first to coauthor and introduce a censorship bill in Congress. Two other congressmen introduced a bill to control portrayal of sex and violence in films. Bills to censor motion pictures were discussed in thirty-six states during the winter of 1921.

Moral Americans established local censorship boards throughout the United States to protect their communities from the rampant sex, violence, and immorality flowing out of Hollywood. The self-serving National Board of Censorship was shaken.

The scarlet shibboleth

The word *censorship* has become a meaningless catchword in our contemporary society, most often misused by the media to ward off any criticism and to guarantee it the license to distribute anything no matter how perverse, immoral, or obscene. Legally *censorship* means *prior restraint by the government*. There have always been limitations on speech in our society—such as the prohibition against yelling *fire* in a theater, the prohibition against publishing obscene material that meets the Supreme Court's Miller test, and the Federal Communications Commission's restrictions on broadcasting over the public airwaves. The movie industry was considered entertainment and not protected by the First Amendment at all until the Supreme Court's Miracle decision in the 1950s.

Many people look back at the movie industry and think about the wonderful, worthwhile, family films released during the

Golden Age of Hollywood from 1933 to 1966 and forget that during the 1920s and early '30s the moral caliber of many Hollywood movies was extremely coarse and corrupted.

While the documentary video *Hollywood Uncensored*[4] is biased against the moral perspective, it contains excerpts from some of the more salacious and immoral movies of the '20s and early '30s, including: the notorious 1933 film *Ecstasy*, wherein Hedy Lamarr appeared nude on screen for several minutes, and the infamous *Babyface*, wherein a father prostitutes his young daughter to pay his gambling debts. Of course, the film and storytelling techniques of these movies were not as sophisticated as the techniques used in current movies so they do not have the same emotional intensity. However, the immoral content of these early films enraged the American people, who reacted by taking legal action against the perverse product from Hollywood.

Where there's a Will there's a Hays

By 1921, Hollywood was the "Movie Capital of the World." Many of the motley crew of independents were now in charge of motion picture studios in Hollywood. Nickelodeons were replaced by theaters seating 3,000 people or more. The star system was developing and executives from Hollywood studios even sat on the boards of Eastern financial institutions.

Local censorship of movies with excessive sex, crime, and violence increased, spurred by the low morals of Hollywood stars. Censorship prompted bankers to refuse to back Hollywood-produced movies.

On December 8, 1921, three prominent men met in Washington, D.C. Two of them were highly placed motion picture executives. The other was William Harrison Hays, a prominent churchman and a politician's politician who had superb connections in both houses of Congress. Hays, a lawyer, was a member of President Harding's Cabinet. The motion picture executives had a proposal for President Harding that was designed to fend off the censors.

On January 14, 1922, Hays resigned his job as Postmaster General of the United States, giving up a salary of $12,000 per year to become the motion picture industry's first movie czar, receiving a three-year noncancelable contract at $100,000 per year plus $15,000 per year for expenses. In addition, he retained his membership as a partner in the law firm of Hays and Hays.

On March 10, 1922, Hays and seventeen leaders of the movie industry incorporated the Motion Picture Producers and Distributors Association of America, Inc. (hereafter referred to as the MPPDA). To preempt the censorship movement, article I, section 3 of the association read, "The object for which the Association is created is to foster the common interests of those engaged in the motion picture industry in the United States by establishing and maintaining the highest possible moral and artistic standards in motion picture production."[5]

Rumors ran rampant that Hays was a bag man attempting to peddle some $200,000 worth of Sinclair Consolidated Oil Liberty Bonds to pay off the debts left over from Harding's successful 1920 campaign for the presidency. As the new movie czar, he was quoted as saying, "Right is right and wrong is wrong."[6] Under his administration, motion pictures:

> Would maintain the highest moral and artistic standards that the industry must have toward that sacred thing, the mind of a child, toward that clean virgin, the unmarked slate—the same responsibility, the same care about the impressions made upon it that the best clergymen or the most inspired teacher of youth would have; that films would go forth from this country abroad, and present to the world the proper manner, the purposes, the ideals, and the life of America.[7]

The primary purpose of the MPPDA was to prevent congressional censorship. The executive committee of Hays' public relations effort previewed motion pictures and recommended what pictures the public was to patronize. They could make specific objections to certain scenes from specific pictures and bad-mouth in monthly bulletins motion pictures the preview committee considered morally corrupt.

In 1921, the Massachusetts State Legislature passed a Motion Picture Censorship Law. Hays spent about $300,000 to buy votes, and censorship of motion pictures in Massachusetts was defeated.

Democratic Congressman William David Upshaw of Virginia, a well-known Baptist layman, introduced a bill in Congress that would create a Federal Motion Picture Commission in the Department of the Interior to be composed of the Commissioner of Education and six commissioners elected for life. The bill described standards of morality to govern the production of films entering interstate or foreign commerce. The penalty for violation was to be the confiscation of all offending films.

Resurrecting his campaign slogan, "Give the motion picture producers a chance to regulate themselves,"[8] Hays flooded Congress with a host of volunteers from his committee on public relations. Congress buried Upshaw's bill.

In 1924, many of the sixty-two national organizations that constituted Hays' committee on public relations left him, referring to his work as a "smoke screen, a camouflage, an approval stamp for salacious film and for questionable, if not criminal, conduct of the industry and its employees."[9]

Censorship boards in major cities cut thousands of scenes from Hollywood-produced films. Hays hired a prominent Baptist layman, lawyer, former members of both houses of Congress and a former state governor to con Protestants into believing the Hollywood producers would regulate their own films. The President of the United States defended Hays and his work in a lengthy published article.

In 1930, after six months of painstaking research, a respected Protestant publication accused Hays of lulling the church to sleep with his soft speeches and of hiding behind a Presbyterian front while the movie producers merrily made money out of muck. After eight years of the Hays administration, Protestant reformers, who had previously hailed Hays as a conscientious churchman, now held him in contempt as a blind for the movie industry's rotten pictures.

The Catholic crusade

In 1930, the Roman Catholic Church took a stand against the industry and movie moguls almost went bankrupt. Wall Street stock and bond brokers met with Roman Catholic cardinals to beg for mercy. A Roman Catholic priest then wrote the Motion Picture Code based on the Ten Commandments.

At first, Hollywood producers ignored the code, prompting the Roman Catholic hierarchy to form the Roman Catholic Legion of Decency. Millions of Roman Catholics joined and signed a pledge to boycott movie theaters, thereby severing the most sensitive nerve in the movie industry body—its pocketbook.

On July 1, 1934, Hays and The MPPDA set up a Motion Picture Code office in Hollywood and gave Joseph Breen, a rough Roman Catholic Irish layman, the power to enforce the code. Hollywood studios set up censorship departments to deal with Breen.

Hollywood got the message. The film producers would have cast out their casting couch before casting aspersions on the Roman Catholic Church, its beliefs, priests, and nuns, not to mention the Pope. For the next fifteen years or so, Hollywood movies, with the exception of the bitter fight over the word *damn* in *Gone with the Wind*, provided good, clean entertainment, giving wholesome pleasure to the whole family.

From 1935 to 1947, Hollywood produced nine feature films with a Roman Catholic theme. One received an Oscar as "Best Picture of the Year."

As a result, Protestants discovered that protests in the form of more warnings, meaningless pronouncements, and supporting federal and state censorship of motion pictures was a poor substitute for a favorable portrayal of their religion and its ministers.

On February 3, 1948, a small group of prominent ministers and laymen from New York and Los Angeles, including three motion picture executives, held a secret three-day conference in Hollywood, and then announced to the press that they were opening a "Hollywood office to represent Protestant denominations of 200,000 churches, able to speak for 54 million Protestants, and encourage production of films of high moral and artistic standards. Furthermore, the office would work with the Breen office and producers by reading scripts and making corrections when the Protestant religion and its ministers are portrayed."[10]

The Protestants formed the Protestant Film Commission (or Fort Hollywood) for the purpose of:

1. Producing pictures for Protestant churches.
2. Acting as a liaison between The MPPDA and Hollywood producers.

Cecile B. DeMille said, "I have been waiting for thirty-five years for this day, for some body to be formed to favorably oversee that the dignity of the church is upheld on the screen. Very often, Protestant ministers are presented as ludicrous figures. This organization will remedy this and see that they, as well as the Protestant church itself, will be clothed in dignity."[11]

During this time, Will Hays resigned and was replaced by Eric Allen Johnston, a Protestant, Republican, president of The United States Chamber of Commerce, and public relations expert with excellent connections in both houses of Congress and the White House. In accepting the position, Johnston said, "There is only one satisfactory way, in my judgment, to meet the issue of political censorship in our country. That is to go to the highest court in the land for a head-on test of the constitutionality of motion picture censorship."[12]

In 1950, the National Council of Churches was formed and Fort Hollywood became the Department of Broadcasting and Film Commission, the communications arm of the National Council of Churches.

In 1952, a Supreme Court decision stopped state censorship of motion pictures, and in 1953 George Heimrich took over as the director of Fort Hollywood. Screenplays, story treatments, and books submitted by major studios, independent producers, and the Breen office having to do with the portrayal of the Protestant religion and its ministers were reviewed under Section 8 of the Motion Picture Code, which read:

1. No film or episode may throw ridicule on any religious faith.
2. Ministers of religion in their character as ministers of religion should not be used as comic characters or villains.
3. Ceremonies of any definite religion should be carefully handled.

The reason why ministers of religion may not be comic characters or villains is simply that the attitude taken toward them may easily become the attitude taken toward religion in general. Religion is lowered in the minds of the audience because the lowering of the audience's respect for the minister. Particularly disturbing screenplays submitted for evaluation were *The Soul Merchant, The Revival, The Money Changer,* and *Elmer Gantry,* all of which denigrated and made fun of evangelism and evangelists. Many of those in the film and TV industry were nonreligious, agnostic, and even atheists. A number of producers and writers had great dislike and even fear of the Bible Belt and hated the Roman Catholic Legion of Decency.

In *The Money Changer* a well-known actor becomes famous evangelist. In the last scene his worshipers find out that he is a phony and beat him to death with their Bibles. After weeks of negotiation, the producer abandoned the project with the parting shot, "Heimrich, you—, either you, or Billy Graham, or both of you, cost me $65,000."[13] Evangelists like Billy Graham were so popular that producers saw ridiculing them as a way to make a fortune.

When Breen retired in 1954, Geoffrey Shurlock, a Protestant, replaced him. In his talk at the annual meeting of Broadcasting and

Film Commission, Shurlock said, "In our files we have this description of the book *Elmer Gantry*: he is a degenerate preacher who uses the pulpit in the same way he would use a procurer to get a woman."[14] He asked the audience to back the fight against *Elmer Gantry*.

In 1959, Burt Lancaster, who purportedly came to Jesus Christ thirty years later on his death bed, formed his own company and produced *Elmer Gantry*. It was a direct slap at evangelists and Billy Graham. Lancaster baited Fort Hollywood in *Variety*, saying, "I don't see what the Protestants are worried about. Elmer Gantry is just an all American guy interested in money, sex, and fun. Just because he is a minister doesn't make him un-American."[15]

The old double-cross

In 1959, Heimrich mounted a campaign to clean up Hollywood entertainment. Eric Johnston, the president of the MPPDA, wrote a letter to the director of social action of the National Council of Churches to complain. The NCC replied, "There is no need for Mr. Heimrich's horror over the possible filming of *Elmer Gantry*. There is no need for Protestants to be defensive about *Elmer Gantry*. It might be good for us in a time that oversentimentalizes the minister to have such a caricature shown."[16]

The NCC had spoken and Burt Lancaster yelled "Amen."[17] Afterwards, the NCC tried three times to close Fort Hollywood.

The NCC killed the Motion Picture Code in 1961. Fort Hollywood worked for more than four years with one of the most respected directors, producers, and writers in the history of Hollywood to develop a feature film on the life of Christ. In 1966, NCC's film awards committee turned down the film on the life of Christ for an award and recommended awards for two independent feature films, one brazenly depicting nudity and the other blasphemy, in direct violation of the Motion Picture Code.

Following presentation of the awards, an executive of the BFC NCC said:

Mainstream attitude among Protestants no longer is principally concerned with condemning sex and violence or immorality and futility, but are interested in films which are honest in their portrayal of the human and humanist situation.[18]

In 1966, Eric Johnson resigned as head of the MPPDA (which was soon renamed the Motion Picture Association of America and is now called the Motion Picture Association) and was replaced by Jack J. Valenti.

In 1967, a major Hollywood studio produced a feature film, the dialogue of which was laced with profanity. In addition, there were several highly questionable sex scenes. Shurlock refused to approve it. The movie received one of the NCC's coveted awards in 1967.

After thirty-three years, the back of the code was broken—"Thanks in great part to the NCC,"[19] one Hollywood executive noted.

The NCC had won. Fort Hollywood was closed. It was the end of an era.

That hideous strength

A few months after the Protestant Film Commission was shut down, Anton LaVey opened up a Church of Satan film office. Soon thereafter a plethora of political groups, from the Gay-Lesbian Task Force to radical feminists, opened up film offices to lobby the entertainment media for their points of view. After 2,000 years of fulfilling the Great Commission to go into all the world, the church halted, turned around, and effectively abandoned the most powerful communications center in the world to unregenerate paganism.

The consequence of all this is that the believers have abdicated all responsibility and turned over numerous battlefields to the left. In the case of the Protestant Film Commission, we gave up the cultural war, allowing the libertines to seize control of the most powerful media of communications. The result has been disastrous for our civilization as sex and violence have flowed from the screen to the street in the form of murders, suicides, rapes, venereal disease, sodomy, divorce, and a wholesale destruction of the family—the basic building block of civilization.

It is not too late to reclaim control. The key is to stand together to redeem the values of the mass media by supporting good movies and entertainment and rebuking the bad. This was the very method that originally gave the church leverage in the Hollywood community, and it is the method that the leftists borrowed to exercise their muscle in the entertainment industry.

Who filled the vacuum?

Today scripts are read by feminist, Marxist, and homosexual groups. These groups award pictures and television programs that communicate their point of view and condemn movies and programs that disagree with it. An antichurch, anti-American, anti-everything attitude prevails in Hollywood today because the church has retreated.

Karl Marx had only four goals in his *Communist Manifesto*: abolish property, abolish the family, abolish the nation, and abolish religion and morality. It is evident that the movie industry today, divorced from the influence of the church, is proclaiming an antibiblical, prohumanist agenda that appeals to an adolescent audience and undermines the fabric of our civilization.

A sensitive subject

Surveys show that Christian teenagers see the same films and watch the same television programs as pagans. World Vision reported that Christians spend $6.60 out of every $100 on entertainment.

Denouncing the media is illogical since movies and television programs are merely tools of communication, just as the telephone is a tool of communication. Like other tools, the movies may be used for good or for evil.

A hammer may be used to build a church, or to hit someone. Either way that it is used, the hammer is not responsible. A telephone may be used to communicate between family members separated by many miles, or to communicate pornography to impressionable children and susceptible adults. We are not called to stop using the telephone because someone is using it for dial-a-porn, rather we are called to redeem the medium by stopping the evil use of it.

Discernment not denial

Denial is part of the problem because it separates the Christian's entertainment choices from his or her moral discernment. By viewing television and movies surreptitiously Christians insulate themselves from moral judgment. Too often they believe that a violent movie or television program will not affect them, although they know that it will affect others.

Denial short circuits the ability to choose good entertainment and reject bad entertainment, and it is through this process of informed choice that we can make a difference. The movie industry needs money to survive. If we redirect our entertainment expenditures from the bad to the good, the industry will change to making more good movies and fewer bad ones.

The pocketbook

The movie industry is the primary cash register of the mass media. If Christians would vote for the good and against the bad at the box office, the mass media would turn from its present course toward a course that would include, not exclude, Christians. Christians are the largest group within the United States, but we have been overshadowed in influence by other groups because we have not acted according to biblical principles in our daily lives.

The reasons: sin, peer pressure, curiosity, deceptive advertisements (especially on television), and a lack of guidance. Many in the church today do not fear the Lord, because they have compromised with the world system. Many are attracted to the lust of the eyes and the lust of the flesh, and movies and television programs are a sanitized way of indulging their sinful natures. Many churches are infiltrated with false doctrine because many of the clergy have not been preaching the Gospel in all its power.

The other side understands the battle

The other side understands what is at stake. Feminist, homosexual, abortion, and other groups have banded together to lobby the entertainment media to establish an anti-Christian, antihuman agenda in the entertainment industry. An instructive article in the April 8, 1988, *Wall Street Journal* discussed Norman Lear's success in opposing the "religious right" and promoting socialism through the entertainment media.

An in-depth portrait, which appeared in the April 1988 *American Family Association Journal* noted that Mr. Lear has united the rich, famous, and powerful against Christianity, morality, and freedom. These dilettante revolutionaries pour millions of dollars into campaigns aimed at destroying our free society and Christianity.

No way out

We cannot escape as some have tried to do. We must take a stand and resist. We are the body of Christ, and He takes His stand in us. For too long, His body has not responded to the directions of the Head, Who is Jesus Christ. Now, He is cleansing and disciplining His body.

There is a growing attack on the body of Christ. The forces of the adversary are marshalled against His people. God has called us to stand for Jesus.

That is why we have established the Christian Film & Television Commission (CFTVC). The CFTVC employs a two-pronged approach to redeem the values of the entertainment industry. This approach was originally developed by the Christian leaders who wrote and monitored the Motion Picture Code. It is now used by many groups to lobby Hollywood.

One prong involves educating moral Americans through MOVIEGUIDE® so that they can make discerning choices at the box office and thereby influence the entertainment industry financially and through their correspondence.

The other prong involves helping media leaders understand the concerns of moral Americans. Like the church offices that inspired the Golden Age of Hollywood, the CFTVC reviews scripts and helps those in the media to work out creative solutions to moral questions so as to improve the dramatic and the moral quality of the movies and programs they produce. The CFTVC also helps them portray religious people in a realistic and wholesome light.

More than conquerors

Through Him we are more than conquerors. We must repent of any apostasy and take a stand for Jesus Christ. It is critical that Christians take every thought captive in the mass media for Jesus Christ.

Endnotes

1. Luke Timothy Johnson, Emory University professor, *Atlanta Journal/Constitution*, (April 7, 1996): R2
2. Gregory Peck, speaking at the Cognac Film Festival, *The Viewer And Listener*, (Summer, 1996).
3. George Heimrich, *The Entertainment Game*, unedited and unpublished manuscript. George Heimrich was the director of the Hollywood office of the Protestant Film Commission from 1953 to 1966. His Protestant Film Commission files were donated to the Christian Film & Television Commission by his estate.
4. *Hollywood Uncensored*, International Video Entertainment, (1987).

5. Heimrich, *The Entertainment Game.*
6. *Ibid.*
7. *Ibid.*
8. *Ibid.*
9. *Ibid.*
10. *Ibid.*
11. *Ibid.*
12. *Ibid.*
13. *Ibid.*
14. *Ibid.*
15. *Ibid.*
16. *Ibid.*
17. *Ibid.*
18. *Ibid.*

WORLDVIEW

BY DAN SMITHWICK

Do not conform any longer to the pattern of this world, but be transformed by the renewing of your mind. Then you will be able to test and approve what God's will is—his good, pleasing and perfect will.
Romans 12:2 (NIV)

I often wonder: Do movies influence the world, or does the world influence movies? What's influencing us more than we know is MTV.
Matthew Broderick[1]

Pluralism destroys reason.
Ravi Zacharias

Fact: Households earning $15,000 to $20,000 a year watch the most TV. Breadwinners in the $40,000 range watch the least. Most children spend more time with the television set before the age of six than they will spend with their fathers during their entire lives.

O ne of the most important aspects of developing discernment is understanding a biblical worldview. Although I have taught on this subject for many years, I asked Dan Smithwick to write the bulk of this chapter because I respect his work in this area.

In 1986, Dan founded Nehemiah Institute[2] to provide Christian worldview assessment and training services to Christian educators. Dan is the author of the PEERS test, an internationally used assessment program for evaluating comprehension of Christian worldview principles, and the author of a new self-paced study course titled Developing a Biblical Worldview.

Dan and his family reside in Lexington, Kentucky, where they are members of Porter Memorial Baptist Church.

What follows are Dan's personal observations on this important topic.

Perspective

Who (or what) is God?

Who (or what) is man?

What is their relationship?

The struggle to answer these three questions has defined the history of the Christian faith and the Christian church. As the answers to these questions have changed over the course of time, they have reflected the significance and influence of the church of Jesus Christ. When the accepted answers to these questions were biblically oriented, the church held a position of respectability and wielded substantial influence in the world. This was certainly the case with the first-century church whereby in Acts believers were said to have "turned the world upside down." The church's influence was felt until the fall of the Roman Empire in A.D. 476.

The Christian church also wielded major influence politically and economically, as well as spiritually, in the Reformation period under Luther and Calvin's leadership. The church's influence on society (primarily through the teachings of Calvin) significantly impacted and shaped most of the northern European countries, England, and eventually America.

Further evidence of the positive influence by obedient Christians is given by men such as American evangelist Billy Sunday. Early in this century saloons and gambling halls closed for lack of business as a result of Sunday's proclamation of the Gospel.

When the answers were other than biblical, the church had little or no impact on the world and evil prevailed. This was most notable during the Dark Ages of A.D. 700 to 1200 when the church gave way to false worship and gross immorality among its numbers. Abuses in the church and in society at large remained until the Gospel was once again held up as the only objective standard of righteousness.

A modern-day example of what happens when the church ceases to be salt and light is the moral decline of young people when God was formally exiled from public life, beginning with the Supreme Court's disallowing prayer in public schools in 1962,[3] and continuing in 1980 when the Supreme Court pulled the Ten Commandments from a classroom bulletin board in Kentucky and thus from all bulletin boards in all public schools throughout the nation.

Without a comprehensive biblical view of life the church retreats into a pietistic mode and focuses only on spiritual and eternal matters while social life deteriorates.

Until recently, *worldview* has been a foreign term for many Christians. My interest in worldview thinking began with the reading of Francis Schaeffer's *A Christian Manifesto*.[4]

At the beginning of his book, Schaeffer lists three other manifestos: *The Communist Manifesto* (1948),[5] *Humanist Manifesto I* (1933)[6] and *Humanist Manifesto II* (1973).[7] Each promoted a worldview in the sense of a comprehensive way at looking at how the world should function. Serious-minded people thought and wrote on such matters, but I was typical of the person Schaeffer described in his opening comments:

> The basic problem of the Christians in this country in
> the last eighty years or so, in regard to society and in regard
> to government, is that they have seen things in bits and

pieces instead of totals. They have very gradually become disturbed over permissiveness, pornography, the public schools, the breakdown of the family, and finally abortion. But, they have not seen this as a totality—each thing being a part, a symptom, of a much larger problem. They have failed to see that all of this has come about due to a shift in worldview—that is, through a fundamental change in the overall way people think and view the world and life as a whole.[8]

I had never thought in terms of an overarching worldview to shape my philosophy or behavior. Since reading Schaeffer's writings and many others related to Christian worldview thinking, I have come to see not only why society is coming unraveled, but why it necessarily has to unravel without the Christian worldview as the basis for personal and corporate behavior in all disciplines of life.

Definitions of different worldviews

Yale scholar Harold Bloom analyzes the emergence of a post-Christian America in his book *The American Religion* and says that the god we worship is ourselves. He says the real religion of America is Gnosticism, an elitist Christian heresy that combines mystical Greek and oriental philosophies and claims that a person needed special knowledge to get to the highest heaven. Christianity posits that you need no special knowledge because Jesus Christ offers salvation to all who believe in Him by faith, which is a gift from God.

Considering the plethora of worldviews presented in the mass media, it is important to have a basic knowledge of them and how they differ from orthodox Christian beliefs. *Orthodox* does not refer to any denominations, but to *right doctrine*, as opposed to heterodox or heresy which refers to wrong doctrine or other doctrines.

The more you understand these worldviews and how they differ from the Good News of Jesus Christ, the better your discernment in all areas of life, including the mass media. As you read about these worldviews, try to discern what they believe about the nature of reality, which is their ontology, and what they believe about how you know about reality, which is their epistemology.

How many worldviews are there? In a strict biblical sense, there are only two—Christian and anti-Christian, otherwise known as paganism. This would be the meaning of Jesus' words, "He who is not with me is against me, and he who does not gather with me scatters" (Matthew 12:30 NIV).

In practical terms, there are many worldviews but not all attempt to give answers to the major questions of life. Those important worldviews that have addressed comprehensive life issues include:

Atheism

Atheism is the disbelief or denial of the existence of God or an intelligent Supreme Being. Atheism is a ferocious system that leaves nothing above us to excite awe, nor around us to awaken tenderness.

Because the atheist rejects any belief in the supernatural, he must view man as an evolutionary creature with no objective basis of morality. Ethics can only be subjective and self-defined, leading to the survival of the strong and destruction of the weak. Abortion, infanticide, and euthanasia are common practice in an atheistic culture.

Deism

Deism is the belief or system of religious opinions of those who acknowledge the existence of a transcendent God, but deny revelation and the personal immanence of God. Deism is the belief in natural religion only, or in those truths in doctrine and practice that man is to discover by the light of reason, independent and exclusive of any revelation from God. Hence deism implies a disbelief in the divine origin of the Scriptures.

While a deist would believe that there is a God Who started things out, the deist would also contend that God is no longer intimately involved with creation. Therefore, there is no purpose in seeking God, or expecting Him to meet our daily needs.

Secular humanism

Secular humanism pertains to the present world, or to things not spiritual or holy. Thus, it relates to things not immediately or primarily respecting the soul and the spirit, but only to the body and the physical world. The secular concerns of life include making provision for the support of life, the preservation of health, and the temporal prosperity of men and of states.

Secular power is that which superintends and governs the temporal affairs of men, the civil or political power, and is distinguished from spiritual or ecclesiastical power.

The humanist looks only to man for solutions to our problems. There is no room for supernatural revelation or miracles as humanism is atheistic. Humanism breeds despair and fatalism.

During the Renaissance, humanism was a cultural and intellectual movement that focused on human beings and their values, capacities, and worth, and emphasized the rediscovery and study of the literature, art, and civilization of ancient Greece and Rome. Thus, humanism dealt with the humanities, a conscious return to classical ideals and forms, and a rejection of medieval religious authority. Boccaccio, Erasmus, and Petrarch were the leading Renaissance humanists.

Pantheism

Pantheism is the doctrine that the universe is god, or the system of theology in which it is maintained that the universe is the supreme god, as well as a belief in or worship of all gods.

Logic and rationale are discarded by the pantheist. Anything goes because nothing is supreme. Ultimately, a pantheistic society embraces chaos as normal behavior in its attempts at attaining liberty.

Furthermore, without a god who is good and determines the laws of nature, the pantheist sees the world around him as chaotic and threatening and is not likely to become an explorer or scientist.

Materialism
The doctrine of materialism that matter is the only true reality and that everything in the world, including thought, will, and feeling, can be explained only in terms of matter. Thus, there is nothing beyond what we can observe. Philosophy is a game of language. Since matter is all there is, comfort, pleasure, and wealth are the only or highest goals or values.

Materialism holds that matter is the final reality. Democritus, Epicurus, and the Stoic conceived of reality as material in nature. The theory was renewed and developed beginning in the seventeenth century, especially by Hobbes. This worldview was developed further from the middle of the nineteenth century, particularly in the form of dialectical materialsim and logical positivism.

Marxist/Leninism
The political and economic ideas of Karl Marx and Friedrich Engels, which Marx called "the ultimate humanism,"[9] as applied by Vladimir Lenin. It is said that Lenin asked God to forgive him on his deathbed.

This system is based on the atheistic assumption that all human experience, behavior, and history are the product of purely material forces acting upon the individual. It was believed that the state should plan and control the lives of individuals to achieve a classless society with total equality of goods.

Marx said that to achieve this classless society the dictatorship of the proletariat must: abolish private ownership of property (which God ordains in the Bible to protect the weak individual such as Naboth from the greedy ruler), abolish religion (which gives man the assurance of things hoped for), abolish the state or nation (which God established to regulate commerce and protect the family), and, to abolish the family (which God ordained as the basic unit of government, education and procreation). In communism, driven by the politics of envy and greed, what a man cannot do on his own to achieve equality of life, he looks to the state to make happen.

There are two Marxist refinements on materialism: Dialectical materialism, which views matter as the sole agent of change and all change as the product of a constant conflict between opposites arising from the internal contradictions inherent in all events, ideas, and movements, and application of the principles of dialectical materialism to the study of history and sociology, which is called historical materialism.

Dialectical materialism is the official philosophy of communism. The obverse of Hegel's dialectical idealism, it holds that men create social life solely in response to economic needs. Thus, all aspects of society reflect the economic structure. Growth, change, and development take place through a struggle of opposites, a process that individuals cannot influence.

Historical materialism regards material economic forces as the foundations on which social and political institutions and ideas are built.

This philosophy has many noncommunist advocates and has undermined morality in the United States and has led to a societal drive toward consensus and compromise even where right and wrong is at stake.

Nihilism

According to this doctrine all values are meaningless and baseless, and nothing can be known or communicated. Nihilism is an extreme form of skepticism that denies all existence, rejects all distinctions in moral value, and refutes all previous theories of morality. This worldview holds that the destruction of existing political or social institutions is necessary for future improvement.

Nihilism started as a revolutionary movement in mid-nineteenth-century Russia that scorned authority and tradition and believed in materialism and radical change in government through terrorism and assassination.

Romanticism

Formalized by Jean Jacques Rousseau and derived from pantheism, this doctrine holds that God is immanent in nature and ourselves. Therefore, self-fulfillment is the basis for morality, and whatever enriches self must be good, while whatever diminishes self must be bad.

Romanticism exalts the senses and emotions over reason and intellect, admires the heroic and the individuality and imagination of the artist, and is interested in the medieval, exotic, primitive, and nationalistic.

This worldview is defined by a heightened interest in nature, an emphasis on emotion and imagination, and rebellion against established social rules and conventions. Today, *romantic* is often used in a derogatory sense and implies unrestrained sensuousness, vague imagery, lack of logical precision, and escape from reality.

Romanticism inspired several streams in philosophy such as a return to occultism and the present new age movement, national socialism (Nazism), fascism, and communism.

English literary romantics like Lord Byron, John Keats, and P.B. Shelley focused on the individual's highly personal response to life. The gothic romantics like Sir Walter Scott became enamored of the cult of medievalism. The German romantics like Goethe, Schiller, the brothers Grimm, and Wagner eventually inspired Nietzsche and then Adolf Hitler. In America romanticism birthed transcendentalism.

Existentialism

This doctrine is that there is no inherent meaning in life and that natural laws are meaningless. Since meaning for an existentialist is a purely human phenomenon, humans can create meaning for themselves, but no one can provide meaning for someone else.

A twentieth-century philosophy, existentialism centers on the individual and the individual's relationship to the universe or to God.

Søren Kierkegaard developed a Christian existentialism wherein concrete ethical and religious demands confront the individual, who is forced each time to make a commitment. The necessity and seriousness of these decisions cause him dread and despair.

Jean Paul Sartre held that existence precedes essence, and that there is no God and no fixed human nature, so each person is totally free and entirely responsible for what he or she becomes and does. It is said that Sartre cried out to God on his deathbed.

Albert Camus, Karl Barth, Paul Tillich, Reinhold Niebuhr, Martin Buber, and Karl Jaspers are often treated as existentialists.

An offshoot of existentialism is contemporary relativism, which holds that every meaning one chooses whether religion or worldview is equally valid.

Nominalism

This doctrine is that reality and God are concepts in name only, convenience of language and thought. Everything is imaginary, which the Hindus call *maya* (illusion). Therefore, magical thinking can change this ephemeral reality.

Originally, nominalism was a doctrine of the late Middle Ages saying that all universal or abstract terms are mere necessities of thought or conveniences of language and therefore exist as names only and have no realities corresponding to them.

Contrasted to idealism and to realism, this philosophy is appropriate to materialism and empiricism.

Realism

This doctrine says that universals have objective reality (ontology), as opposed to nominalism, and that material objects exist in themselves, apart from the mind's perception or consciousness of them (epistemology), as opposed to idealism, which holds that reality exists only in the mind.

Orthodox Christians and Jews have a real ontology and epistemology.

Socialist realism

This is a Marxist aesthetic doctrine that promotes the development of revolutionary social consciousness through didactic use of literature, art, and music.

Idealism

This doctrine says that the objects of perception are actually ideas of the perceiving mind and that it is impossible to know whether reality exists apart from the mind as opposed to realism and materialism. Idealism attempts to account for all objects in nature and experience as representations of the mind and sometimes assigns to such representations a higher order of existence.

Plato conceived a world in which eternal ideas constituted reality. Modern idealism refers the source of ideas to the individual's consciousness. In Kant's transcendental idealism the world of human understanding opposed the world of things-in-themselves. Later German idealists like Hegel treated all reality as the creation of mind.

New age

The new age is a complex of recent spiritual and consciousness-raising beliefs and doctrines that cover a range of themes from a belief in spiritualism and reincarnation to advocacy of holistic approaches to health and ecology.

Much of the new age worldview is neoplatonist, which was a mystical philosophy based on the later doctrines of Plato. It was developed in the third century A.D. by Plotinus, who saw reality as one vast hierarchical order containing all the various levels and kinds of existence. At the center is the god, an incomprehensible, all-sufficient unity that flows out in a radiating process called emanation, giving rise to the divine mind, or logos. The logos contains all intelligent forms of all individuals.

Later neoplatonists incorporated such disparate elements as eastern mysticism, divination, demonology, and astrology.

St. Augustine was a neoplatonist before his conversion and incorporated some elements of this doctrine into his theology, although not to the detriment of his orthodoxy. Elements can also be found in St. Thomas Aquinas and Hegel.

Occultism

Occultism is a belief in occult powers and the possibility of bringing them under human control. It includes spiritualism, sorcery, divination, astral bodies, spirit bodies, ethereal bodies, spirit manifestation, ectoplasm, telekinesis, poltergeists, spirit-rapping, automatic writing, spiritualistic apparatus, Ouija boards, psychical research, transcendentalism, esoteric, cabbalism, reincarnation, theosophy, Rosicrucianism, alchemy, astrology, fortune-telling, and palmistry. It implies having a secret or hidden meaning.

God's word is clear about occultism: "Let no one be found among you who sacrifices his son or daughter in the fire, who practices divination or sorcery, interprets omens, engages in witchcraft, or casts spells, or who is a medium or spiritist or who consults the dead. Anyone who does these things is detestable to the LORD, and because of these detestable practices the LORD your God will drive out those nations before you" (Deuteronomy 18:10-12 NIV).

Revisionism

Revisionism advocates the revision of an accepted, usually long-standing view, theory, or doctrine, especially a revision of historical events and movements. Revisionism is a recurrent tendency within the communist movement to revise Marxist theory in such a way as to provide justification for a retreat from the revolutionary to the reform position.

Biblical theism

Theism is the realization that the Creator God created the universe. Therefore, we can explore and study science because we know that the universe was made according to a plan and is not haphazard. Unlike the pagan belief in many gods that causes fear and uncertainty about the nature of the world, biblical theists understand that the world has order, so they can develop science and technology. Furthermore, biblical theism realizes that God reveals Himself and His order in the universe (Romans 1) so the universe is knowable. The biblical theist also understands that God is good and that man has been given stewardship over the earth. Finally, the theist knows that he has fallen short of God's glory, but that God has revealed Himself in Jesus Christ to reconcile man to God and bring us into the fullness of His kingdom.

Biblical theism gives man the liberty to pursue knowledge and understanding, the assurance that good will triumph, and the opportunity to enter into the grace of a relationship with our Creator and be delivered from the alienation, confusion, and demons of our fallen condition.

Christian worldview

The Bible provides the definitive answer to the meaning of the Christian worldview, which is biblical theism. God has revealed Himself in creation so that no person can say, "I didn't know there was a God" because: ". . . what may be known about God is plain to them, because God has made it plain to them. For since the creation of the world God's invisible qualities—his eternal power and divine nature—have been clearly seen, being understood from what has been made, so that men are without excuse" (Romans 1:19-20 NIV).

He chose to reveal Himself most completely in written word. For this reason, ultimately, the Christian worldview and the biblical worldview are synonymous.

Other Scriptures that provide the basis of a Christian worldview (viewing all things in life through the lens of Scripture) include:

> "For my thoughts are not your thoughts, neither are your ways my ways," declares the LORD. "As the heavens

are higher than the earth, so are my ways higher than your ways and my thoughts than your thoughts" (Isaiah 55:8-9 NIV).

Do not conform any longer to the pattern of this world, but be transformed by the renewing of your mind. Then you will be able to test and approve what God's will is— his good, pleasing and perfect will (Romans 12:2 NIV).

We demolish arguments and every pretension that sets itself up against the knowledge of God, and we take captive every thought to make it obedient to Christ (2 Corinthians 10:5 NIV).

These Scriptures help us see how critically important it is that we think as God thinks to the degree granted by Him. This is a fundamental meaning of the Christian worldview.

There are other questions that must be answered to more fully understand every worldview. Some are:

What is the origin of man?

How was man created?

Is there purpose in life?

Why do I exist?

Why is there evil in the world?

Does God care about my suffering?

Is there an afterlife?

Are all religions that believe in God valid?

Will there be an end to life on earth as we know it?

Most people ask themselves these or similar questions while thinking about God.

Importance of Christian worldview thinking

Understanding Christian worldview thinking is the greatest issue facing our culture today. It is a more important issue than poverty, racism, AIDS, immoral entertainment, low SAT scores, the budget deficit, divorce, illegitimate births, domestic violence, and even abortion. While each of these is a serious problem they are simply the fruit of bad worldview thinking. To the degree that we understand and embrace biblical thinking in all areas of life the social ills of our nation will subside.

Dr. Ronald Nash, a professor at the Reformed Theological Seminary, said about the importance of the church teaching a Christian worldview:

> America's mainline denominations were lost to liberalism and unbelief because in the century following the American Civil War the Christian church lost the battle in the world of ideas. The most important step for Christians is to become informed about the Christian worldview, a comprehensive systematic view of the life and of the world as a whole. No believer today can be really effective in the arena of ideas until he or she has been trained to think in worldview terms.[10]

Yes, Christians have the truth that sets people free, but if this truth, the Word of God, is not understood and applied, it is of little help to those in bondage. Jesus said, "You are the salt of the earth. But if the salt loses its saltiness, how can it be made salty again? It is no longer good for anything, except to be thrown out and trampled by men. You are the light of the world. A city on a hill cannot be hidden" (Matthew 5:13-14 NIV).

When the church loses its focus (not seeing biblically), its ability to be salt and light to a hurting world diminishes. Even more serious, when the church stops being the true biblical church, as commissioned throughout the Old and New Testaments, it is entirely possible for the church to offer, unknowingly, a counterfeit gospel with "another Jesus" to lost sinners.

On nearly all fronts—education, economics, crime, family, marriage, and others—we are losing the cultural battle. Why is the ever-growing church not turning America upside down? Or better stated, right side up?

First, the army of the Lord is not getting as many new recruits as church rosters would indicate. The easy-believism, nonconfrontational Gospel is only applying a veneer coating to sin-darkened hearts, not replacing them.

Second, even for those who are coming to Christ through true regeneration, most are not being enrolled into serious-minded Bible studies equipping them to be effective soldiers for Christ. They have assurance for eternal life, but not the arsenal for victorious living.

For the most part, today's church is simply not delivering the goods.

Powerless Christianity

David Wells, in his book *No Place for the Truth* said, "The vast growth in evangelically minded people in the 1960s, 1970s, and 1980s should by now have revolutionized American culture. With a third of American adults now claiming to have experienced spiritual rebirth, a powerful countercurrent of morality growing out of a powerful and alternative worldview should have been unleashed in factories, offices, and boardrooms, in the media, universities, and professions, from one end of the country to the other. The results should by now be unmistakable. Secular values should be reeling, and those who are their proponents should be very troubled."[11]

The Bible says, "You will pursue your enemies, and they will fall by the sword before you. Five of you will chase a hundred, and a hundred of you will chase ten thousand, and your enemies will fall by the sword before you" (Leviticus 26:7-8 NIV). With the odds 100 to one against them, God's people defeated the enemy. So with today's ratio of only two to one (unbelievers to believers, supposedly) why isn't the church winning?

Wells continued, "This surely is an odd circumstance. Here is a corner of the religious world that has learned from the social scientists how to grow itself, that is sprouting huge megachurches that look like shopping malls for the religious, that can count in its own society the moneyed and powerful, and yet it causes not so much as a ripple. And, its disappearance, judged in moral and spiritual terms, is happening at the very moment when American culture is more vulnerable to the uprooting of some of its cherished Enlightenment beliefs than ever before, because it knows itself to be empty. Thus, it is that both American culture and American evangelicalism have come to share the same fate, both basking in the same stunning, outward success while stricken by a painful vacuity and emptiness in their respective centers."[12]

What the church is serving is a shallow and saltless Gospel. Though delivered with deep compassion for lost sinners and with a burden for a hurting culture, the message is lacking comprehensive truth to shape the minds of believers and redirect their behavior. Without biblical principles for all areas of life, especially in critical areas such as the structure and role of civil government, economic policy, education curriculum, church/state relationships, health care, entertainment, arts, foreign affairs, and crime, new believers stay off the battlefield.

A Gospel that only gets one ready for heaven upon death and asks converts only for help in getting others ready for death is not biblical. This is a "What's in it for me?" message of which the church's martyrs knew no part. Early church converts were not martyred for "believing in Jesus" in their private thoughts, but for challenging the secular anti-Christian authorities of their day.

That people could ask Jesus into their hearts by "faith," and believe their destiny is heaven and be totally wrong is confirmed by Jesus Himself: "Not everyone who says to me, 'Lord, Lord,' will enter the kingdom of heaven, but only he who does the will of my Father who is in heaven. Many will say to me on that day, 'Lord, Lord, did we not prophesy in your name, and in your name drive out demons and perform many miracles?' Then I will tell them plainly, 'I never knew you. Away from me, you evildoers!'" (Matthew 7:21-23 NIV). Their religion was abhorrent to God because they sought to save themselves apart from God's sovereign grace. I am convinced that the chief reason why most Christians don't think in worldview terms is because of the self-centered mentality of how one becomes a member of the kingdom of God.

Man's redemption comes by grace: "By grace you have been saved, through faith, and this is not from yourselves, it is the gift of God" (Ephesians 2:8 NIV); ". . . to those who believed in his name, . . . children were born not of natural descent, nor of human decision or a husband's will, but born of God" (John 1:12-13 NIV). Even so, Jesus identified the redeemed: "For whoever does the will of my Father in heaven, is my brother and sister and mother" (Matthew 12:50 NIV).

The local church must began identifying itself by fruit producers rather than just by decision makers.

In thousands of churches each week, tens of thousands are acknowledged as converts into the kingdom, yet instead of the church becoming more powerful and gaining victories against Satan's assault on society, one would think that the church at large is on an extended retreat.

With the church not in sight, the enemy is ransacking the entire camp. Antibiblical philosophy abounds at all levels of government, schools are failing everywhere, marriages and families are coming apart faster than new ones are being formed, immorality of the worst kind is being flaunted openly, and, horror of horrors, this immorality is being sanctioned from certain segments of the body of Christ.[13]

With the high-growth "accept Jesus" evangelism, the Christian church is experiencing a metamorphosis, transforming itself into a civic religion based on community needs. Families are looking for a place of weekly fellowship that provides marriage ceremonies, baby dedications (or baptisms), day care, youth activities, mom's-day-out, counseling services, twenty- to thirty-minute nonconfrontational messages, all designed to fit the tolerance-based climate of our day. What they are not looking for is sacramental worship, serious theological Bible study, pastoral confrontation over personal sin, or commitment.

By responding to the "market demand," church services are becoming anthropocentric rather than theocentric. Apart from a return to solid Christian worldview focus, a new day in Christendom is arising.

A lost generation

That we are missing the mark with young adults is of little surprise to most pastors, Christian educators, and parents. They are painfully aware that a high percentage of young people stop attending church after leaving home, and many live in a manner highly displeasing to the Lord. One recent study of more than 3,500 incoming freshman at various universities who identified themselves as born again Christians found that by their senior year between one-third and one-half said they no longer considered themselves as such (decisions that defected!).[14]

The lack of presenting a Christian-worldview Gospel makes the church and the Christian faith seem irrelevant to young people. While the church was the dominant force in building our universities and hospitals, producing scholarly statesmen who drafted state constitutions and later the federal Constitution, creating charitable organizations to care for the poor and widows, today the church has been pushed, or voluntarily retreated, back into a nondefining role for how society should function. Contrary to the Christian worldview at work 200 years ago, the agenda for today's public square is clearly shaped by secular and anti-Christian forces. The church's job is mostly viewed as getting people ready for heaven.

To young men and women who are thinking about living rather than dying, this makes the church appear unimportant. They see a church lacking forward thinking, with no desire to create or influence culture-shaping institutions such as schools, legislative assemblies, and courts. They see a church without a Christian worldview.

Christian worldview uncovered

All creedal Christians believe God made the world and "so loved the world that He gave His only begotten Son." All faithful Christian churches want to impact the world with missionaries as much as possible. And, what church-attending person wouldn't say that he or she believes in biblical principles for the whole of life? So why the charge that the church is without a Christian "world" view?

The issue gets a little clearer when we substitute *civilization* for worldview. To say that the Bible gives principles for all areas of life, and that Jesus has authority over all things, and that the church has been given the keys to make disciples of all nations, is to say: "Our goal is nothing less than a Christian civilization." Are not these biblical views saying that the bride of Christ will be glorious and victorious for the return of her King?

This means that God is to be obeyed and glorified in all aspects of society, particularly in government, commerce, entertainment, education, and the arts. Impossible? Not for the God Who created everything in the universe out of nothing, simply by speaking it into existence. And, it is not impossible for "You, dear children, are from God and have overcome them; because the one who is in you is greater than the one who is in the world" (1 John 4:4 NIV). With God's power and with clear, comprehensive instructions in His Word, the church can and will bring Christian thought and behavior to all aspects of world civilization. We need to know this and work accordingly. By the empowering of Holy Spirit, we will overcome.

How are Jesus' enemies defeated? Paul gives the answer: "The God of peace will soon crush Satan under your feet. The grace of our Lord Jesus be with you" (Romans 16:20 NIV). *"Under your feet."* This is the church crushing the head of Satan, destroying anti-Christian thinking day by day, mile by mile.

What must we do?

We must think and behave biblically in all areas. We start with prayer, asking God to forgive us for being shortsighted and of little faith. We ask Him to equip us for the battle of life.

Read books on Christian worldview thinking. Also read of the Christian impact on the founding of our nation. This is history that is being denied to students in public schools. Examples of the providence of God have been systematically removed from text-books for the past several decades.

Support Christian education, financially and/or as a volunteer on a committee of a local Christian school.

Support a mature Christian candidate for a political office.

Introduce others to Christian worldview studies; start a study group in your church.

Most important, thank the Lord for your life in Him. Thank Him for redeeming you and the opportunity to work in His kingdom.

Then, take joy in knowing that at the end of a productive life, formed by a Christian worldview, you will hear, "Well done, good and faithful slave . . . enter into the joy of your master" (Matthew 25:21 NASB).

How your theology shapes your worldview

Here are some key doctrinal questions for you to use to evaluate different worldviews. These doctrinal questions are adapted from those asked by Michael S. Horton in an article in MOVIEGUIDE®.[15]

The doctrine of God

Does God have all power and authority over the universe, or is history a battle between good and evil forces (dualism)?

Is this world rational and ordered? What is justice, goodness, truth, beauty? How are these reflections of God's character?

What is the significance of the affirmation that "the Word became flesh" for our view of our humanness and the importance of this world?

Is God the separate, sovereign, Creator of the universe as in theism? Or is God part of the universe as in pantheism, polytheism, and monism?

The doctrine of man

Is man a product of chance? Are we part of God or distinct creations of God? What distinguishes humans from the rest of creation?

What is the "image of God"? Do people still possess that image even if they aren't Christians? What does this mean for the arena of life we share in common with non-Christians (work and play, etc.)?

Are humans basically good or evil? How are we dead in our sins? How are we cut off from God? What does original sin mean?

What does this mean for government and law? How do we balance liberty and justice? Can we expect to build an ideal society?

The doctrine of salvation

Is salvation eternal or temporal?

Do people really need saving? From what?

Of what does the Christian doctrine of salvation consist? Is salvation the work of God entirely, or the work of God and man, or man alone?

How can man save himself? If man can save himself, why did Jesus Christ need to die on the cross and be resurrected?

The doctrine of the church

Are we saved *from* the world, or saved *in* the world? Is the church a community that is separated from the world or to God in the world?

Is the church a community of only those who are truly saved, or is it a mixed body of Christians and hypocrites who will only be sorted out on the last day?

How important are the earthly sacraments of bread, wine, and water in our Christian experience?

What are my responsibilities to the church as well as to my calling?

The doctrine of history and the future

Is God's history of salvation, from Genesis to Revelation, a story of escape from this world and normal human history, or a story of providence and redemption in real time and space history?

Are we wasting our time getting involved in this world when it is going to pass away at our Lord's return?

The doctrine of the nature of reality—ontology

Do we live in a real world—ontological realism?

Or do we live in a great thought or imaginary world that can be shaped by magical thinking—ontological nominalism?

The doctrine of knowledge—epistemology

Can we know that something exists such as a tree falling in the forest—epistemological realism?

Or can we never know with certainty anything and so must make believe that reality exists—epistemological nominalism?

Endnotes

1. Matthew Broderick, quoted in *The Hollywood Reporter*, 63rd Anniversary Edition, (Fall, 1993).
2. The Nehemiah Institute is a nonprofit foundation with headquarters in Lexington, KY. The institute provides a unique Christian worldview assessment and training service to Christian schools, homeschoolers, and churches. The institute has also developed a precinct-based program for use by local churches in coordinating various tasks to curb evil and restore righteousness in their community. The program is called *The Nehemiah Plan*. The institute may be contacted at (800) 948-3101. PEERS and NEHEMIAH are registered trademarks of the Institute.

3. *Engel v. Vitale*, 370 U.S. 421 (1962).

4. Francis A. Schaeffer, *A Christian Manifesto* (Westchester, Il: Crossway Books, 1981).

5. Marx, Karl, *The Communist Manifesto: English edition of 1888* (New York: Bantam Classic Books, 1992).

6. *Humanist Manifestos I & II* (Buffalo, NY: Prometheus Books, 1973).

7. *Ibid.*

8. Schaeffer, *A Christian Manifesto*, 17.

9. Marx, *The Communist Manifesto*.

10. Ronald H. Nash, *Worldviews in Conflict* (Grand Rapids, MI: Zondervan Publishing House, 1992), 9.

11. David F. Wells, *No Place for Truth* (Grand Rapids, MI: Eerdmans Publishing Co., 1993), 293.

12. *Ibid.*, 293-294.

13. A recent example was the United Methodists' 1996 General Conference held in Denver, CO, which included a report by "fifteen dissenting bishops" over their "pain" about the church's present standards on homosexuality.

14. Gary L. Railsback, *An Exploratory Study of the Religiosity and Related Outcomes Among College Students* (A dissertation submitted in partial satisfaction of the requirements for the degree, Doctor of Philosophy in Education), 1994.

15. Adapted from an article written by Michael S. Horton, "My Father's World," MOVIEGUIDE® VII:22: 921116.

THE LAST ACTION HERO

They shall teach my people the difference between the holy and profane, and cause them to discern between the unclean and the clean.
Ezekiel 44:23 (KJV)

In Hollywood, if you don't have happiness, you send out for it.
Rex Reed

Today, as you know, I am famous and very rich. But when I am alone with myself, I haven't the courage to consider myself an artist, in the great and ancient sense of that word. I am only a public entertainer, who understands his age.
Pablo Picasso[1]

Fact: A report on "Sex and the Mass Media" funded by the Kaiser Family Foundation found that 40% of the sexual behaviors depicted in prime time TV would be illegal in real life. The report also showed that many "family-hour" shows, such as Martin, talk about sex 50% of the time.[2]

M inisters and parents must develop strategies to facilitate the process of training young people to think biblically. This task is difficult because today's Christian youth in America live in a quandary of ideas. They are both secular and religious. They do not know where paganism and pragmatism intrude on the boundaries of Christianity. They are taught by modern culture to synthesize their value and belief system through the grid of a godless, egocentric rationalism.

We must inform students of the other philosophies and enhance their biblical education to reinforce Christian theism, which means the church must battle the prevalent secular mindset and worldview by training students to think and live biblically. We must also prepare students to be aware of and reject the subtle messages of the media. We must teach and model a godly, disciplined lifestyle.

Thus, parents must be equipped to teach their children discernment. Many, of course, have no idea how to do so beyond removing the television set. While that may be a good idea, stories abound of children who became addicted to the worst sex and violence across the street at a neighbor's house, or who were the victims of someone else who was addicted to sex and violence.

There are no quick fixes in this matter of teaching discernment. You have to teach your children what the problem is, why there is a problem, what the impact of entertainment is on each of them, how to look at different media differently, and how to ask the right ascertainment questions in order to understand what is going on in a given entertainment product. In other words, you must equip your children with the intellectual, cognitive, and spiritual tools to deal with the mass media.

Too many people tend to reduce the entertainment media issues to immoral sex and violence, even though sex and violence are only important parts of the problem. False gods and doctrines, which beckon to us with so much deadly appeal, are often more dangerous.

Describing the elephant

To teach discernment, you must understand that many parents primarily look at the entertainment media semantically in terms of the amount of sex, violence, nudity, and profanity, while many children just look at the entertainment media syntactically in terms of the rhythm, action, adventure, and special effects. So parents and children talk at each other about the entertainment media, not to each other.

A father might say to his son, "Did you hear the horrible lyrics in that music?" The son might reply, "No, but did you hear the riff, the rhythm, and the beat?"

Children are not immune to the messages of the mass media, but it is the syntactical elements of those messages that influence them. Try asking a younger child what he or she is watching on television. Quite often he or she will say, "I don't know." Ask the child what the program is about and often he or she will repeat, "I don't know."

However, pay attention to the child's actions, and you will often see him or her mimicking the behavior he or she is watching. Or later he or she will mimic the behavior or ask for a product that was advertised with the program.

Thumbs up

One set of keys to media literacy is to teach your children to deconstruct[3] the mass media product by deciphering, decoding, and detecting meaning in the mass media communication and then to compare and evaluate that meaning with a biblical world-view so as to understand and discern. Once they learn the right questions to ask, you can help your children broaden their perspective and develop discernment by having them review, critique, and report on the mass media they see and hear.

One of the most important keys to developing the biblical discernment needed to choose the right entertainment is asking the right questions. The entertainment media are loaded with messages. Learning how to discover these messages helps you appreciate the movies and television programs you watch, the games you play, the music you listen to, and the mass media information sources upon which you rely.

Asking the right questions about the entertainment media requires media literacy and a working knowledge of how the medium in question communicates and entertains. Developing discernment requires comparing the messages you discover from the questions you ask with the standards and principles presented by a Christian worldview.

There are two types of questions presented:

Ascertainment questions—which help us isolate elements, evidence, meaning, point of view, and worldview in a particular mass media product.

Discernment questions—which help us to compare the answers to our ascertainment questions with the biblical standard.

A Christian worldview requires the wisdom that comes from a fear of the Lord, the understanding that comes from a personal knowledge of Jesus Christ, and a solid knowledge of Scripture.

We will look briefly at those elements that make up powerful, dramatic entertainment. This analysis will be framed as a series of questions to guide you to ask the right questions about the entertainment product you, your children, and friends view. These questions will help you look beneath the surface of an entertainment product to determine whether you and God's Word written[4] agree with the messages the media product communicates.

This is a call to action, including active viewing and listening. It is beneficial to discern the subtle ways in which seemingly innocuous material molds our thinking through explaining its elements to others. This is especially important for Christian parents to consider.

For the reasons stated in the introduction, I will focus on

movies and videos, but the principles apply and are easily adapted to other media. Stimulating children to interact with their entertainment media experience rather than simply absorbing it is crucial.

But first . . .

On the way to the theater and before the video brainstorm with your child for prior knowledge about the story or content matter. This gives you an opportunity to share a short description of the movie's plot and characters. Before the film begins you can encourage children to imagine the characters and what could happen. If the child's thinking is activated prior to the passive activity of watching, they can engage in the story and learn from the plot on the screen.

Prior to viewing, to facilitate active viewing:

Talk about the title, images, and ideas about the plot.

Predict the character types and action in the film.

Ask what your children know that they can bring to the film.

Use MOVIEGUIDE®'s "In Brief" as an introduction to the film.

Plan to stop the video for predictions of a character's actions or plot twists, but too much stopping is not recommended as it may disrupt the rhythm of the film.

HINT: Set the VCR timer so that if you or older children see something worth discussing in the video, you can easily return to that section after the movie.

ELEMENTAL AND EVIDENTIARY QUESTIONS

The first set of questions we will ask are known as elemental and evidentiary questions because they deal with elements of the mass media product that are easily ascertained. Most of these questions help us to find out the facts of the mass media product about which most thinking people will agree. It should be clear after reviewing these questions that there are many other questions that we can and should ask in order to be media literate and discerning to choose the good and reject the bad.

These are key questions to ask your children after watching a movie. They're sure to help launch an animated discussion. It is important to set a tone that supports their responses and creative impressions of the story.

ASCERTAINMENT QUESTION: Who is the hero?

Usually the easiest question for anyone, including children, to answer about a movie, television program, computer game, stage play, book, or story is Who is the hero or heroine? Of course, when we are confronted by some modern literature wherein the reader has to realize that he is the hero (or the hero doesn't exist), or if we probe beyond the character's name to find out his characteristics, then this question becomes much more complex.

Many dramatists[5] talk not about the main character in the story whom most people would consider the hero, but rather about the character who forces the action, whom the dramatists call the protagonist. From a dramatist's point of view the villain, such as Judas in the Passion story, can be the protagonist if he forces the action, whereas the hero, Jesus, may be the antagonist because He opposes the protagonist. Even so our main character, in this case Jesus, remains the Hero because He triumphs over His opponent(s).

For our purposes, we can conclude that in most cases, especially as far as popular entertainment is concerned, the hero is the main character who is the focus of the story. Using this insight, most children can find the hero in most entertainment media products.

However, knowing the name of the hero is not enough to be discerning. To understand who the hero is we must analyze the hero's bone structure. The bone structure of any character is the combination of all the characteristics that make up the character. In analyzing a character's bone structure we need to look at the following: his physical characteristics, his background, his psychological characteristics, and his religious characteristics.

As a guide to the impact a hero has on a story, the following reminder of the archetypal story genres are helpful:

In the mythic story, such as *The Ten Commandments*, God triumphs, or the hero triumphs because of an act of God.

In the heroic story, such as *High Noon*, the hero triumphs because he or she is superior.

In the high ironic story, such as *Forrest Gump*, the hero triumphs because of an quirk of fate or circumstances.

In the low ironic story, such as *Death of a Salesman*, the hero fails because of a quirk of fate or circumstances.

In the demonic story, which includes not only many horror films but also psychological movies and political films such as *The Diary of Anne Frank*, the hero is hopelessly overwhelmed by evil.

During the next movie, television program, story, or game with which you interact, locate the hero or heroine and describe his or her character traits.

DISCERNMENT QUESTION: What kind of a role model is the hero?

After locating the hero or heroine in the entertainment product and identifying his or her character traits, you need to discern whether or not he or she is a worthy role model. It is not safe to assume that the heroes of today's movies are the positive role models we want for our impressionable children. Even where the premise is positive and the morals in the entertainment product reflect a Christian worldview, we must ask the question: Is the hero compatible with the biblical role model?

Comparing three of action star Sylvester Stallone's characters—Rocky, Rambo, and Cobra (one of his lesser known, later characters)—illustrates the different messages that a hero can communicate through his or her character traits in movies with basically the same premise:

> Rocky is an ironic hero who loves his family, prays, and tries to do the right thing, although he is reduced to using brute force to prove his worth and win in our complex modern society. Rocky's use of force in the boxing ring is mitigated by the fact that he prays before each fight, demonstrating his reliance on God and not on his own prowess. (Note that in *Rocky IV*, Rocky steps out of character and pursues vengeance for its own sake.)

> Rambo is a haunted man who strikes out at the country (U.S.) that abandoned him to die in Vietnam and tries to rescue his buddies who have suffered a similar fate. Rambo has lost faith in everyone and ends up by asking why the rug of faith was pulled out from under him by the country he loved. He uses brute force to triumph out of anger and frustration.

> Cobra is a killing machine who sets himself up as judge and jury. He is the ultimate humanist, a product of Ayn Rand, Nietzsche, and Hobbes, who exhibits the solipsistic heresy of titanism.

The Last Temptation of Christ pushed the desecration of the hero one step further. Never before in history had moviemakers declared war on Jesus. Here are excerpts from notes taken by Evelyn Dokovic of Morality in Media at a screening of *The Last Temptation of Christ*:

Judas berates Jesus for making crosses that are used by the Romans to kill Jews. As they talk, Jesus indicates that he is struggling. (Viewer observation: Jesus is weak, confused, fearful, doesn't know who he is, from time to time falls on the ground in a faint after hearing voices. He doesn't know if the voices come from God or the devil.)

Jesus seems to be helping them crucify the man. He revives and says he wants God to hate him. He makes crosses because he wants God to hate him.

The viewer sees a bare-breasted woman sitting at a well. Jesus proceeds on his way to Mary Magdalene's house. He has to wait in line to get in. When he does the room is filled with men sitting down, watching Mary have sex with a customer. Jesus sits down and watches, too.

Jesus says: "I'm a liar, a hypocrite, I'm afraid of everything. Do you want to know who my God is? They're fear. Lucifer is inside me. He tells me I am not a man, but the Son of Man, more the Son of God, more than that, God."

Jesus is walking with his wives (bigamy) and children, and stops to listen to a preacher—St. Paul. He is telling the people that Jesus of Nazareth was the Son of God, that he was tortured and crucified for our sins, and that three days later He rose from the dead.

Jesus screams: "Liar." Jesus tells Paul that he is Jesus, asks why he is telling these lies. Jesus says: "I was saved. I have children." Paul tells him to look around him and see how unhappy the people are. Their only hope is the resurrected Jesus. Paul says: "They need God. If I have to crucify you, I'll crucify you. If I have to resurrect you, I'll resurrect you. My Jesus is more important than you are. I'm glad I met you. Now I can forget about you."[6]

This hero is evil and this movie is blasphemy. To think that Jesus, the Word, Who was in the beginning, through Whom all things were made, Who is God, was lusting in His holy heart for one of His creations is grotesque and horrifying (see John 1). This film desecrates the sinless Lamb of God Who cleansed us through His death and resurrection. *The Last Temptation of Christ* is the ultimate desecration of the hero, even though the premise says that good triumphs over evil.

Subsidiary discernment questions:

If the hero is not a moral character, how would the story change if the hero were a moral character?

How would you tell the story from another character's viewpoint?

Do you know anyone like the hero?

Is there a character in the Bible who is like the hero? Who is it? What is his or her story?

ASCERTAINMENT QUESTION: Who is the villain?

As in the case of the hero, you need to identify the villain and his character traits. In most entertainment product the villain is easy to identify, but there are exceptions.

To identify the villain, it is helpful to recall the four basic plots:

Man against man.

Man against nature.

Man against himself.

Man against the supernatural or the subnatural.

In the remake of *Cape Fear*, the villain does not say he is a Christian, but does have Bible verses tattooed on his body and spouts contemporary Christian code words in a malevolent manner. Therefore, you need to look at all the attributes of character to see if he is supposed to be a Christian.

Once you have identified the villain, you should list his character traits in the same manner that you did with the hero. You will want to list physical characteristics, background, psychological characteristics, and religious characteristics.

Since the demise of the motion picture and television codes, there have been many media products portraying those who are moral as prudes, nerds, kooks, and psychopaths. One of the first was *Midnight Cowboy* (1969), which portrayed a street preacher as a sleazy homosexual who leads the hero into homosexual prostitution. The movie *Criminal Law* (1989) went further by portraying pro-lifers, who do not think that babies should be murdered in their mothers' wombs, as psychopathic killers.

In *Shirley Valentine*, the working husband is the villain, while the heroine is the wife who runs off with her bisexual friend to have a series of adulterous affairs in Greece. In *Dances with Wolves*, the villains are the American settlers and the U.S. cavalry. The heroes are the Indians. In *The Bear*, the villains are the hunters and the heroes are the bears. In *Old Gringo*, the Americans are the bad guys and the Mexicans are the good guys.

Although white males should not always be the heroes, they should not always be the villains either. The modern politically correct position in that they are always the villains.

In contrast, in the 1996 film adaptation of *Richard III*, the archetypal villain is truly evil, so much so that his mother tells him that he has abandoned God.

DISCERNMENT QUESTION: What kind of a message does the character of the villain communicate?

As Christians, we need to analyze the character of the villain to determine whether he, she, or they are being used to attack a religious, biblical worldview. If they are being so used, we may want to protest this anti-Christian bigotry and, perhaps, even boycott the movie in question.

ASCERTAINMENT QUESTION: How much violence is there in the mass media product?

Violence in the entertainment media is a critical problem because of its influence on children and susceptible individuals, so it is important to know how much violence is in a mass media product. Many contemporary movies and television programs push the limits of violence.

Looking at the content of some movies will help you to understand the severity of the situation:

In *Freddy's Dead: The Final Nightmare* there were:

Multiple grotesque murders and violence in dream sequences.

A wooden rod rammed through a man's ear.

The deforming and exploding of a character's head.

A man impaled on bed of nails.

Blood dripping or gushing from doors, ceilings, and a television set.

Stabbings and slashings.

Amputation of fingers and ears.

Recurrent intense depictions of child abuse and molestations by parents.

In *People under the Stairs* the content included:

Sadistic violence, including a woman bound by wrists inside a torture chamber.

People hit with cement blocks.

A tongue cut out.

Chasing a girl with meat cleaver.

Woman impaled in stomach by knife.

A pit bull attack on intruders.

Body mutilation.

A gory corpse hanging on rack.

Electric shock.

A man shot and hurled down stairs.

The forcing of a child into boiling water.

Punching a man in the groin.

Pouring gasoline inside an inhabited chamber and setting it aflame.

Dog impaled by a sword.

Poking a man in the eye.

Crude references to genitals.

Sexual jokes.

A child likened to a prostitute.

Talk of "tricks," tarot cards, and voodoo dolls that embody the souls of victims.

Crack and drug addicts.

Distortion of the Twenty-third Psalm.

Breaking and entering.

Sadomasochistic dress.

Cannibalism.

Something must be done to curb this level of violence in movies. The most effective stand you can make is to know before you go by reading MOVIEGUIDE® and then to avoid movies with such abhorrent material. Since teenagers are the most likely to attend these types of movies, it is important to help them understand why they need to make godly choices before they use any of the modern mass media.

DISCERNMENT QUESTION: How is the violence presented in the mass media product?

The emotive heart of drama is conflict and the ultimate conflict ends in violence. The Bible is full of violence and the Gospel story has one of the most violent scenes imaginable: the crucifixion of Jesus Christ. The presentation of violence in the entertainment media is not always bad and is sometimes necessary. It is, however, critical to protect young children from such violence and to identify how it is presented in the entertainment product so you can discern whether it is necessary and furthers the good and the true.

Ron Maxwell, director of *Gettysburg*, said that while violence was essential to the storyline of the movie, he purposely avoided porno-violence with its excessive blood, guts, and gore. His discretion made *Gettysburg* a better movie that could reach a broader audience.

DISCERNMENT QUESTION: How is love portrayed?

The beauty of God's love is wonderful, yet most movies reduce love to one night sexual relationships, tedious ordeals, eternal battles, or homosexual coupling. This desecration of love should be an anathema to His people.

The Scarlet Letter contends that adulterous love is honorable. *Kids* suggests that promiscuous sex posing as love is acceptable among young teenage children. *War of the Roses* suggests that marriage is war. *Skin Deep* starts out with the hero sleeping with one woman after another. The Disney movie *Ruthless People* has the husband trying to murder his wife, while the wife is trying to blackmail the husband. *Desert Hearts* has a woman who is getting a divorce find out that lesbian love is better than heterosexual love. *The Accidental Tourist* proves the despicable premise that self-indulgence is more important than love. *Naked Lunch, The Incredibly True Adventure of Two Girls in Love, Bound, Philadelphia,* and *Birdcage* present homosexual lust as love.

Many horror movies capture an audience by luring them with the thought of forbidden lust, such as necrophilia (fornication with the dead) and bestiality (fornication with animals).

However, horror films are not the only films that extol forbidden fruit. The Disney comedy *Splash* lifts up bestiality in a humorous way by having the hero fall in love with a mermaid. Bestiality is not funny and is condemned by God.

Many movies suggest, or even promote, the idea of sex with a child.

The most memorable and most profitable movies are usually carefully crafted character studies that portray love in a wholesome, biblical, uplifting light, such as *Tender Mercies* and *Sense and Sensibility*.

ASCERTAINMENT QUESTION: How much sex is in the mass media product?

In 1995, there were thirty-six movies produced that had excessive sexual content. These films earned on average less than $1 million at the box office. Two of the biggest-budget Hollywood sex films, *Showgirls* and *Striptease*, bombed at the box office and lost millions of dollars despite mammoth advertising campaigns. In 1996, the average box office for the six movies with strong homosexual content was a pitiful $705,302. Since the average Hollywood movie costs $54 million to produce and market, one has to wonder why the industry continues to try to force such product on the public. Movies with strong Christian content in 1995 earned on average 2,400% more at the box office than movies with excessive sexual content.

An example of the excess of sexual content in some Hollywood movies is the critically acclaimed movie *Naked Lunch*. This disgusting movie contained twelve obscenities and six profanities, a woman shooting insecticide into her breast, grotesque giant bugs with talking anuses, a woman ripping open her body, women shot in the head, "mugwump" monsters with dripping and squirting phalluses on their heads, graphic fornication, adultery, reference to sexually transmitted diseases and fellatio, transvestitism, homosexual kissing, lesbian and homosexual copulation, male and female nudity, surrealistic and overt depictions of genitalia, witchcraft, graphic drug use, drug-induced hallucinations, and alcohol consumption.

Many such movies garner the applause of the secular critics and film festivals around the world, but do not get much of an audience.

DISCERNMENT QUESTION: How is the family portrayed?

Contemporary movies that build up the family, such as the prolife, profamily, promarriage, profatherhood *Father of the Bride*, are rare.

Instead, today's movies tend to lift up homosexuality, promote free love, tear down marriage, portray motherhood as psychopathic, and show husbands and dads as irresponsible. These types of movies attack the basic building block of our society: the family.

The content of two antifamily movies with family MPAA ratings is very instructive:

In *Addams Family Values* (PG-13), the content includes:

children dropping a cannonball on their baby sibling, dropping a guillotine blade on their baby sibling, dropping their baby sibling from roof of house, burning summer camp, and starting to burn a girl at the stake;

a nurse trying to electrocute her husband, trying to bomb her husband and trying to electrocute the family;

extreme graphic violence in a scene at a camp;

sadomasochism, sadism, and perverse sex and fornication are suggested;

occult references throughout the movie; and

blasphemy and mocking of Christianity.

In *The Brady Bunch* (PG), there is:

frequent sexual innuendo;

an older woman flirts with young boys;

a lesbian girl has a crush on unsuspecting friend; and

the family's nonreligious, clean-living morality is mocked.

The Bible is very clear about the importance of the family. The family is the focal point of God's economy and governance. God created the family and ordained it as basic unit of government along with self-government, the church, and civil government. The family is much more important than the state.

ASCERTAINMENT QUESTIONS: Is religion, the church, people of faith, and/or Christians in the mass media product?

Being able to identify religion, the church, people of faith and/or Christians in the entertainment media product is an extremely important aspect of discerning viewing. Religion is alive and well in the entertainment media, especially on prime time network fiction television, but it is not the predominantly Christian faith of our founding fathers. It is, instead, a cacophony of ill-conceived religions such as materialism, consumerism, eroticism, hedonism, naturalism, humanism, cynicism, stoicism, the cult of violence (that used to pay homage to the war-god Mars), and a multitude of other modern variations on pagan practices. These religions, many of which can trace their roots back to long discredited ancient cults, have their rituals, beliefs, values, signs, significations, metaphysics, cosmologies, ontologies, epistemologies, and ultimate meanings played out with ritualistic regularity on programs, commercials, and music videos. On any given night on television we may find happy Hollywood stars touting the virtues of astrology and Madonna embracing a religious statue that comes alive.

Many in Hollywood recognize the religious significance of their work. Joe Eszterhas, author of the sleazy movie *Showgirls*, claimed that his pornographic film was a religious experience.

Theocentric religions are underrepresented in the mass media and especially on prime time entertainment television, though there has been a significant increase in their presence in the last few years in popular programs such as *Touched by an Angel* and even *Dr. Quinn, Medicine Woman*. In fact, there has been an increase in television programs that focus on Christianity and Jesus Christ such as *Christy, 7th Heaven,* and even some episodes of *Walker: Texas Ranger* and other popular series.

DISCERNMENT QUESTION(S): How are religion, Christians, and the church portrayed?

All too often in contemporary movies, religion, individual believers and the church are portrayed as evil, weak, insincere, obsequious, rotten, or foolish.

Though it had nothing to do with the premise, a series of morning prayer meetings were inserted into the mediocre movie *Head Office*, which caricatured Christians as neo-Nazis who prayed for world conquest with German accents. In Woody Allen's movie *Hannah and Her Sisters*, Christianity, Roman Catholicism, and even Hinduism are mocked.

As Christians, we may think mocking other religions is funny, but the truth is that mocking false doctrines is a sign of hubris and not of a godly desire to lift up the Truth, Who is Jesus the Christ. Furthermore, as history has constantly proved, mockery will lead to disaster. For example, Hitler began his campaign against the Jews by mocking them in grotesque cartoons.

The good news is that there are more and more movies that lift up Jesus Christ and commend the church, such as *Dead Man Walking* and *The Preacher's Wife*.

Subsidiary discernment questions:

Does one or more of the characters play the role of God?

Did you see anything supernatural? Who was the source: God or Satan? Or were you not sure? (Ask God to show you.)

Does good win over evil?

Does the winning side use spiritual power not from God? (Remember, if supernatural power is not from God, it is demonic. Frequent exposure tends to bring unquestioning acceptance, so be careful.)

Are magic, spells, fortune-telling, spiritism (contacting the spirit world or functioning as a medium between the living and the dead, as in *Ghost*) presented as a helpful means to happy living? Might they build a dangerous fascination with paganism and a desire to experiment?

ASCERTAINMENT QUESTION: How is the world or the environment in which the story takes place portrayed?

The environment in which a story, song, or entertainment event takes place has an immense impact on the audience. Because every communication excludes what it does not include, its omissions create powerful secondary messages in the minds of the audience. Editing, close-ups, reverse shots, and other camera techniques can distort the meaning of a scene and the way we look at the world.

To understand how the media influence by excluding material, look through the viewfinder of a camera and note how you can completely changed the mode and the message of a scene by what you include and what you exclude within the frame of the picture. Let your children do the same and you will help them to develop a critical media literacy skill.

One college student wanted to become an anthropologist because of a beautiful picture of a temple in Bali. When I recognized the location and told the student that the temple was surrounded by a gas station and urban blight, his perspective changed.

Research has shown that the background environment of an entertainment media product has a tremendous impact on the worldview of the children.

It is important that we are aware of how the media product is portraying the world so we can counter any misconceptions the product might create.

Since a camera excludes everything beyond its field of view, television journalism is technically biased in its reporting, yet the viewer interprets what he or she sees as the truth. The camera is typically used to implode the subject matter by focusing tightly around one aspect that makes the shot appear larger than life. This distorts the real world environment.

In other words, the camera does lie.

The entertainment industry often distorts the way we look at the world. The next time you watch a movie or television pay close attention to how the world or environment in which the story takes place is portrayed. Although the environment in which the story is set may not be the focus of your attention as you watch or listen to most media product, the environment will send you distinct messages that influence how you look at the world and the subject matter of the entertainment product.

Subsidiary ascertainment questions: Where did the story take place? How do you know?

Children need to be aware that movies are staged—that props and scenery are used to set a story in a particular time and place. These questions help determine if your child realizes that, say, a horse and carriage signals a story set in the past. When children notice details, movie viewing will be a richer experience.

Subsidiary ascertainment question: How is language used in the mass media product?

Closely related to the environmental ascertainment and discernment question is the question of how language is used in a mass media product. A definitive study by Professor Timothy Jay on *Cursing in America*[7] found that only 7% of American people curse on the job and only 12% in their leisure time, yet many movies and television programs would lead us to believe that Americans cursed all the time because they are so full of profanity and obscenity. It may be rare to hear cursing in your local grocery store or mall, but turn on your TV, or radio or go to the movies and you will hear a constant barrage of cursing.

One school of Marxist thought considered language as a weapon with which to attack the bourgeois society in which we live.[8] Playwright David Mamet belongs to this school.

In the years MOVIEGUIDE® has been tracking language in movies, we have found that the more foul language included in a movie, the worse it will do at the box office.

Subsidiary ascertainment question: What special effects were used to create the setting and environment of the entertainment product?

This question helps demystify the entertainment media product so that children can see that it is pretend—that it is all created. Children can be unsettled by even seemingly innocent things in a entertainment media product, so it is important to emphasize that some movies, television programs, and other mass media product are fantasy.

If your child is very young, you might ask questions like:

How do you think they made that character fly without getting hurt?

What pretend things were the characters doing?

A lot of young children want to duplicate what they see, so it is wise to point out what is not real.

DISCERNMENT QUESTION: How are government and business portrayed?

This question belongs as a subset of the question "How is the world portrayed?" but because so many movies attack Republican governments and promote socialism and communism, it behooves us to pay close attention to the way a movie portrays government. Furthermore, to really analyze what worldview is being foisted upon us by a motion picture, we should also ask in conjunction with the question, "How is private enterprise portrayed in the movie?"

The Lichter, Rothman, and Lichter studies show[9] the vast majority of those involved in the entertainment industry believe in socialism, which believes that the state, not God, is the savior of the mankind.

At the very root of socialism and communism is a negation of God's law, the Ten Commandments, particularly the first, since the state is being elevated to a position higher than God; the eighth, because the redistribution of property by the state is stealing from those less powerful than the state who are forced to give up their property against their will; and the tenth, because the whole premise of socialism and communism is based on the politics of envy or coveting that which belongs to someone else. A movie that lifts up the state as savior and attacks the individual and his God-given rights is, in fact, promoting a very anti-Christian worldview.

Salvador is a particularly coarse example of a movie aimed at promoting the goals of socialist revolutionaries. The rebels are a nice bunch of young people with no weapons except their good cause, and the hero makes it clear that he hates all authority, especially American.

Another extreme example is *Remo Williams: The Adventure Begins*, a fascist fantasy wherein mystical, humanistic violence is used to defend the Big Brother state from unscrupulous free enterprise capitalists. The savior is an ancient Korean martial arts master who can walk on water. Regrettably, this savior is dedicated to serving Big Brother and death. Many people become infected by the virus of the corrupt mystic statism in such movies, so we need to be aware of these deceptions and be prepared to rebuke them.

The opposite view, that the state is always the villain, as represented in the movies *JFK* and *Nixon*, is also wrong. In a similar vein, *Fat Man and Little Boy* suggests that the United States government was immoral for creating and employing the atomic bomb to end World War II. *Independance Day*, for all its many good points, goes in the opposite direction and suggests that internationalism is the key to harmony and world peace.

Statism, in whatever form it takes—whether fascism, communism, or national socialism—is a punishment for rejecting God and seeking salvation from men. This is the key to the impoverishment of every totalitarian state, including the former Soviet Union with all its natural wealth. Salvation can never be found in the state, but tyranny can.

Forrest Gump and *Braveheart* are two very successful examples of movies that adhere to a biblical view. *Forrest Gump* shows the foolishness of the self-appointed revolutionaries; while *Braveheart* demonstrates the principle of Lex Rex, which holds that even the king has no right to violate God's law.

Asking how government and private enterprise are portrayed will help us to cut through the hidden political agendas that are in too many films.

DISCERNMENT QUESTION: How is history treated in the media product?

Any familiarity with world history will convince us that those who forget the past are doomed to repeat it. When the media revises the past to suit their worldview, it is a very serious issue for the future of our civilization.

Much revisionism has been devoted to whitewashing the Holocaust. Those who deal in this area of revisionism are anxious to remove the memory of the Holocaust from the annals of history by claiming that the gas chambers could not have killed so many people and that the death camps were actually work camps with good sanitary conditions.

While *Schindler's List* accurately portrays the horror of the Holocaust, *The English Patient* whitewashes the real history of its Nazi hero, extols adultery, and promotes euthanasia.

Any thinking person understands the threat of revising history to remove the memory of the Holocaust, but few object to the wholesale revision of history that supports our republican democracy and Christian heritage. Historian Catherine Millard has chronicled the removing of Christian quotes and information from our national monuments by the U.S. Park Service and the removal of the Christian writings of our founding fathers from the Library of Congress in her book *The Rewriting of America's History*. Reading her book gives a frightening look at how the revisionists are trying to remove any trace of Christianity from our society.

WORLDVIEW QUESTIONS

We move out of the evidentiary world toward the philosophical foundations and perspectives that the mass media feed us over the impulse waves. In order to discern meaningful biblical agendas, we need first to distinguish between the differing worldviews and man's relation between himself, his world, and his God.

The term *discernment* has a much deeper meaning than identifying discrepancies between "good" and "bad" viewing, which is to see the differences between the two elements and to make an educated decision. We are here to build discernment, and discernment involves our entire process of thinking, feeling, and knowing so that we are able to recognize a pieces of media or information as moral, ethical, and holy or as information that does not follow the laws of God and His plan for our lives.

Therefore, the second set of questions that we will ask is known as worldview questions because they deal with the underlying elements of the mass media product that must be ascertained by looking at the dynamic interfaces between the evidentiary elements. These elements help us to understand the philosophical and theological messages that the mass media product is communicating and are critical to making discerning decisions.

ASCERTAINMENT QUESTION: What is the premise of the movie?

If you understand the premise of the entertainment product, then you understand the ultimate message the product is communicating to the audience. The premise drives the story to its conclusion. Whether or not the audience is conscious of the premise, it implants its message in the minds of the audience.

The storyline logically proves the premise. If the premise of the mass media product is "good triumphs over evil," then the storyline has to tell in a logical manner how the good hero triumphs over the evil villain or the story will fail to capture the audience.

Without a clear-cut premise, no idea is strong enough to carry a story through to a logical conclusion.[10] If there is no clear-cut premise, the characters will not live. A badly worded or false premise will force the mass media–maker[11] to fill space with irrelevant material. A mass media product with more than one premise is confused because it is trying to go in more than one direction. A premise that says too much is ambiguous and, therefore, says nothing. A premise that does not take a position is ambivalent and, therefore, says nothing.

In most cases, a mass media–maker will not be able to produce a successful entertainment product based on a premise that he or she does not believe. No one premise expresses the totality of universal truth, and every premise is limiting. For example, poverty does not always lead to crime, but if the mass media–maker has chosen the premise that poverty leads to crime, it does, and he or she must prove it.

Here are some sample premises:

God's love triumphs over death (*Dead Man Walking*).

Great faith triumphs over death (*Lady Jane*).

Love conquers death (*Romeo and Juliet*).

Great faith triumphs over despotism (*Braveheart*).

Ruthless ambition destroys itself (*Macbeth*).

Strength defeats evil (*Rambo*).

Cunning defeats evil (*Alien*).

God triumphs over self-centeredness (*The Preacher's Wife*).

God's call triumphs over bondage (*Trip to Bountiful*).

The premise can be found by analyzing the story. In *Driving Miss Daisy*, an elderly woman has alienated all those around her. Motivated by his Christian faith, her black chauffeur gives his life to help her, ignoring her cruelty and demeaning barbs. In the end, she recognizes that he is her only friend. This heart-warming story has the incredibly powerful premise that Christian virtues bring reconciliation and love into an old woman's life.

Finding the premise will help your children develop cause-and-effect thinking, which is so important in understanding a story. Another way of finding the premise is to ask: Why did the story end the way it did?

DISCERNMENT QUESTION: Does the premise agree with, or conflict with, a biblical worldview?

Once you find the premise, you need to evaluate whether or not the premise is consistent with a biblical worldview. If the premise of the media product does not square with a biblical worldview, then you need to question the message the product is leaving in the minds of the audience.

The premise of *Rambo* has led to senseless violence and bullying because too many impressionable viewers end up believing that might makes right, since Rambo demonstrates that strength, not goodness, triumphs over evil. The eternal truth is that God's love alone secures the victory over the forces of evil, which the classic movie *Ben-Hur* clearly demonstrates.

ASCERTAINMENT QUESTION: How is the premise solved?

It is quite possible that the premise can agree with the biblical worldview, but the way that premise is solved may be anti-Christian, immoral, or evil. If that is the situation, then the media product is not acceptable viewing for Christians.

In many movies good triumphs over evil but only by means of magic. So while the premise ("good triumphs over evil") agrees with the biblical worldview, the method by which the premise is solved (magic) is antibiblical. These movies are suspect for anyone who does not understand that all magic is evil. If the magic were a literary device to point away from the manipulation of the supernatural for personal gain toward Jesus and God's grace, as in *The Chronicles of Narnia*, then there would be a redemptive aspect to the story that would make the movie acceptable.

The premise can be perfectly biblical, while the solution is immoral or demonic.

Subsidiary ascertainment question: What is the plot of the media product? What is the mass media product about?

Part and parcel of identifying the premise is to identify the plot. To do so you need to identify the five W's: who, what, where, when, and why. Always attempt to identify in the film as many of these as you think need to be answered. Often, it is a good idea to try to do this in one or two sentences.

Identifying the plot will help you to identify the premise and help your children to understand stories. Asking this straightforward question helps you find out whether your children understand a movie's main ideas. This question will also prompt children to recall details and incidents in sequence, which are two important thinking skills. Concerned about question formation techniques and the taxonomy of thought, education specialists stress the importance of asking questions deeply and not widely to explore knowledge, comprehension, application, analysis, synthesis, and evaluation.

Subsidiary discernment question: What image/sounds would you say best summarize the media product?

A sound-image schema can help you discover recurring themes and underlying principles in the media product. Ask your children to state one sound or image that relates to the story and discuss different suggestions from the family.

The subconscious sounds and images recite themselves over and over in the mind like an unwanted mantra. (Of course, no

Christian wants any mantra, especially one placed in our minds by a media product.)

Children constantly repeat songs from commercials such as McDonald's advertisements. Ask them to think about the songs and what they mean. Most children will come to the conclusion that they do not want to be singing songs that manipulate them.

If these ideas are presented into the conscious, only then can we make decisions about their appropriateness in our hearts and heads. We can choose to accept the song and dance or demand that the negative images leave in the name of God.

ASCERTAINMENT QUESTION: What are the moral statements in the media product?

and

DISCERNMENT QUESTION: Do the moral statements agree or conflict with a biblical worldview?

Besides having a premise that drives the story to its logical conclusion, many media products make one or more moral statements. *Batman Forever* has the premise "Cunning intelligence (as represented by Batman) triumphs over evil" and the biblically sound moral statements that "A double-minded man is unstable in all his ways" (James 1:8 KJV); "Pride goeth before destruction, and an haughty spirit before a fall" (Proverbs 16:18 KJV); and "Do not take revenge, my friends, but leave room for God's wrath, for it is written: 'It is mine to avenge; I will repay,' says the Lord" (Romans 12:19 NIV).

Sometimes the premise of a media product is anti-Christian while the moral agrees with a biblical worldview. The premise of *Labyrinth* that "a strong will defeats evil" is contrary to the biblical worldview; however, the primary moral statement of *Labyrinth* is that "possessions are worthless when compared to the value of the life of another human being," which agrees with God's Word written.

ASCERTAINMENT QUESTION: How is evil portrayed?
and
DISCERNMENT QUESTION: How does the portrayal of evil in the media product compare with the biblical view of evil?

Heretical doctrine can most often be traced to an incorrect view of evil, as is the case with humanism that sees man as basically good and minimizes evil and sin, or new age religions that see evil as simply an illusion, or occultism and Satanism that view evil as strong as, if not stronger than, the ultimate good Who is God. It is critical of an orthodox Christian worldview that evil be presented for what it is—real, not illusory or imaginary, and that it is clear that Jesus won the victory over evil on the cross.

Sweet Liberty is the archetypal humanist view of evil: neither God nor evil is a factor; everything is okay in the right context; and man's actions don't have consequences. *The Craft* portrays evil as having tremendous power and says that the teenage heroine can succeed only by participating in the occult power wherein the evil witches also draw their strength. The *Star Wars* movies show evil as being simply the other side of the good, with the Force, the god of *Star Wars*, being ambiguous and ambivalent. *Agnes of God* distortes the Gospel by making evil good and by portraying the nun Agnes as a spiritist who talks to departed spirits and who worships the powers of the air. All of these movies demean the reality of our sinful situation and negate the truth of God, His sovereign goodness, and His victory on the cross.

However, there are many movies that take a biblical view of evil and good, from classics such as *The Sound of Music* to more recent movies such as *First Knight*, which has one of the best portraits of a biblical view of good and evil ever presented in a movie.

ASCERTAINMENT QUESTION: How is reality portrayed? and

DISCERNMENT QUESTION: How does the presentation of reality in the media product compare to the biblical norm?

The question as to how reality is presented in the media product is the classic ontological question (ontology is the study of the nature of being, reality, or existence). That is, how is the very nature of being, which is reality, presented in the mass media product?

For Christians and Jews the biblical view toward reality is that we live in a real world, created by the real God, wherein there are real problems, pain, and suffering that we can not ignore or wish away. For those of us who are Christians, the Creator God has saved us from real evil, sin, and death through the real death and resurrection of His Son, Jesus the Christ, Who was really God and really man. Any other ontology, or view of the nature of being, denies the Gospel.

Classical Buddhism considers reality to be an illusion and the ultimate reality to be nonbeing, which means that there is no evil and no need for redemption.

In Christian Science, the sinful, fallen world as we know it is only mortal mind, while reality is divine mind, which is similar to the good universal consciousness of new age religions.

In like manner, Hinduism and many new age and pagan religions see reality as an illusion or *maya*. The ultimate reality for these nominalists (which means that the things in the world are only names not real things) is merely a fiction and not the real creation of a real theistic, separate God of the Bible. This nominalistic ontology denies the reality of sin and the need for salvation.

A nominalist premise blurs the line between imagination and reality. Evil is real and denying its reality by saying that it is only a dream or an illusion denies the need for Jesus' death on the cross to save us from our sins and from sin itself.

Hindus ignore the sick and hurting people around them because they believe that such sickness is *maya* and nothing is real. Therefore, Hindu holy men will pass a dying street urchin, with the explanation that his suffering is only an illusion and his karma, while Mother Teresa will pick the child up and take him to a hospital.

A Universalist worldview suggests that Jesus is not the only way to salvation. If that were the case, then it was futile for Jesus to suffer a vicious death on the cross. The Universalist worldview makes a mockery of the reality of His suffering, death, and resurrection, and reduces Jesus to a liar or a madman, rather than the "way, the truth and the light" (as C. S. Lewis so aptly noted).

Another branch of the new age and pagan religions see the world as made up of many gods and spiritual forces, a polytheistic ontology that sees reality as a cacophony of a myriad spiritual forces.

While Christians and Jews believe they live in a real world, they do not subscribe to the materialistic view of humanists and communists—that all that exists is the material world and the spiritual world is merely an invention of deluded minds.

Every movie has an ontology whether the producer, writer, or director knows it or not. The funny, poignant movie *Groundhog Day* presents a nominalistic ontology that is contrary to the Word of God, though it has a moral conclusion that makes it worth watching. Movies with magical thinking, such as *Aladdin*, usually have a nominalistic ontology. However, it is interesting that the movie *The Lion King* has a real ontology where there are real consequences for young Simba's actions, real death, and real solutions that require taking responsibility.

Subsidiary ascertainment and discernment question: How does the media product present knowledge and how does that presentation compare with the biblical norm?

How do we know that anything exists? This question is often phrased: How do you know that a tree fell in the forest if no one, including yourself, sees it?

Christians and Jews believe in a real epistemology, which means that they know because God tells them. He has told us that His laws govern all creation, including the forest, so we know that the life and death of trees occurs because trees are subject to His laws.

Many media products, especially horror films, posit that you cannot know and therefore are trapped in an unpredictable and frightening world. Other media products, such as Sartre's famous play *No Exit*, take an existentialist perspective that you cannot know so life is essentially meaningless.

In *Groundhog Day*, there is the unique combination of ontological nominalism and epistemological realism. So even though the days repeat themselves in a very unreal fashion, the hero knows that they repeat themselves and can adjust his actions accordingly, which, by the way, no one else can, so the other people are trapped in the nominalistic universe.

Subsidiary ascertainment and discernment question: What is the cosmology of the media product and how does that presentation compare with the biblical norm?

Christians and Jews believe God created the universe, therefore the universe is governed by His laws of creation. Since He has informed us that He is good, we can trust those laws of creation and explore the universe with confidence.

In contrast, many media products have an evolutionary cosmology, which means that nothing is certain and everything is ultimately pointless. You need to understand the cosmology of a media product to make discerning entertainment choices.

ULTIMATE ASCERTAINMENT QUESTION AND DISCERNMENT QUESTION: What is the worldview of the media product and how does it compare with a biblical worldview?

Developing a biblical worldview involves much more than a particular perspective or filter over a lens. Your worldview defines your approach to all areas of thought, including mass media, education, politics, religion, law, and government. It is the task of the viewer to examine the messages and assumptions that the entertainment industry imparts and to ask the kind of questions that pierce through thinking that is inconsistent with biblical principles. Parents have this opportunity to teach their children how to probe beneath these assumptions to test their truth or validity against the Word of God.

When looking at a media product, ask the basic philosophical questions, such as:

What is the nature of reality?

What can we know about reality?

What is the nature and purpose of humanity?

How do we decide what is good or evil?

In what does a human find value?

What is the relationship of the individual to God? To self? To nature?

Is truth relative or the same regardless of the era or culture?

How does the hero live his life justly?

Every media product is a reflection and a projection of the broader culture in which we live. The entertainment industry often regards the problematic elements in their media product as a problematic element of our society as a whole.

The entertainment industry evades criticism by appealing to the First Amendment and by claiming that we cannot judge a media product out of the context of our culture. Clearly, these are specious evasions. We need to judge the righteous judgment and view the world through God's Word, not God's Word through the eyes of the world. We need to be media literate and familiar with a biblical worldview and then compare the worldviews of the media product we encounter with that biblical worldview.

Subsidiary ascertainment and discernment question: Who are the stars, the director, and the other important production people, what are their worldviews, and how do their worldviews compare with the biblical norm?

Biographical criticism is not always a viable or even productive way to examine a media product. On the other hand, the creative people behind the media production often influence the communication. Many excellent communicators make it a point of proclaiming false gods, including sex, money, and even the forces of darkness, in their movies. For example, George Lucas, in talking about his successful films, said, "*Raiders [of the Lost Ark]* will be the most action-oriented of the *Indiana Jones* movies—the others should deal more with the occult."[12]

Ever since a miraculous recovery from a childhood injury, Lucas has had a mission to proclaim an occult force. We must make it a point to rebuke and boycott such antibiblical communications.

Oliver Stone, who directed *JFK*, *Nixon*, and *Salvador*, always inserts a political bias into his movies. He has said bluntly, "I think America has to bleed. I think the corpses have to pile up. I think American boys have to die again. Let the mothers weep and mourn."[13]

Paul Newman is very active in humanist/socialist liberal causes and was in the movie *Fat Man and Little Boy*, which distorts history to blast America, and *Blaze*, which mocks Christians and morality.

Jane Fonda's hatred for America was vented in her movie *Gringo*, which bombed at the box office despite her heavy public relations push. The director, Costa-Gravas, an avowed communist, designs his movies to attack what he abhors, such as Christianity in *Betrayed* or anticommunism in *The Music Box*.

Charlton Heston has taken a very clear stand for traditional American republican democracy, which is reflected in the roles he plays—even the remake of *Treasure Island*.

Barry Reardon, the president of Warner Brothers Distribution, is a Christian who every year tries to release some strong Christian films. He has been responsible for distributing *Chariots of Fire*, *The Mission*, *A Cry in the Dark*, and *Driving Miss Daisy*, along with numerous other wholesome films.

If you follow the careers of any of the stars, directors, and the other important motion picture production and distribution personnel, you will quickly discern in many cases a pattern to their communications. The biases of key people could be catalogued, but that would run on for several pages and not be as effective as each of us developing our own discernment by noting the preferences of individual members of the media and understanding how those preferences influence their communications.

There are many talented individuals who have been able to separate their work from their personal preferences and prejudices. Horton Foote wrote the screenplays for *To Kill a Mockingbird*, *Tender Mercies*, and *Trip to Bountiful*. He is one of the greatest screen writers of all time and many of his movies have a solid, biblical Christian worldview. In fact, his best known movies have biblical Christians as the hero or heroine. These Christians are not suffering from some heresy. Their theology is totally biblical. However, Foote himself is not a Christian. He is a Christian Scientist, whose theology is distinctly different from biblical Christianity.

"I don't think that a real artist is a proselytizer," he said. "An artist tries to be honest and truthful. My characters are involved with the problems of faith and how to proceed in life. However, I don't think that many films are based on life—they are proselytizing."[14]

Foote said his films have not been studio financed and that they are distributed modestly. His films seem to break conventions, but that is not his purpose. His purpose is to capture a sense of truth and to be intellectually respectful. He said that to a large degree he is reporting on the people he knew as a child, many of whom were committed Christians. We can only pray that these influences in his past will bring him into the kingdom of God in the future.

Many members of the entertainment community, unlike Foote, believe it is their responsibility to proselytize. The very lifestyle of the stars and the media leaders communicate profound messages to the general public. Goldie Hawn has said marriage is ridiculous. The unwed Jessica Lange has given birth to two children fathered by two different famous men. With role models like these, it is no wonder that so many babies are illegitimate.

If you undertake to track the careers of most of the names receiving credit on a motion picture's advertising, you will quickly note how many fall into the socialist/humanist pattern. This situation should mobilize all of us who call ourselves Christians to witness to these lost men and women and help them to understand the saving message of the Gospel. If we don't, then we are not only disobeying the Lord's command, but we are also abandoning the entertainment industry to the adversary.

ASCERTAINMENT QUESTION: Is there any redeeming value?

A media product can have many of the above-mentioned worldviews going against it and still be redemptive. *Nothing in Common* starts out focusing on the story of an egocentric young advertising executive who pushes everyone around and plays with every woman he meets, but ends with him giving up his job and his fast life to take care of his sick father. He makes a decision for love that costs him everything in the world's eyes, but gives him back his father and a new appreciation of life.

Surprisingly, his boss lets him leave work to take care of his father with the insight that "there has been only one perfect son," or so he had been told. Therefore, *Nothing in Common* tells the story of a man who has been moved by the power of love from selfishness to selfless giving—a very redemptive message.

It is very rare that a film can have a redemptive element that will transcend the negative elements. Some children's films such as *The Dirt Bike Kid* do transcend their negative parts because those parts are treated lightly, with deference and a lack of conviction as storytelling devices, while the redemptive element of love, courage, or integrity are emphasized. If a motion picture does transcend its parts because of some redemptive element, then we need to be aware of the good and the bad in the movie so that we can discuss it honestly and rebut any negative elements that may be detrimental to our Christian worldview, or the worldview of those we hold dear who see the film.

REFLECTION QUESTIONS

REFLECTION QUESTION: Would you be embarrassed to sit through the movie with your parents, your children, or Jesus?

When we are alone, or with a friend, we often deceive ourselves regarding the true nature of a movie (or television program). If we ignore the faults in a movie we are watching, then we will slowly be conditioned to condone, if not accept, a non-Christian point of view.

There are many other questions which we could ask to help evaluate a motion picture, but they may be boiled down to, How would we like our loved ones to be inundated by the messages being communicated by the movie?

REFLECTION QUESTION: What was your favorite part? Why did you like that part so much?

Here you're guiding children to think about how the mass media product relates to real life. Most important, you're boosting a child's self-esteem. Any time you ask children their opinion, you build their confidence tremendously.

REFLECTION QUESTION: If you were an actor in this movie, what character would you be?

Children usually love to think about the character they feel most like, or would most like to be. Your child's responses, of course, can give you insights into his or her wishes and concerns. Children are prone to accept role models and to accept the underlying belief systems that these models exercise and demonstrate. In this discussion, a parent can expose worldviews and value systems that are inconsistent and even dangerous.

Subsidiary reflection question: Would you do just what that character did, or do you think you would have done things differently?

This question gets children thinking about the plausibility of characters' actions. It's important to invite your child to consider whether a character's action was the right choice—because sometimes mass media product makers manipulate a character's choice just to make the entertainment product more exciting. Children should know that kind of thing goes on in Hollywood.

REFLECTION QUESTION: What did you like about the hero/heroine? What things were important to the hero/heroine? Are those things important to you?

Get children to explore the association between the character and their own lives. Children become aware of why they like a character—because the character made them feel good or because he or she did something they could do. Mass media product made for children oftentimes communicate positive values of honesty, loyalty, and so on. So hopefully, your child will respond to your questions with answers like, "Well, she was a good friend to him and believed in him no matter what," conveying to you that your child is picking up on values. Together, you can also discuss a full range of solutions to the problem this character faced and possible remedies for their future problems with biblical guidance.

REFLECTION QUESTION: What feelings did you have as you watched or listened to this media product? When did you feel sad, mad, or scared? What part of the media product made the feeling change?

Can your child identify what he is feeling? Does the child realize that it is the media product and the storyline that is making him feel that way? It is important for parents to explore this because children need to put a name to their feelings—especially younger children who might not know from where their feelings are coming. Asking children questions such as these after seeing a movie helps them identify the source of their emotions.

There are many other questions we could ask to help evaluate a mass media product, but they all boil down to how we would like our loved ones to be inundated by the messages being communicated by the mass media. If we care about others and about the Lord Jesus, we will take a stand against anything being communicated that undermines a biblical worldview and mocks our Lord and Savior Jesus Christ. Anything less than standing on His Word written denies our relationship with Him.

FOUR SEASONS

Through their eyes and ears

Beyond asking the right questions to help your children develop discernment about the mass media of entertainment, you need to understand the perspectives or methods of evaluative media viewing and listening that your children possess. You will then be able to guide them through the different levels of critical viewing.

Our perspectives shape the way we look at and understand a media product. By viewing the media through these various perspectives or filters, we are better able to comprehend and analyze its message and how the message influences those who have a particular perspective.

Our children continue to develop different perspectives of critical viewing that reflect their cognitive levels as they grow and mature. A young child in the imagination stage perceives and extracts a different message from mass media than older children in the concrete stage and even teenagers growing into adulthood.

Try to picture what they are seeing through their eyes at the various cognitive levels and introduce them to other perspectives appropriate to each child's cognitive level. You can use these methods of critical viewing with your children to understand how they examine media messages and teach them to dissect the message. This is an opportunity for you and your children to better understand the workings of the mass media of entertainment together.

Role model

The first stage of cognitive development, as we have discussed, is the **sensation stage** (approximately ages birth to two years old). During this time the child's sole means of processing reality is his senses. Children in this stage think that they are the center of the universe and that everything around them serves them.

Most younger children in the sensation stage of cognitive development look at the entertainment media:

Aesthetically—in terms of how interesting and attractive it is to watch or hear.

Young children may not pick up on the emotional elements in a movie or television program and certainly will miss the message of the lyrics of a song. They will quite often toddle around while a very emotive scene is occurring in a television program, much to the chagrin of their parents. However, they will note and respond to the emotional state of their parents.

Though not cognizant of the various aspects of a particular media product, they do absorb what they see and hear and can repeat songs and remember images, so they need to be protected from those mass media products that will leave negative images in their minds. Furthermore, the mass media will model behavior for them, and they will copy that behavior, so the parent has a responsibility to be careful about the mass media to which they are exposed.

If you are watching or listening with a very young child during this stage who can talk, ask him or her:

What do you see?

What do you hear?

Then, help them understand what they are seeing and/or what they are hearing.

For parents, this is often an easier stage than the next stage because it is clear to the parent that a child at this stage sees the world differently, so most parents are attuned to being careful in their guidance of the cognitive development of these young children. Regrettably, when the child starts to talk fluently, the parent can often forget that the child perceives the world differently, so the parent starts to treat the child like an adult.

Imagine

The next stage of cognitive development is the **imagination** or **preoperational stage**, which spans the period from two to seven years of age. In this stage, the child's cognition is dedicated to the acquisition of representational skills such as language, mental imagery, drawing, and symbolic play—and limited by being serial and one-dimensional. During this stage, the child has a very active imagination, often confusing fact and fiction.

While the terms *real* and *make-believe* are used by younger children, they do not understand the implications of these terms. Thus, the notion that a character or an event is *not real* should have little impact on a younger child's emotions.

Younger children in the imagination stage of cognitive development look at the media aesthetically and:

Syntactically—in terms of the characters, the action and the special effects.[15]

Emotively—in terms of how it excites and amuses them.

Younger children focus on the individual elements of a movie, such as acts of violence, a character's costume and outward appearance, landscape, or setting while watching a program on TV or a movie or a video. They tend to see each image as isolated, so each event in the program is taken at face value.

At this cognitive stage, the child is not integrating the images to create a dramatic story with a moral and a happy ending. They are viewing the movie syntactically by looking at each element such as action, then special effects, then camera angles. The picture tells the story, much like an advertisement page in a magazine. Therefore, most documentaries and lectures do not hold their attention no matter how amusing or interesting the topic.

Advertisers are aware of this, so they produce toy-product advertisements to reflect an imaginative cognitive level with quick camera clips and sharp angle transitions. If they can keep your child's attention long enough, the child will remember their product. This means you will hear about this product the next time you enter the store.

The mass media serve two functions in a household: to inform and persuade. The media are extremely adept at persuasion and commercialization. Therefore, as the audience, we must become more savvy in our resistance and critical thinking. Commercials use icons of the family to sell a long-distance carrier, the power of survival protection to sell a new recreational vehicle, even the desire to attract a future mate with the right toothpaste is not an uncommon sight. Though many of these tactics are identifiable, we can be caught up in viewing the media emotionally by allowing the message to sway our opinions or make us vulnerable to new interpretations.

At a young age children can develop an awareness of the emotive quality of critical viewing. Television programs, movies, the Internet, and news media are all worthwhile places to get meaningful information, but much of this information is saturated with an emotive influential agenda.

Christians need to discern when this agenda is sincere or when it is used as a manipulation. The difference being that manipulation tries to change our feelings or persuade us away from the truth, while sincerity comes from the liberating truth of God.

Since younger children actively view a movie or program for its presentation, encourage them to look at the film for its aesthetic value as well. You can ask them to describe the different camera angles and lighting in a scene:

Why was this scene so bright and happy?

Why was another scene so dark and gloomy?

Discernment grows in your children as they observe what you appreciate and find to be attractive in a video. Videos are helpful because you can stop the tape and go back to places that you feel were presented honestly and well-produced.

Viewing a program aesthetically means understanding its presentation. Now is an appropriate time to interest your child in what are artistic media and what are not. If the presentation is honest and not biased, as a parent you can use this opportunity to instill these ideals in your children. When they are older, you will be able to hear them share these ideals back to you.

Some examples of television programs that are worthwhile viewing for this age are:

Mr. Rogers' Neighborhood (PBS)

Sesame Street (PBS)

Welcome to Pooh Corner (Disney Channel)

Some examples of movies that are appeal to this age group are:

Babe

Charlotte's Web

Lassie

Mickey's Christmas Carol

The Muppets Take Manhattan

All these movies are friendly, low violence, and positive role model. Regrettably, most of them are animation or fantasies, which are categories that play upon the child's inability to separate fact from fiction. Therefore, you need to ask your children discernment questions, such as "Can animals talk?" to help them develop an understanding of the difference between fact and fantasy as they move into the next stage of cognitive development. Some children persist in the imagination stage longer than others, and some develop patterns of thought that are conducive to ontological nominalism or magical thinking based on what they view and their susceptibility.

It should be kept in mind during this stage that even the psychologically healthy preschool child tends to indiscriminately imitate all that he see and hears, whether the characters are good guys or bad guys, and whether the long-run consequences of the actions are positive or negative. There is very little power to pick and choose what is imitation-worthy and what isn't. For this reason, in choosing entertainment product for young children, we want as many imitation-worthy acts as possible, and we also want as few nonimitation-worthy acts as possible, regardless of who does them and whether good wins out over evil.

Children do need to learn to deal with tragedy and to deal with bad people eventually, but the more their preschool years, particularly the early preschool years, can be filled with positive models, the better off they will be.

In this regard, it is extremely important to avoid exposing young children to acts of violence that are very easy to imitate. In *The Wizard of Oz*, Dorothy's killing the witch by accidentally getting water on her is not an aggressive act that seems to inspire much real-life imitation in young children. The kicks and karate chops of *Teenage Mutant Ninja Turtles*, by contrast, are easily imitated by young children.

Just the facts

The next stage is the **concrete operational stage**, which spans ages seven to eleven. In this stage the child acquires the ability of simultaneous perception of two points of view so he or she can master quantities, relations, and classes of objects. At this stage, there is such a strong correspondence between the child's thoughts and reality that he or she assumes these thoughts about reality are accurate and distorts the facts to fit what he or she thinks.

Children in the concrete stage of cognitive development look at the entertainment media:

Conceptually—in terms of the storyline, character motivations, and basic concepts

Emotionally—in terms of the emotional response of the characters in the entertainment product

Realistically—in terms of the realism of the events portrayed

Legalistically—in terms of whether the perpetrator is rewarded or punished

In this stage, the child is starting to appreciate the nonvisual threat. In this regard, younger children are likely to be frightened by visually frightening creatures like witches and monsters, while older children will focus more on conceptual qualities, such as the motives of a character.[16] Indeed, older children are likely to be more upset by an evil, normal-looking character or by an unseen threat than by a benign but grotesque character. Thus, younger children are more likely to be frightened by *The Wizard of Oz* and *The Incredible Hulk*, while older children are more frightened by movies such as *Poltergeist* and *Jaws*, which rely more on nonvisual threats.

Children in this stage are more attuned to realism in the plot and the victim's emotional reactions to the threat.

Violent depictions for which the aggressor is rewarded are most likely to produce imitation effects or foster attitudes supportive of aggression.[17] Also, as long as there is no punishment associated with a violent act, young viewers have been shown to imitate such depictions.[18]

Children in this stage are more likely to respond to characters who are attractive.[19] In determining whether the character is "good" or "bad," this age group tends to focus more on the character's motives.[20]

Violence that is justified is more likely to be imitated,[21] such as the hero who is forced to be violent because his job demands it (e.g., *Dirty Harry*) or because he must retaliate against an enemy (e.g., *Batman*).

Children in this stage are more likely to imitate models who are portrayed as similar to themselves,[22] especially if cues in the program are similar to those in real life.[23]

Children in this stage need to be helped to compare what they see with the biblical model. Therefore, ask questions of them that will cause them to make these comparisons, such as:

How does the character relate to what God teaches is right and wrong to do?

Some examples of television programs that are worthwhile viewing for this age group are:

3-2-1 Contact (PBS)

Animal Crack-ups (ABC)

Adventures from the Book of Virtues (PBS)

Something Else (Family Channel)

K.I.D.S. (ESPN)

Older children in the reflection stage

In the **reflection stage**, which spans ages twelve to fifteen, abstract thought gains strength. In this stage there is still incomplete differentiation as a result of the adolescent's inability to conceptualize the thoughts of others—exemplified by the assumption that other people are equally obsessed with his or her behavior and appearance (such as a pimple). Since the adolescent still has difficulty conceptualizing the consequences of his actions, he will often take risks without regard to consequences.

In this stage, the adolescent will perceive the media product:

Semantically—by looking at the individual elements such as words, nudity, and violence and their meanings

Propositionally—by looking at what the program or movie is communicating as summarized in the premise

Thematically—by looking at the themes that are present

Sociologically—by looking at how it relates to culture and society

Systemically—by looking at how it relates to other productions in a similar genre

The **reflection stage** is an excellent time for helping your children develop critical viewing habits. At this age, they can look deeply at the content of a story and learn about plot, character, and setting, which will strengthen their reading skills throughout their lives. They can also learn to look at a movie's language and make decisions about what is appropriate and what is out-of-character or not useful for a character.

In the reflection stage, the child desires deeply to make decisions and solve problems but wants approval from his or her parents in the process. As a parent, you have a prime opportunity to help lay a valuable foundation for your children to rely on as they grow.

As children grow older they begin to be able to evaluate entertainment media through higher levels of critical thinking. Children at the reflection stage of cognitive development are beginning to understand content, language, and drama of the story. Since older children are developing the ability to make inferences between a sordid cowboy's black hat and dark nature or actions, parents can foster this progress by discussing a story semantically. Adults tend to overlook some elements of a story because they know this story has a happy ending.

Such is the case in the Walt Disney animation *Aladdin*. The main goal of the story is to have love triumph over all evil, including Aladdin's own deceit, but Aladdin is a thief in the animated version of the story. Therefore, a good discernment question to ask your child is; Is it wrong for Aladdin to steal? Most younger children will say no, but your adolescent should begin to understand the complexity of Aladdin's character and be able to condemn the stealing while understanding that he learns that he has to be honest in order to achieve his heart's desire.

From the story's plot, characters, and setting, we can summarize its premise. Children at this cognitive level are just developing the ability to integrate the elements of a story to deduce its basic assumptions or to view the program or movie propositionally.

Although this is a challenging task for many children, you can use a video box to help. Have your children read the description of the movie on the video cover before they view. What do you already know about the story? The characters? What is the conflict that needs to be solved? How will the conflict be solved? Here is a way to quiz your children and yourself about the nature of the movies you bring into your home. Does the solution to the conflict have a biblical answer or secular, ungodly answer?

Many plots are not written by Christians or people with a biblical belief system, which is the reason we have many stories that end without a redemptive or positive resolution. The basic assumption of many of today's writers is that there is no escape from evil, no release from sin, and no true hope. Though I suggest that you do not subject your family to this type of mass media of entertainment on purpose, there is a valuable distinction between the light of God and the darkness of the world. If you choose to view a movie and then through critical analysis discover the story's premise to be lacking in biblical grace, here is a wonderful time to share with developing minds what God can do with this situation. Now you are set to discuss the ways God could influence the characters to change hearts. How would you solve this conflict? What do you feel is a Christian response?

While older children are looking for the meaning of a story, you can help them use the themes inherent in a program or movie to draw out the overall premise. Themes, such as color (a dark character dressed in black or a positive character dressed in white), are beneficial to children in the cognitive stage. Directors use lighting and foreshadowing to disclose information that aids the audience in discovering a story's meaning. By critically viewing the program or movie thematically, you will be looking at how the program's themes shape our impression of the premise.

Teenagers in the reflection stage

In the **reflection stage** the adolescent grows into a mature adult and there is progress toward complete differentiation. As a result the adult understands that others are different and accepts those differences by learning to relate to others. Furthermore, the adult is able to conceptualize the consequences of his actions and take the necessary steps to reduce his risks.

Teenagers and adults can view the media product:

Ontologically—by looking at how the media product deals with the nature of being

Epistemologically—by looking at how it deals with the nature of knowing

Morally—by looking at its moral perspective and content

Philosophically—by looking at the philosophical perspective and the worldview

As children grow older, their cognitive powers of reasoning and thinking grow tremendously and they become capable of using the concept of *not*. If all has gone well, when they become teenagers they will be able to appreciate the fact that in works like *Hamlet* and *Oedipus Rex* the violent acts are tragic and horrible with terrible consequences, and perhaps have their repulsion for violence increased rather than decreased. The teenager should have the maturity of thought processes to be able to identify with certain characters in a work of fiction, and to want to become more like them, and to want to become less like other characters. This is the stage at which all our previous questions come into play and when full media literacy and discernment can be achieved.

However, because teenagers are still immature in many ways other than cognitive development, they are still susceptible to the appeal of today's movie theaters, rental VCR tapes, and multiple cable channels. It is advisable, therefore, to help them understand the impact of the mass media on them and to have them reflect on biblical principles that apply.

Teenagers hate to be manipulated and need to understand that Satan is trying to manipulate them in his quest for their minds and hearts. He is constantly endeavoring to get them to think his thoughts and act his ways. From gratuitous profanity in otherwise innocuous story scripts, to rock and roll radio, to spicy and even steamy scenes in dramatic films, to vulgar comedy, it is a humanistic philosophy that is presented. Christian young people need to recognize it and shun it.

Before they rent a video, plop down in front of the TV for some mindless entertainment, or even consider going to a theater with the friends who are pressuring them to see the latest violent film, (in a theater you have almost no control over what comes before your eyes) consider these helpful hints:

Weigh the impressions:

Does good triumph over evil?

Is the primary appeal to the flesh? (1 Peter 1:13-16)

Will this use of the media allow them to control what they watch and hear, and thus bring every thought under captivity of Christ? (Proverbs 4:23-27)

Will there be antibiblical philosophy, unwholesome music, and compromised standards that will wear them down or make them doubt what they believe or tempt them to sin?

Will they be tired when they are watching or listening? Does the potential exist for letting their mental guard down?

Perhaps substitution of another medium such as good music or a good book would be more to the glory of God? (Philippians 4:8)

While the rest of society is making TV and movies the standard against which they measure and make moral choices, Christians should not. Because someone else tries to legitimize an action or practice by positively presenting it in an attractive package does not lessen the Christian's responsibility to make the Word of God the main source of his values.

By and large, the mass media is discretionary. We are able to control what we put before our eyes by the way we use it or don't use it. Some guidelines to follow include:

Don't watch just because the television set is there or the tape box looks good.

Don't watch out of boredom; instead, read, exercise, play a game, listen to good music.

Set the proper priorities and make the media less of a priority.

In previous centuries, entertainment was a once-in-a-while thing. Someone might read aloud or play a musical instrument and there might be an occasional visit to the theater. Today's use of the media has no relationship to those occasional happenings. It is not separate from the daily routine, it *is* the daily routine.

God's standards have not changed. His expectation for us is that we will try to bring each thought into captivity and be good stewards of the time He has given us on this earth. Remember, the goal is to bring every thought into captivity. It is a lifelong challenge and an eternal command.

By ourselves, we can't resist the devil's schemes. However, God, who is far greater than Satan, has already won the war. When we know and follow Him, He makes us "more than conquerors" in Christ.

Endnotes

1. Pablo Picasso, *Le Spectacle du Monde* (November 1962), reprinted in Duncan Williams, *The Trousered Ape* (1971), ch. 2.
2. *Media Update* (March/April 1996).
3. Though not in the philosophical sense.
4. God's Word is Jesus Christ (John 1). God's Word written is the Bible. God's Word written was used often by the Reformers to emphasize the relation between God the Father, God the Son, and His Holy Scripture.
5. Such as Lajos Egri, who wrote the definitive text about scriptwriting, *The Art of Dramatic Writing* (New York: Simon & Schuster, 1946, 1960), which is must reading for anyone interested in scriptwriting. *The Art of Dramatic Writing* is the text used at USC, UCLA, and other premiere film and television schools.
6. Evelyn Dokovic, *Morality in Media* newsletter (August 1988).
7. Timothy Jay, *Cursing in America* (Philadelphia: John Benjamins Publishing Company, 1992).
8. The famous Marxist Professor Marcuse, at the Sorbonne, advocated using language as a weapon. He inspired many of the most renowned communist revolutionaries in the twentieth century. Even Jane Fonda studied with him.
9. See S. Robert Lichter, Stanley Rothman, and Linda Lichter, *The Media Elite* (Maryland: Adler & Adler, 1986). Also see Donald Wildmon, *The Home Invaders* (Wheaton, Illinois: Victor Books, 1985) pp. 18-23 for an excellent analysis of the Lichter Rothman studies.
10. Egri, *The Art of Dramatic Writing*, 6.
11. Note that *movie-maker* is being used here to refer to all those people who are responsible for authoring a movie, including the screenwriter, the director, the producer, the executive producer, et al.
12. Michael Sragrow, "Raiders of the Lost Ark," *Rolling Stone* (June 25, 1981): 22.
13. Oliver Stone, quoted by William B. Guidry, "Masterful Theater, Spurious History," *New American* 8:2 (January 27, 1992), Cultural Currents.
14. Telephone interview with Horton Foote on June 23, 1986.
15. Of course, from a media producer's point of view the syntactical aspect of the media product refers to how the elements come together and how the pieces and characters relate to each other, but herein we are focusing on how these elements relate to the young view or listener.
16. Barbara J. Wilson, Daniel Lynn, and Barbara Randall, "Applying Social Science Research to Film Ratings: A Shift from Offensiveness to Harmful Effects," *Journal of Broadcasting & Electronic Media* 34:4 (Fall 1990): 443-468, citing C. Hoffner and J. Cantor, "Developmental Differences in Responses to a Television Character's Appearance and Behavior," *Developmental Psychology* 21 (1985): 1065-1074.
17. *Ibid.* citing A. Bandura, "Influence of Models' Reinforcement Contingencies on the Acquisition of Imitative Responses," *Journal of Personality and Social Psychology* 1 (1965): 589-595; A. Bandura, D. Ross, and S.A. Ross, "Vicarious Reinforcement and Imitative Learning," *Journal of Abnormal and Social Psychology* 67 (1963): 601-607; M.A. Rosekrans, and W.W. Hartup, "Imitative Influences of Consistent and Inconsistent Response Consequences to a Model on Aggressive Behavior in Children," *Journal of Personality and Social Psychology* 7 (1967): 429-434.
18. *Ibid.* citing A. Bandura, "Influence of Models' Reinforcement."

19. *Ibid.* citing A. Bandura, *Social Foundations of Thought and Action: A Social Cognitive Theory* (Englewood Cliffs, NJ: Prentice-Hall, 1986).

20. *Ibid.* citing W.A. Collins, "Interpretation and Inference in Children's Television Viewing." In J. Bryant and D.R. Anderson (Eds.), *Children's Understanding of Television: Research on Attention and Comprehension* (New York: Academic Press, 1983), 125-150.

21. *Ibid.* citing L. Berkowitz, "Some Aspects of Observed Aggression," *Journal of Personality and Social Psychology* 2 (1965): 359-369; T.P. Meyer, "Effects of Viewing Justified and Unjustified Real Film Violence on Aggressive Behavior," *Journal of Personality and Social Psychology* 23 (1972): 21-29.

22. *Ibid.* citing A. Bandura, *Social Foundations of Thought and Action.*

23. *Ibid.* citing M.A. Liss, L.C. Reinhardt, and S. Fredrickesen, "TV Heroes: The Impact of Rhetoric and Deeds," *Journal of Applied Developmental Psychology* 4 (1983):175-187.

12

CHILD'S PLAY

IN COLLABORATION WITH ELIZABETH CHAMBERS

> **But the fruit of the Spirit is love, joy, peace, patience, kindness, goodness, faithfulness, gentleness and self-control. Against such things there is no law.**
> Galatians 5:22-23 (NIV)

Having a thirteen-year-old in the family is like having a general-admission ticket to the movies, radio, and TV. You get to understand that the glittering new arts of our civilization are directed to the teenagers, and by their suffrage they stand or fall.
Max Lerner[1]

The futility of everything that comes to us from the media is the inescapable consequence of the absolute inability of that particular stage to remain silent. Music, commercial breaks, news flashes, adverts, news broadcasts, movies, presenters—there is no alternative but to fill the screen; otherwise there would be an irremediable void. . . . That's why the slightest technical hitch, the slightest slip on the part of the presenter becomes so exciting, for it reveals the depth of the emptiness squinting out at us through this little window.
Jean Baudrillard[2]

Fact: You burn more calories lying down doing nothing than watching television.

Introduction
While the last chapter helped you ask the right questions to help your children understand their media diet and develop discernment, this chapter will show you how to make a game out of helping your children develop discernment. Although I have taught on this subject for many years, I asked an education specialist, Elizabeth Chambers, who teaches at Oglethorpe University to collaborate on this chapter because I respect her insights in this area. She will give you practical ways to have your children become your allies in the battle against immoral entertainment.

Have you ever noticed your reaction when a child in your life says, "I'm bored"? Oh, to have time to be bored! There is always the lawn to mow, that book we've never read, the friend with whom we'd love to have coffee, and the work left undone. We live in a era of increasing options and so little free time to exercise those options. The pace of modern life seems to have accelerated at the same degree as the inventions designed to make life easier. So why do the children seem bored with life?

For one thing, today's children are accustomed to being entertained every minute of their lives. As a culture, we have dismissed the practices of daydreaming and discourse.

This change in how we conduct our daily affairs has been assisted by the media. All the news that never was fit to print will interrupt our lives with minute-by-minute updates all evening long. Worse, we don't have to interact with our children, just buy them the latest toy or video game.

Children today are not heard or seen. Many are in their rooms on their own phone, their own television is tuned to *Beverly Hills 90210*, and they're playing a computer game for a few hours before they go to sleep. If, by an act of God, the power goes out, they do not know what to do with themselves.

By entertaining them from infancy, we have short-circuited their ability to use their own time creatively. All of this is compounded by living in a culture accustomed to three- and two-second sound bites.

Although we live in a frenzied, media-saturated culture, we do have choices. Understanding those choices will enable us to make better ones. We can find a wholesome way to live in the world and not be consumed by it.

If we want to raise children to be thoughtful and compassionate adults with good moral values, we must begin to be accountable for the modeling they encounter. With attention to how they absorb the values of the larger culture, we can teach them to discern what is "of good repute."

We do have the power of the *off* button! In order to be guardians of those in our care, we must choose not only what to use of the media, but must prepare our children not to drown in its ever-present input into their lives.

It is important to reinstitute the mechanism for shielding children from information they are not mature enough to handle. With the advent of television, all the content and taboos of adult life are available to everyone at all hours. The result is children who are left unprotected from the adult world. They are seeing all these things that they know are bad, but no one is trying to shield them.

Children may make the assumption that since their parents allow certain programming into the home, they must approve of it. This covers the menu from hate-mongering neo-Nazis to date rape to gratuitous violence.

MEDIA LITERACY

The definition of *media literacy* is the ability to access, analyze, interpret, and create media messages.

The ability to **access** must include everything from owning media delivery devices (TV, radio, computer, VCR, etc.) to understanding how to turn them on and use them to deliver messages. One cannot "access" a VCR if one does not know how to plug in the various wires and set it to tape, then playback.

Analyzing includes being able to comprehend not only the storyline or language of a program, but also how it may have been put together. Understanding the media requires some exposure to and comprehension of the way it was made.

Interpretation requires that we have a basis for both the story and the agenda, which may be part of its underlying message. If the program is sponsored by the XYZ company, one can assume it expects its views to be promoted, probably not only in the advertisements but also in the story. Some networks (particularly Fox) have stated that the programs they produce are intended to appeal to the "real world" of singles who live together, adults who accept a standard of divorce, and homosexual viewers. They try to stretch the bounds of acceptable programming every season.

Creating the media helps everyone understand what to look for in the media we watch. When teenagers use a video camera to make a ten-minute film, the camera angles, script, actors/actresses, sets, and scenery all become important decisions.

Who are you?

A good place to start building the wholesome pattern of media consumption is documenting what we do. A diary of a week's media use is a great place to begin. Log the amount of time each family member watches TV, what is watched, and the reaction. All forms of media should be logged. Keep track of radio, video games, CD and tape use (even in the car), computer on-line time, and what the computer user was exploring. Don't be overwhelmed by the log, but do understand, all of this is media input. Someone else has control over what you are during the time you are consuming this media. It would also be helpful to note what and for how long each family member reads.

When you have begun to be aware of how you use the media, you can begin to make conscious choices. Many households turn the TV on the minute everyone comes home, especially to keep the children occupied while supper is prepared. This is a difficult habit to break, so pay close attention to the programs chosen during this time.

Most news programs are not fit for children under ten. From five to seven P.M., most stations are broadcasting the news, so another choice is advised. Discuss and predetermine the channel choice. This way whoever turns on the TV doesn't immediately see the latest murder or airplane crash. Attention to details like channel preselection or a schedule taped to the set can save your children nightmares. Before going to a movie you probably talk about what film to see and where it is playing. Do the same with TV.

Television is designed to capture our attention and deliver that attention to advertisers. Everything about a TV show, from the choice of actors and actresses to where the commercial breaks are, is designed for the most impact on viewership. If a station can document that it has a large percent of the viewing audience, it can charge more for commercial time during that show.

Discernment

There are three necessary steps in teaching discernment to your children:

We must inform children of other worldviews and philosophies and enhance their biblical education to reinforce Christian theism.

We must prepare them to think about and reject the subtle messages of the media.

We must teach and model a godly disciplined lifestyle.

The church must battle the prevalent secular mindset and worldview by training students to think and live biblically.

CRITICAL THINKING

Note: Critical thinking depends on the stages of cognitive development, which we have discussed earlier and you should review at this point.

The imagination stage

Parents need to protect children in this stage. *Cinderella* is an example of a film that seems appealing but can terrify young children.

Don't dazzle your younger children with mesmerizing images and quick cuts that leave them little time to absorb and understand the story.

Look for programs based on storybooks that encourage them to go to the books. Children might not understand the dialogue in the video, but with the book they choose when to turn the page.

To further avoid passive viewing, question young children about what they watch and create activities that bridge the book to the video.

Were the characters changed to make them more exciting?

Which character is more real, the book character or the video character?

To examine children's understanding of the plot, setting, and characters, have them do the inquiring. Children should practice questioning the story, then they will be more apt to ask questions about video production as they move into the concrete stage.

The concrete stage

In the concrete stage, stories with distinct and immediate causes and effects will give children a clear frame of reference. Science and game shows are good examples of causes and effects that are immediate and quickly established.

When older children watch a scary story like *Pinocchio*, they find the happy ending reassuring. Also, at the end they feel a sense of accomplishment for having stuck with it. They have survived and developed a sense of *real* versus *imaginary*.

After helping the child to understand the foolishness of wishing upon a star, Christian parents can use this story with older children to relate the power of God as expressed in the biblical story of Jonah.

Children in the middle years will accept and watch poor-quality programming, even though they are fully aware that it is not worthy of their attention. It is important to educate them about questioning the mass media.

Fourth, fifth, and sixth graders will benefit from reading a book, watching the video, and then carefully breaking the story into smaller pieces (**analyzing**)—comparing the strengths and weaknesses of each.

Teenagers in the reflection stage

Evaluating, analyzing, and even investigating the facts after viewing a program, movie, or news broadcast is more beneficial to teenagers than interrupting the viewing. Since teenagers are exposed to all forms of media and its persuasive forces, their cognitive ability needs to be stimulated in order to formulate personal decisions about what to accept as valuable information.

The media instruct us to "turn on, tune in, and drop out,"[3] which inhibits the ability of teenagers to make a choice. We are set up by the media to buy the lie or to keep watching until we embrace what they are selling.

Summary

Discernment cannot be mechanically transferred into our minds. Discernment is allowing God to influence every area of your life, even your entertainment media.

Children in the imagination stage look to their parents to protect them from outside elements they are not equipped to understand and least of all to confront. Older children in the concrete stage need their parents' resolve in establishing habits to make appropriate decisions and valuable judgments about interacting with all forms of mass media.

Teenagers have matured into a cognitive level of understanding, but not of discernment or active decisiveness. At this stage, they want to be stimulated and to offer their opinions and feelings. While many teenagers are uncomfortable talking about themselves and their immediate friendships, parents can use the issues in the entertainment media to explore responses and reactions.

DISCERNING VIEWER MODEL

Production—M	V—Cognitive Development
Genre—U	I—Knowledge
Language—I	E—Media Literacy
Violence—D Personal	W—Utility
Sexuality—E Interpretation	E—Character
Special Effects—M	R—Attitude

VALUES ORIENTATION
Christian Worldview

Biblical Principles

Salvation

Media Awareness

Familial Relationships

This discerning viewer model exposes the underlying structure of what enables a child or an adult to discern the messages of the media. These elements construct the framework for developing discernment in your life and the lives of your children.

As discerning viewers, we need to understand:

(1) the medium of the entertainment industry,

(2) the cognitive processes of the viewer, and

(3) the values orientation that supports our understanding of both the medium and the viewer (ourselves).

If the mass media run counter to the Christian worldview they should be refuted. If the medium portrays appropriate familial relationships, even avenues toward salvation, it should be commended.

Medium

Within the realm of the medium the **production** includes the presentation of the story, characterization, setting, scripting, and editing. Directors and producers make judgments about the value and quality of their product, such as the extent of the violence and/or sex that is used. The values orientation of a particular person in this role can strongly affect his or her decisions in creating the film piece.

To correctly appreciate the elements of a visual story, consider the source or include its **genre** in the equation. Opposing genres will present different conflict resolutions differently.

Language can demonstrate a character's passion. Profanities are strong terms, but are not meaningful and are often much less descriptive. When a character uses profanity and blasphemies to drive a point, he or she loses the opportunity to clarify and support the argument.

Violence has found a level of acceptance in American television, subjecting children to intense and destructive images. Children may develop a casualness about pictures that don't scream or cry. Action violence increases viewer anxiety level and the desire to watch for a calm conclusion.

Sexuality attracts viewers through passive means. Sexually imbibed dialogue and licentious images heighten awareness and cause a viewer to attend more closely to the medium.

Special effects can take an illusory image and present it as truth. The power of a strong image, be it fearful or seductive, is very persuasive.

Viewer

Children at the imagination level of cognitive development will interpret the message of a program in a manner different from their parents. It is difficult to comprehend what your children are gleaning from the media's messages without talking to them about what they see and what they understand. This continual exercise will bring meaning to critical viewing and stop negative images from taking over their minds.

Knowledge gives the viewer a basis from which to accept or reject facts or stories that are changed by the production team for cinematic enhancement. If children know American history, they are less likely to accept a made-for-TV movie that presents an altered story.

Media literacy assists viewers in conceiving of the ways that media are manipulated and distributed to people. The goal of television programming is to keep the attention of viewers long enough to present them with a product. Advertisers create visual commercials that slip easily into one's memory and are hard to resist, especially for children with less cognitive maturity.

Viewers are responsible for how media are utilized. Regulated by a family's moral standards the entertainment media can be beneficial. Parents must augment media literacy by presenting and modeling the values orientation and moral character that endows the viewer with discernment.

The discerning viewer responsibly accepts only what is consistent with God's law from the mass media. Here is an opportunity to teach your children character and integrity based on biblical principles. If you choose to turn off the television or walk out of a movie and demand your money back, you are displaying a character that is conducive and even productive for your children to practice.

Values orientation

Developing discernment runs parallel to developing a **Christian worldview**. Christian interpretation of philosophies and behavior is radically different from the viewpoints of non-Christians. Any philosophy other than that which emanates from the Bible is suspect and should be refuted, not reconciled with Christianity.

The entertainment industry depicts several conflicting world views in their story plots. A character might resolve his or her conflict in a self-promoting, humanist manner. Understanding the differences between the world's distorted and confused views and a biblical view provides valuable lessons for a discerning Christian.

Discernment would be lost without salvation. We are unable to perceive the world's messages without the grace of God to do the work for us. The wisdom of the Lord is intrinsic and necessary to every meaningful action.

The viewer works to develop media awareness. Critical viewing involves discipline, controlling and evaluating what we accept.

ACCESS

Media awareness

When we draw a picture or look at beautiful art, we see the picture as a whole, complete product, even though the picture is constructed of several parts. Media literacy teaches us to deconstruct[4] the different elements—from hiring actors to choosing scripts and selecting camera angles, so we can understand the process.

Critical beginning

The first media sharing parents do with young children is usually reading books that are mostly pictures. Habits of questioning and being aware will carry over to prereading and viewing if these are pleasant times spent with Mom and Dad. Before reading a new book go through the book from cover to cover looking at the pictures together. Ask questions like:

What do you think this book is about?

What do you see in the pictures?

Where does the story take place?

Who do you think would like this story?

After reading the story go back and review the pictures again.

Were your ideas correct?

Do the pictures give you a good idea of the story?

What would you like to change about the story?

Critical viewing log

The PTA (Parent Teacher Association) provided this activity in its guide to critical viewing for parents and children.

Encourage children to look for patterns in their viewing habits.

How do you decide what programs to watch?

What do you do while watching a program or a video?

Do you always watch the same shows and at the same times?

How much do you remember about the shows, such as the setting or a character's name?

How do you respond to the programs?

Was it a good way to spend time? Why or why not?[5]

You might begin a kind of science experiment to investigate your family's viewing habits. Draw a chart for everyone, including parents, to "sign on" and "sign off" as they watch television. This can be placed by each television set in the house. At the end of a week, compare what is being watched and the amount of time involved. If you can find one time when the entire family is watching media, even if no one is watching the same thing, this can become a great time to do alternative activities together.

Make the diary as simple as follows:

Your Family TV Viewing Diary

Who Watched	Day	Date	Program Watched	Amount of Time
_____	___	___	_____	_____
_____	___	___	_____	_____
_____	___	___	_____	_____
_____	___	___	_____	_____
_____	___	___	_____	_____

(*Taking Charge of Your TV*, National PTA)

Discussion

Discernment of good and valuable entertainment can be achieved during the exchanges between parents and their children. Explain to your children why you are dialoguing about your entertainment media and how the discussion will help them discern the media.

Research shows that discussion completely changes a child's perception, modeling, and mimicking.

Inquiring minds

Dialoguing with your children can be a reflection of what goes on in your thoughts. Children can experience this process and develop a habit of "talking back" to the television. Parents can offer their values and point of view through a conversation about a scenario or issue presented in a film and ask family members to find places in the film that support or counteract the position.

This exercise from *Television Awareness Training* gives them a clear example of critical thinking in action:

How do people work out problems?

How are different kinds of people presented?

How real are the programs to you?

How do you know when things are real or not?

What do you like and dislike about certain characters?

Do you ever wish you could be like some TV characters?

How truthful are commercials?

Do you ever worry about things you see on television?[6]

Who? What? Where? When? Why? How?

Children must understand the television program or story before they are able to compose interesting questions. Through forming questions themselves, your children will acquire the meaning of active viewing.

Have your children write questions about a section of a video with the question words *who? what? where?* and *when?* This will change the focus of media literacy activities from passive answers to active inquiry. Older children and teenagers will enjoy being the teacher.

After children are comfortable with fact-finding questions from the questions above, have them explore more discussion-type questions beginning with *why?* or *how?* Questions of this nature require a different style of thinking and a different type of response.

Listening

Children are open to all kinds of influences and images of which they are not aware. Encourage your children to listen to people, television, radio, and music actively to build understanding.

Listening is an autonomic behavior. Whether we like it or not, we are always listening and deciding what to remember and what to discard from our memory. As a person matures he or she develops the skill to choose or resist a message, but a young child has not learned to discriminate between necessary, beneficial information or hurtful messages.

We cannot monitor every image and thought our children encounter, but we can teach them how to listen purposely to the good while resisting immoral messages Hollywood packages through musical undertones meant to raise our emotional state. Helping them identify the special technology and subconscious opinions that Hollywood promotes carries them out of the realm of passive believers into discerning decision makers.

Begin your discussion of active listening with these questions:

What is a good listener?

Are there times when listening is easy?

Is it ever hard to listen?

Name that sound

Everyone can collect different sounds from around the house, such as the doorbell, running water, washing dishes, footsteps, etc. Record the sounds and play them to see who can identify them first. You can also extend this game to sounds found in the neighborhood.

If your children enjoy different styles of music, you can make a cassette of the beginning notes of songs or commercial jingles. It is surprising how much easier a product is to remember because of a catchy jingle or musical tune.

Image-sound skim[7]

After viewing a program ask children to recall the first image or sound that comes to mind. Children will recall useful points about the images and story that can be discussed in depth. You will be surprised at the messages they receive and to which they attach meaning. This activates the child's thought process and brings meaning to the discussion.

Movie producers and directors hide images that adult minds factor into the whole of the message or theme, but children think by accepting distinct segments in order to create a framework from which to reason. Children experience the framework as it is being laid in their minds. This is why many children enjoy structured activities and follow them rigidly step-by-step.

Children are able to detect hurtful and inconsistent images that the adult mind passes over as part of the whole. The reward of this lesson will return when your children discriminates against negative messages you taught them are wrong or hurtful that you did not realize they understood.

What did you say?

Practice listening to others. Invite a friend, child, spouse, or parent to take a "talk-walk" with you. As you walk around the neighborhood, role-play different characters you know or act like strangers and reintroduce yourself.

How well do you really know this person? Ask questions about the person's favorite ice cream, funniest thing you've done, best friend and why, what would you do in ten years or with $5,000.

Voice mail

Don't rely on listening alone for a clear message. Use all sorts of media to practice pronunciation and voice intonation and mimicry.

Have everyone write a phone message script. Make them interesting by adding accents, sound effects, and special themes. Friends will soon begin calling just to hear your messages.

Family standards and rules

It is essential to develop a set of rules and standards that everyone understands and adheres to for family media literacy. Parents will want to monitor their children's media input and reactions to what they are seeing and hearing. Since it is impossible for parents to accept this responsibility for the rest of a child's life, the child must devise acceptable standards for viewing.

Children will probably set a higher standard than parents for the evening news. Bringing a child into the decision process puts him or her in a place to own his or her standard. Allow your children to turn off the TV or change the channel when a particular show becomes too violent or uses negative language, such as bad words or language hurtful to a group of people.

The format provided cannot be used for all children at every level. Choose the elements that you feel your children can comprehend and appreciate.

Devise Acceptable Standards[8]

IMAGINE

The criteria for choosing and showing movies and television programs have disappeared in your country. There are no criteria or standards governing the movies people of differing ages can see. Moreover, there are no standards regulating what can be shown on TV.

The President has just announced the formation of a Bureau of Movie and Television Standards, which has the job of establishing a ratings system for movies and TV. These TV standards will apply to entertainment and news programs. You should try to be specific so that there will be no confusion.

I. TELEVISION STANDARDS Choose the level that applies to each answer.

A never to appear
B appears under certain circumstances (give specific circumstances)
C appears without restriction

Language

Obscene language	A	B	C
(define obscene)			
Any reference to sexual body parts	A	B	C
Dirty jokes that do not use obscene language	A	B	C
Statements supporting the violent overthrow			
of government	A	B	C

Violent Scenes

People hitting or killing animals	A	B	C
Adults hitting children	A	B	C
Adults hitting other adults	A	B	C
People using weapons to hurt each other	A	B	C
Torture	A	B	C
Murder	A	B	C

Sexual Scenes

A man and a woman holding hands			
Married	A	B	C
Unmarried	A	B	C
A man and a woman kissing			
Married	A	B	C
Unmarried	A	B	C
A man and a woman in bed			
Married	A	B	C
Unmarried	A	B	C
A man nude	A	B	C
A woman nude	A	B	C
A man and a woman nude	A	B	C
Homosexuality	A	B	C

List five programs you have seen on TV which cannot appear on your TV station.

1.
2.
3.
4.
5.

II. MOVIE STANDARDS
Define the following terms:

Young Children—ages (   )

Children—ages (   )

Young people—ages (   )

Adults—ages (   )

Movies that can be seen by everyone including children must not contain:

Movies that can be seen only by adults (not by young people or children) include the following types of content:

Management

One solution to regulating television fixation and other forms of mass media is to make children barter for their media time. Moviegoers pay directly at the box office, but commercial TV and some other forms of the mass media have a hidden cost that children don't readily understand—the cost of the advertising that is built into every product we buy.

An easy way to help your children understand the value of the time they spend in front of television is to make them pay for every half hour of television. Since Jesus Christ spoke more about money (nine times) than salvation (twice) in the Gospels, our children should be prepared to deal with money in a biblical manner. Children can earn any trinket or currency to represent free time, e.g., tokens, for doing extra chores and volunteering their assistance to others. They should also lose time for not obeying or not doing what they have been asked to do.

Instead of rewarding children with TV time, let them host a neighborhood party, sports carnival, or ice cream social.

Parents will have to be firm and loving with children to help them develop discernment, values, and responsibility.

Control devices

There are many devices for controlling the use of your television and the Internet. These devices are being improved and new devices are entering the marketplace almost daily. MOVIEGUIDE® has tested several of these devices, but recommends that you seek current information about these options.

One device, TIME-SLOT attaches to your television set and enables you to program the amount of time each child can watch. Each child receives a credit card that can be run through TIME-SLOT as he wishes although certain times of day and certain channels can be blocked. The parent card allows the parent to program the time and hours for each child.

Dr. Baehr has used this device and says, "ABC-TV came to our home to see how [TIME SLOT] was working and was impressed that our children felt that they had better things to do than watch television, such as homework, playing games with their parents, and reading."

Another simple and inexpensive device is a lock for your television power plug, which can be bought at any hardware store. One of these is called the plug. The inexpensive cost of this device is a big plus. The negative is the fact that these types of devices require more parental involvement.

With regard to the Internet, there is an abundance of new software and devices to control what your children can access. Regrettably, these must be updated frequently because of the constant flood of new websites. Please seek current information on these devices and software.

There are, of course, other devices, but some media management systems need to be installed in every home.

ANALYZE

Plot

In order to analyze, parents need to become familiar with each element of a story. Begin teaching your child about the plot. The plot tells the reader or viewer what is happening, when the story is beginning, and when it has ended. The plot provides understanding of the story's overall meaning. Start young children with simple plots that do not have many changes or twists.

The plot can be encapsulated in three events:

(1) Conflict

(2) Climax

(3) Resolution

This structure should be elaborated on as children develop cognitively, such as including rising action and falling action and even plot twists. Young children may need help learning this approach to stories, but they will be relieved to know that most stories have a happy ending when the character's conflict is resolved.

Knowing the plot of a story makes it easier for children to make predictions about a story's ending. Active analysis and critical thinking skills involve guessing what might happen. Instead of simply allowing the story to lead its audience until the end, the critical thinker and discerning mind will search for a viable answer to the problem, then test their answer against the solution of the character.

If your child likes fantasy or science fiction, ask if these events could really happen.

If you have not approached the topic of luck, this is a good time to refute the notion of being a lucky or unlucky person. Persistence and work, not luck, propels people into being a hero or heroine. In addition, people are graced by God, not sleight of hand or a twist of fate.

A new image

When watching a favorite television show, have your children create a new title they feel describes the show better than the original. If your children have trouble with this exercise, come up with one title for them. Use the main character or the location to design a new name. This activity will help children play with words and ideas that they receive from the message in the show.

Silent movies

After seeing a video once or twice, turn off the audio and narrate the story as one of the characters. This is wonderful way to see **what** is understood and **how well** it is understood by your child.

Conflict resolution

Conflict resolution is a fundamental element of all stories, and these stories essentially contain a lesson or moral. The lesson is taught to us by choices the main character, or characters, make to resolve the problem.

We identify with cartoon superheroes who solve crime and evil through overcoming aggression and force, while Bugs Bunny tries to outwit his opponents. As children, fairy tales help us define what is good or clever and what is right or wrong in the context of a story.

The dynamic conflict makes a story intriguing. Either two characters are in opposition or one person is fighting a flaw in his or her moral and personal development. Without the initial conflict and the final resolution, the audience does not experience the catharsis that a good drama affords.

Television and entertainment media do not simply distract our attention from our personal conflicts, but present us with stories and morals. Christians must search for stories that reflect scriptural morals and values. We can learn from the mistakes of secular characters and use those lessons to teach our children. Our duty is to actively examine the choices of the main characters and the final consequences of those decisions.

Before showing a program, present a problem faced by one of the characters in the story. Write down possible ways to handle the conflict:

Would a Christian have an alternative these characters do not have?

Would a Christian with a similar problem experience the same despair experienced by these characters?

Resolution

In the middle of the action (or during the commercial break), stop the tape and briefly ask everyone to predict the ending of the story. After viewing the video, talk about the actual outcome and how the problem was solved.

What other resolutions would have worked?

Can we improve our resolutions?

Characters

It is difficult for young children to differentiate between a movie character and an actor. When young children see a character wounded, or even murdered, they believe in the pain and suffering they are witnessing. When young children continually see movie or cartoon violence without real-life consequences, they can develop a distorted and false view of cause and effect.

Ask children to imagine the person hurt is someone they know. How can they help that person feel better? What can they do to stop them from being hurt?

For children to care about and relate to the people in a story, the characters must be believable. Have children dramatize a story they know or have seen in a video, because it increases their understanding of the story. Ask children to choose their favorite character and pantomime him or her. This will reinforce the difference between real and pretend for future viewing of more complicated plots and themes.

Character compare

Before watching a video with several characters, write a list of words that describe people positively—such as honest, wise, and responsible.

After seeing the video, repeat the exercise using characters in the story. Ask each child to select one character and suggest they put themselves in the action instead. Ask how they could change the story for the better.

Press conference

As a family you could role-play a press conference to interview a main character from a movie. Have the children be the interviewers and ask questions: Who? What? When? Where? Why? How? This can run smoothly with younger children and older children if they work together.

Instruct everyone to write the names of the movie's characters from a variety of video stories on the left-hand side of a piece of paper. On the right-hand side have them write questions that would be fun or interesting to pose to each character.

What's my name?

After the press conference, you could tape the name of a different character on each family member's back and have each person ask questions to discover who he or she is.

Am I a man or a woman?

A boy or a girl?

Do I live in the U.S. or South America?

Heroism

Jesus Christ is the true heroic figure for all Christians who place their trust and hope in becoming Christlike. Even children can develop the ability to build themselves up as members of the body of Christ, but they need real-life examples to interpret this abstract ideal. Brainstorm together to identify real people with nobility of purpose.

Also have children identify villains or evil characters in the videos they have seen.

What does *evil* mean?

Why is a person evil?

See if children can break down the character's decisions to learn what caused them.

How could they change the character to make him or her better?

Who's who?

Help your children differentiate between genuine heroes and media villains by writing down all the actions that you see people do in one hour of television. You can think up other more Christian actions that your family does, such as being a friend to someone who feels hurt, helping an elderly person cross the street, and talking through a problem with your parents. Then divide this list into two categories, one for genuine heroes and the second for media villains. This will help your children understand that media heroes do not always exemplify the qualities that Christians value and share with each other.

Stereotypes

Stereotypes can cause serious problems for young viewers since they take what they see at face value. As children struggle with their own identities, television preaches a philosophy of physical perfection and endless leisure as the ideal lifestyle.

Most television programs present their characters in mansion-sized houses with high-paying jobs that don't require much work but allow the characters loads of free time to joke, quarrel, and mock each other. With this image in mind, a young child can form expectations of an entertaining adult life without the responsibility and honest hard work needed to obtain such a lifestyle. With no example of a disciplined lifestyle, children will become very disappointed adults and might have difficulty embracing good habits and a strong work ethic when adults.

Most thirty-minute television shows rely on stereotypes to build their character sketches quickly. These stereotypes reinforce differences between peoples of all groups.

No longer does the media ignore minorities in American society, but now the problem lies in the manner in which minorities are portrayed. In addition, children of minority groups (African-American, Asian-American, Latino, etc.) have a hard time picturing themselves as successful members of American society.

Here is a list from *Television Awareness Training* of some common stereotypical minority roles on TV:

Sidekick role, always second in command

Server role

Amusement object or buffoon

Poorly educated, speaks poor English

Linked with criminal activity

Can't manage own life, needs help

Helpless victim[9]

Typecast test

Your family can test the media to check their depiction of American culture against your experiences and biblical teachings. You will need to watch closely to see the subtle messages the media feed us. After viewing ask these questions:

What are men like?

What are women like?

What are children like?

What do the people do for a living?

What do they do for pleasure?

What do they value highly?

What do they believe?

Setting

The setting of a program or movie establishes the parameters of the story. The setting can include the location, culture, era, season, and time of day. It involves more than building a stage with costumes, props, and backdrops. It can manipulate the audience to evoke a particular emotive response.

Some movies are shot entirely in the dark, where the characters and the audience are stumbling through the plot to discover a surprise ending. On the other hand, detergent commercials are shot with bright lights and colorful clothes to reflect light. In both contexts, the audience is being told an important message: either you don't know what will happen or you know more than the truth.

Try to help children make a connection between the weather and feelings, as many films try to make a similar connection. Why do we usually feel sad when we see rain?

Movie sets, scenery, props, and costumes are designed by the production team with the purpose of informing the audience through subtle mood changes. Children are an easy audience to trick, so it is advantageous for them to discuss the type of information the setting conveys about a story.

The setting can be a silent indicator of a character's identity and integrity as well as actions and resolutions. Costumes and colors speak loudly to the audience in cartoons and children's programming: the good guy in white and the bad guy in black.

Musical message

Children love to move, and a video program with a strong musical element often brings this out. Can they sing a song or tune that represents the story or character?

Have children do dances to music in the video, such as a Mexican hat dance, or choreograph their own movements from slow calm to fast and exciting music.

Genre

The habit of noting the genre can influence children's later choices about mass media. They will remember favorite types of stories or authors and look for them both in print and video.

Ask your children to list all the different television shows he or she watches regularly. Then help them divide their favorite shows into various genres, such as comedy, drama, mystery, documentary, etc. This can lead your family into a discussion of the different kinds of television shows and movies.

Category shuffle

On index cards, write as many movies as the family can remember. After you have about twenty to thirty cards, try to group the movies into categories such as mystery, drama, comedy, fiction and nonfiction, etc. Then write the categories on the backs of the cards, so you can create a study guide and reference for action or drama movies.

Here is a list of some different genres:

Action adventure	Horror
Animated	Nature and wildlife
Biography	Musical
Comedy	Mystery
Detective	Religious
Documentary	Romance
Drama	Science fiction
Fantasy	Sword and sorcery
Game show	War
Historical	Western

INTERPRET

Material girl and boy

Television commercials can teach children that materialism brings happiness and satisfaction, which can severely damage a child's developing value system at a time when he or she is not able to understand the consequences of this kind of worldview.

It is important to connect our emotional responses to what we watch in commercials and to help our children identify how their feelings are changing.

Parents should discuss the images that commercials give our children before entering a grocery or toy store.

Many children's shows are meant to hold a child's attention long enough for the next commercial to attract your child to their product. Daytime television programs and commercial breaks are increasingly becoming infomercials targeted toward children who are not able to make decisions about fact and fiction.

Make your children aware of the media industry's ploys and you will have an easier time saying no in the stores. Help children make connections between the show and the products advertised.

After viewing a commercial, ask your children:

How do the images or pictures make you feel?

Do you like the people you see?

Do these people act like people you know?

What do you know about the product?

How can this product help your life?

Journals

Journals are a great place for children, particularly shy children, to share their personal opinions and feelings about the messages they receive from the media. The cognitive skills for listening are similar to the ability to read, whereas the skill of speaking is like the ability to write well.

Although the four abilities come from a need to communicate, the application of them is different. Reading and writing require more literacy practice and concentration, thus journals and diaries are a great way for your children to enhance their ability to be understood in different formats.

If you choose to respond to your children's writings, you can begin a dialogue journal that will be treasured throughout your life. If your child enjoys writing, you can begin the process with the first letter. The point is to have children write in order to pull together their ideas.

Free writing

Younger children will need help and instruction to make a personal movie notebook. They might not be able to write full sentences or pages at first, but they can draw pictures and have parents write the story while they dictate. They gather an incredible amount of language ability through seeing their parents record their words.

Older children will have a place to write that is not only associated with school assignments. If they are able to dialogue with their parents in writing, then they can discuss intimacies with their parents they don't want to share face-to-face.

Teenagers can use this space to develop a sense of trust with their parents. With a well-written journal entry, parents can be certain their teenager went to the right movie without having to sit next to them and their friends.

Reviews

Write and illustrate your own book of reviews. Dr. Baehr has used this process with his family. Have your children report on the programs and the movies they see.

Dr. Baehr asked his younger children to give verbal reports and his older children to give written reviews. The minimum they need to tell is: the hero, the villain, the plot, the quality, and the good and bad elements in the program or movie. In effect, they need to ask the right questions about the program or movie and evaluate their answers according to biblical standards.

This process has been a great blessing to Dr. Baehr's children. Giving oral reports and writing reviews are excellent exercises that help children to learn and grow cognitively.

Many years ago, Dr. Baehr taped a religious radio series with one of the best preachers in America, the Rev. Terry Fullam. He was so good at giving a sermon in the allotted time limit with no errors that the recording engineer came to Jesus Christ (The engineer had been recording radio sermons for over ten years, but they never touched him as Terry's did). Very few preachers have had such a powerful delivery of a solid, well-reasoned Gospel sermon when given odd times such as fifteen minutes and twenty seconds within which to preach.

When Dr. Baehr asked Terry how he did it, he said that he was inspired by God and that his mother was a speech teacher who made all her children tell stories or reports at the dinner table. Every night, she had them give a report on a surprise subject for a specific period of time (i.e., ninety seconds, two minutes, 150 seconds, and so forth). These exercises helped Terry to develop into a great preacher.

These same exercises have helped Dr. Baehr's children to become very competent public speakers. When his son Peirce was eight years old, he starred with Rick Schroder in an ABC Movie of the Week, *A Son's Promise*, and later that year in a play. Not only was his delivery in both excellent, but he memorized the thirty pages of dialogue for the play in two days.

To write the rough draft, collect a variety of movie reviews you have written and choose a genre, such as mystery, and publish the collection in a magazine. It will be fun to design advertisements, covers, and articles by sketching some pictures for each page. To publish your magazine neatly copy and transfer onto construction paper for the cover or wrap around.

Summary/response

Story: comment on plot, story logic, theme

Characters: casting, acting, makeup, costumes

Set: music, location

Production: special effects, camera work, lighting

Response: reviewer's point of view

Letters

Writing letters gives you and your children the chance to transform mental images and thoughts onto paper. Many people write to form their thoughts more clearly. Scriptwriters are responsible for creating a plot and characters that are interesting to others, while producers want stories that make an impression on their audience or cause people to think and react. Professional writers must convey a message to someone for their writing to be meaningful and credible, so they focus on a particular audience and attempt to reach this defined group.

Personal letters carry weight if they reach the right people. If an individual wants to inform, persuade, or create good will, the most effective way is through writing good letters. It is important to try to create good will in your letters, even if you are disagreeing with the person to whom you are writing. To do this, have your children be specific as possible about what they are saying. This will improve as your child's cognitive ability allows for more mature writing strategies, such as compare and contrast, description, and cause and effect.

Our goal in writing to the mass media is to refute the bad while commending the good. It will be helpful for you and your children to practice writing as many complimentary as negative letters.

CREATE

Video Production

Critical viewing skills that prove most useful are those that help provide a rudimentary understanding of how videos are made. Good activities are home movies or short dramas that can include cameras, makeup, costumes, and special effects that can be used to create a program.

Lights! Camera! Action!

It is helpful for children to be introduced to the technical vocabulary used in movies. They can also have fun with phrases or simple commands like "Cut!" and "Roll 'em!" Then you can progress to more advanced elements of video production, such as title, credits, live action, and animation. Through the credits you can introduce young children to the role of a producer and director. Discuss the production value by making note of scenery, costumes, or the presentation of the story.

Bible stories

Costume the entire family as characters in the Bible with a narrator. The characters can be silent with a narrator, or you can write a script for each character to have a speaking part. Older children can draw pictures for the setting, while younger children can color them.

You can choose from many stories, like the obstacles that Daniel might have faced in today's society. For example:

Noah (Genesis 6-9)

Lost Sheep (Matthew 18)

Jonah (2)

Unmerciful Servant (Matthew 18)

Daniel (6)

Workers in the Vineyard (Matthew 20)

Zacchaeus (Luke 19)

Making a movie takes considerable teamwork. Have children carefully watch the opening and closing credits of a video. List each job and appoint committees to research what each person's job entails.

You can design your film's credits with old magazine and newspaper cutouts. Cut and paste phrases, words and/or letters to create messages. If you can't find the right word, cut out a picture.

Character portrait

Have children choose what parts they would like to play in a given story. Ask why they chose that role.

They can draw themselves in scenes with some of the other characters in the story.

Draw a costume as it appeared in the video and then have them draw their ideas for a different costume for the same character, perhaps in a different setting or a different time period.

Special gift

Send a video letter to a family member or friend. This a great way to share family news, show off a new talent, or just brighten someone else's day. Send missed loved ones a special message they will never forget. Make the message meaningful and fun with sound effects and props; also change the location and setting between different shots.

You can make a birthday really special for someone by taking the time to design your very own card. Write an honest verse about why you appreciate him or her.

Use photographs and art, such as drawings or cutouts.

Radio days

Organize a one-minute radio program. Children will choose the type of show (news, commercial, interview, sports event, or dramatic short story), the specific content, and especially the types of sound effects. Talk radio is a great way to introduce them to the idea of listening well and using imagination to picture what the speaker is describing. Create a longer show with the whole family and assign different members different jobs. This could be done in lieu of Christmas cards.

MEDIA-WISE STAGES
The Imagination Stage

Viewing summary (ages three to seven):

Stories with a straightforward plot

Detailed fables with colorful characters

Storylines with some conflict and resolution (with a moral)

Dramas with music and song that utilize their imagination (but not magic)

Inspirational, real-life stories with characters their age

Real characters who solve problems similar to their own

Genre

Most kindergartners and first graders love stories about real-life children who, like themselves, are members of a family and are experiencing school and friends and learning about the intricacies of life.

Animated   *Bambi, Charlotte's Web, Dumbo, Pinocchio*
Comedy   *Follow That Bird, The Love Bug, Pollyanna*
Fantasy   *Muppet Christmas Carol, The Princess Bride*
Musical   *The Sound of Music, Song of the South, Annie*
Nature   *Born Free, Lassie, Swiss Family Robinson*

ACCESS

Media Awareness:

Power shortage

Imagine that the world experiences a power shortage. No one has electricity or refrigeration or television. The children in your neighborhood all come over to your house to find something to do. Everyone is bored and frustrated, but you have a great idea as to what to do. What can you explore without television in the afternoons?

What is scary?

Comfort your children by making them aware of how the media uses special effects and by discussing frightening scenes in a video or program.

What was scary about it?
How did the filmmaker create the scary effect?
Were special effects used?

To make a scene scary, filmmakers create illusions with special effects. It is a good idea to help the children differentiate between real and pretend with use of special effects and costuming. Give them background schema to defend themselves from the horrid images that they are faced with in modern society and the evening news. Role-playing and games that include making and dressing up as another person or character give children experiences they can trust and understand. You don't need to use gory makeup and Halloween costumes to make this point clear.

Discussion:

Realize what you advertise

Parents serve as a model for correct behaviors and attitudes. Children watch parents curiously and adopt their attitudes about the mass media. As these behaviors develop into the healthy habits of their children, the children will develop discerning hearts through God's grace.

Discuss all areas of the media and help children build the foundation for understanding as they grow. Parents, you are your child's best asset and model.

Telemonster

Another form of media about which parents are not always cautious is the telephone. Children love talking over the phone, which is accepted as an essential part of an average day for adults. Set guidelines for using the telephone to which both the parent, as a model, and the child can adhere.

What is good phone etiquette?

How long should you talk on the phone?

How and why should your child interrupt your telephone conversation?

Guidelines and habits for telephone usage will be a real help as children become teens.

Be sure to warn your children of telemarketing calls and the methods used to mislead the consumer. Many families have been hurt financially by their children engaging in these dangerous marketing ploys, especially 900 numbers.

Teach them how to handle a stranger's call.

Listening:

Musical chairs

Young children love to move, and often a video program with a strong musical element brings this out. After viewing a program together, ask your children if they can sing a song or tune that represents the character or the character's mood.

As an alternative, have children do dances to music in the video, such as a Mexican hat dance or choreograph their own movements from slow, calm to fast and exciting music. The symphony version of *Peter and the Wolf* is a good example of music, setting, and character development.

Pages come to life

A wonderful way to increase a children's ability to listen is to read to them and let them read to their parents. Parents don't realize how much passive listening is taught to children. Parents may listen to their children's stories while watching television or while driving down the road with the radio blaring. These activities reinforce the ability to choose what to hear and what to factor out of our thoughts.

When parents read with their children, they need to turn the television off.

The best way to know if a child is listening is to ask each other questions about the story. If a child asks good questions, then he listened and understood the story.

ANALYZE

Plot:

Picture this

Sequencing events is an important skill for young children to understand a story as a whole unit. In order to understand the integration of the characters, the problem, and the solution as they relate together, parents can have their children describe what happens at important places in the program or movie. To increase their

memory, ask children to draw pictures describing:
What happened first (beginning)?
What happened next (middle)?
What happened last (end)?

Scramble these pictures then recreate the story in the proper sequence. Also use the pictures like a wordless book and "read" the story to each other or write captions with dialogue for the characters.

A happy ending

Parents wish every story in a child's life and on their television screen could have a happy ending, but that is rarely the case. If you are viewing a story with your child and the ending offers no resolution, ask your child to offer a solution to the problem.

As Christians, we can look forward to the day we are blessed with happy endings to all of the events in our life, because Christ Jesus provides for His children. Christians will face the fears of this world, but we have God the Father to carry us through these troubles and pain. We are never alone or without purpose in His world.

Character:

Party hats and face lifts

Younger children, who may not be able to distinguish what is real and what is pretend, can recreate characters of their favorite children's television program. If you make puppets, they see the process before their eyes of a character from felt and buttons to fantastic actions.

Parents can help their children make simple paper plate masks or hats using pictures, yarn, buttons, feathers, and scraps of material to decorate. Then, the children themselves can pretend they are the characters and imitate them.

Put on the pantomime for friends and family and have them

guess what is being acted out. You can enjoy acting out nursery rhymes, children's stories, Bible stories, or a family original.

Plentiful puppets

If you can gather a group of younger children together for an afternoon, you can discover many ways to make puppets to put on a puppet show. Here are some choices that could help you make puppets together before the show.

Popsicle stick

• Cut out faces and glue to Popsicle sticks

Sock puppet

• Put your hand in a sock and pull the tip in for the mouth

Finger puppet

• Draw a face on the tip of your finger. You can also add a grass skirt, hats, and rings to dress up the character

Glove

• Create a crowd scene with your whole hand. You can fill the church.

Paper bag

• Use the fold in the bottom of the bag for the mouth

Paper plate

• Staple two plates together with a Popsicle stick and draw a face with hair

Papier-mâché

• Blow up a balloon and cover strips of newspaper with paste to create a head. Paint the face and glue hair to look like the character in your story or a member of your family. Go into your closet and look for clothes that the character would wear in the scene.

Setting:

Diorama

Draw a map or make a three-dimensional diorama of the country, city, town, or area shown in a television program or video. If possible, have children find locations on a map. They can begin to develop schema about places that will help them in their future studies in school and in their adult lives.

What is the weather and climate like?

Write or call the location's chamber of commerce or tourist office, requesting information about the city including maps and kinds of recreational activities.[10]

Outside/inside

Since children at this age sometimes have difficulty identifying real from imaginary images in visual media, it is helpful to walk them through set designs. Many times the outdoor scenes in a show are recorded inside a warehouse by adding lighting, scenery, and props.

If possible, take your younger child on a field trip to a movie set location or a local theater before a play and show them the stage design, scenery, and props. Local high schools generally produce at least one play per year and seeing the neighborhood teenagers as participants would delight elementary children.

Have them meet the characters in their costumes and interact with the props before the play. They will enjoy and remember meeting a character they will see later in front of their eyes.

INTERPRET

Advertising:

Commercial countdown

Through television, advertisers have a direct link to you and your children. How many commercials do you see in a year? A month? A week? Together you can find the sum by counting the number of the commercials you see while watching your favorite shows. Keep a tally sheet by the television and each time a member of the family watches television have him or her mark the number and the product's name.

Advertisers perform market analysis to target a specific audience and purchase air time based on the viewing habits of that audience. Advertisers understand the cognitive levels of children and use this to their advantage. Parents can counter advertising ploys by talking to their children about how advertising operates.

Ask children to take an inventory of the commercials that come on during their favorite show, while parents do the same for their favorite shows.

What kinds of products did the advertisers pitch during a younger children's television show? Adult dramatic movie or program?

Why do some commercials show only with certain programs?

Then, the next time your family is shopping together, you can choose different products and ask each other what shows you think would advertise that product.

Who would buy that product?

This can save parents lots of trouble before their children fall prey to the idea that they have to have a particular object or toy they saw on television.

Journals:

Collage montage

If your younger children do not enjoy writing passages or letters to you, they can create a message with pictures. Movies and visual media engage a series of pictures on film to create a moving image; similarly your children can draw pictures about a program or movie or cut pictures out of magazines and make a collage of a story.

What's in a name?

Titles usually represent the story in a word or a phrase. Older children can cut out different advertisements for television programs and/or movies from the newspaper or television schedule. Then, they can predict what they think the story might be about or write a story for the title with characters and a special location.

After the family views the program or movie together share your idea of the story to see how close or how far away you were.

Would you change the title?

Can you think of a better title for the program or movie?

Badge of color

Cartoon characters are easily identifiable because of their bright colors and symbols. With your younger child, choose favorite cartoon characters such as superheroes and animals and draw a picture of them in your journal.

Try to change the colors and see what differences you can make on the character.

Do they look as interesting?

As strong and powerful?

Do their original colors match or clash?

Your color analysis can also tell you what colors can make the character seem aggressive or passive, friend or foe.

Context clues

Most children's stories teach a lesson or a moral that can be learned from a combination of the plot, characters, and setting. Good stories and programs also include context clues to help the reader understand a moral or lesson that is implied.

Help your children write what they learn from a program or movie.

Have they ever had a similar experience?

How can they apply the lesson a character learned to their own life?

Publisher

Children care more about their work and assignments if they are given ownership of their materials. Help them personalize their notebook with stickers, pictures, and their name, so their journal is different from everyone else's. Use movie clippings from the newspaper, draw pictures, and make your own binding like a glossy magazine.

Review:

Images

Find movie advertisements in the local newspaper and use a highlighter to pick out all the adjectives that are used to describe a film.

Do the movie advertisements describe a movie correctly?

Cartoon carnival

Ask your children to write their opinion of the cartoons on television during a two-hour period. They can compare characters, character goals, settings, and the lessons the character learned.

Do they like the characters?

Which characters are better than others?

Why do they like those characters more?

Would they like to be friends with these characters?

How is life different in cartoon?

If these characters lived in your neighborhood could they do the same things they do in their television program?

What's so funny?

Programs for younger children use comedy to keep their attention, but not all humor is funny and friendly. Discuss the different kind of humor in various programs by pointing out humor when it is hurtful to other people.

Is one character making fun of or mocking another character?

Is it funny to hurt someone's feelings?

Was the other character hurt by what his friend said?

Many adult programs rely on put-downs for their humor, and this has found its way into children's shows. These comments hurt the receiver as well as giver, especially for children who sometimes do not understand satire.

Ask your children if they have ever heard a character make a mean comment about another character.

Have they heard a friend make the comment to another friend?

Have they ever tried to make a joke and no one laughed?

Letters:

Through the eyes of children

Although parents will have to help write letters with their younger children, it can be very rewarding to teach your children about advertising and have them write a letter to respond to an advertisement. Children are drawn to products and acquire an unconscious need for objects they view in commercials with special technology and features that are more attractive on film than in your living room.

If you find an advertisement that your child does not like or a product that does not fulfill its advertised promises, have your child write a letter to the company. Most companies include an address on the package. Your child will develop a lasting opinion about advertising and products.

CREATE

Video Production:

Storyboard

Explain that when filmmakers produce a movie or TV program, they make a storyboard. The storyboard puts together the different scenes from the story. Fold a large piece of paper in four parts and draw a story with a series of events or use a series of index cards. Ask children to draw a simple picture on each card illustrating what they do every morning before they eat breakfast.

In order to prepare a storyboard for a video, use some photographs from a scrapbook. Encourage children to consider the dialogue as well as the music and sound effects that would accompany the scene. Have them write a caption for each picture, then place the pictures in a series to make a story. Children can work together to develop and write the dialogue for their characters.

Ten minutes of fame

Have children produce a dramatic reading of a short story. The family will decide what the script will be, who will play the characters, and how to introduce the story to the viewers.

Or, you can present a series of short poetry readings.

You will need a producer, a camera operator, and the talent, which can be any number of people.

You might try switching roles so everyone gets to be in the other person's shoes.

Who's telling me what?

Use the same set of facts to present two different stories from different points of view. You can create situations.

Have parents and teenagers play each other's roles, then switch and play their own.

How can the camera be used to present the storyteller's point of view?

Should we focus on the adult or the child?

In later discussions about family rules and their importance, it is easier for both sides to see the other's point of view as well as learn that reporters have to decide what angle to use and which set of facts tells the story they want to tell.

Special Technology:

Roll 'em

Have children draw pictures to show the different camera angles, such as "zooming in" for a head shot and then "zooming out" for a full top-to-bottom shot in the second picture. If a child has difficulty with point of view, you can use comic strip frames and discuss the different angles used to draw the picture.

Now is a great time to introduce your child to perspective and color scheme.

Editing is the thing

Allow children to look through a video camera and experiment with different kinds of shots: pan, close-up, head shot, zoom in/zoom out. When the camera is tilted up, the image looks different from when the camera is tilted down.

The Concrete Stage

Viewing Summary (ages seven - eleven):

Stories with many character who solve their problems together

Strong characters with real-life dilemmas and solutions

Information that helps them bring clarity to the world and non-fiction

Stories that ask important questions about life with positive resolutions

Storylines that involve the audience, such as mysteries and game shows

Plots and settings that challenge their sense of real and imaginary

Genre

Nature	*Homeward Bound, Milo and Otis, Black Beauty*
Biography	*The Pistol, Bird, Tucker: The Man and His Dream*
Detective	*Harriet the Spy, Sherlock Holmes, Agatha Christie*
Drama	*Searching for Bobby Fischer, Little Women, Squanto: A Warrior's Tale*
Historical	*Gettysburg, Sergeant York, Chariots of Fire*

ACCESS

Media Awareness:

Watchdog

While watching a scary section of a program, point out the sound that accompanies the scene. Then play the scene again alternating the scary music with recorded happy music instead.

Discuss the differences.

Count the number of times music changes in a video.

Eye (and ear) witness news

News stories and information are presented differently by newspapers, television, and radio stations. To learn the ways information is presented and what we learn from the media, compare the different methods.

Choose a current news story. It can be local, national, and/or international, but should be something that interests your child and you. Read the story in the newspaper, watch the evening news, and listen to the radio together.

How are the stories different?

How are they similar?

Is more or less time devoted to the story in each media method?

Compare the different styles of learning information. Compare the journalist, the anchor, and the radio newscaster.

Who is easier to understand?

Who do you remember better?

What method do you prefer—listening, reading, or watching a story?

Do you remember the broadcast news stories better than newspaper stories?

Discussion:

Prime-time worldview

Since older children make more decisions, be prepared to discuss the values and worldviews of what is presented as acceptable behavior on prime-time television. Television programs claim to have no particular agenda, but the characters must have personality and three-dimensionality to be a dynamic element of a sitcom, drama, or made-for-TV movie.

As you view a favorite evening family show, watch what compels characters to make certain decisions. Do they want to help those around them or help themselves? Are they careful about what they say to another character or do they enjoy ridiculing others?

These two differences reveal two very different worldviews. Characters who are selfish and enjoy humiliating others are based on humanistic principles. Characters who are selfless, watch what they say about others, and seek to help people regardless of circumstances are based on Christian, biblical principles.

What's in and what's out

Older children enjoy being given the ability to make their own decisions almost as much as they do not like being told to do what they do not choose to do. Now is a wonderful age to discuss the family standards and allow your children to show you what they have learned as well as participate in making decisions that affect the whole family.

Use the family guide to devise acceptable standards and actively evaluate programs for family viewing. This can become a regular practice for television programs and movies or videos shown in your house.

Invite a group of your child's friends over and let everyone participate. Then, when your child goes to a friend's house for an evening, he or she can take their family standards with them and show other parents.

At the concrete stage of development, your child will be able to internalize principles that you establish through repeated practice and participation. As your child develops into teenage and adulthood they will take these principles with them as a habit and then discernment.

Listening:

The telephone

The game of telephone or gossip promotes good listening when you are with a group of children. Whispering a word, phrase, or sentence to one child's ear, then allowing the secret to go around the circle can produce some varied and strange final products. Encourage children to pronounce words or phrases carefully.

To strengthen vocabularies, talk about words they hear in videos—big, little, funny, and interesting-sounding words. Good listening is a skill that requires continual practice and reinforcement for children to become active watchers and critical viewers.

This skill will enhance the child's cognitive ability to focus and to learn.

Jingles jangle

Advertisers use music and repetition to create a memorable commercial. These jingles are attractive to children because they have musical rhythm and lyrical repetition. .

Children, particularly, pick up on the singsong quality and in effect memorize the product name. As your family watches television, ask your children to listen for a repetitive chorus and melody during the commercials.

What kinds of products have catchy tunes?

How are the products being used?

What are the words to the songs?

In addition, ask your children to remember other commercial jingles they have heard.

What do they remember about the commercial?

About the product itself?

Are there products in your home that have commercials with a memorable jingle?

ANALYZE

Plot:

Say when

Before watching a movie video together, place the video counter on 0000, and ask your older children to write down the number on the recorder if something occurs in the story they find interesting. Everyone should find at least one scene in the movie they thought was good or bad or scary, etc.

After the movie is over the family will be able to review the plot and check the family's understanding of the story by reviewing their point of interest. Everyone presents his or her point of view and why he or she chose this scene. This gives each a chance to share his or her opinions with the family, then other family members can add their impressions of what happened and how the scene was different and various opinions are good for discussion.

It is not recommended that you stop the video too often in the middle of the story, because this distracts some children from thinking about the story line.

The sequel

Together, the family can outline a sequel to a recently viewed movie. Have your children pretend they are directors and/or producers who must choose one section of the video to recast in a different manner and style.

Be certain to include some elements of the original plot (conflict, resolution, and theme), characters, and setting (history, season, and place). They can change one of these elements, which might change the outcome of the story as well. Encourage new characters and places that might take more investigation and a trip to the library.

This is a very motivating way to read books and to see the immediate results of your work.

Character:

Charades

Older children can still enjoy acting out creative scenes and having everyone guess who they are. Start by making a list of different topics and ask children to list as many specifics as they can, such as characters, settings, and situations. Then, have each child write the detail on separate pieces of paper, which are wadded into little balls. Place all the pieces in a hat and have the actors/actresses choose one to act out.

Places everyone—action

In order to help children understand the work that actors and actresses do for a movie or TV program, you could take the family to a local theater production and meet the cast in their costumes after the show. Local theater is a wonderful place to introduce children to acting and drama.

Setting:

Where am I?
Imagine Spiderman in Gotham City.
Would he be considered a criminal or a friend of Batman?
Where would he eat or spend the night?

It is fun to imagine how well-known characters from different programs might interact in a different setting.

Have your children imagine a favorite character from one program making a guest appearance on another favorite show. Or they can invent a new story in which famous characters meet in different locations, such as in a science-fiction story or a Western.

Can they predict what would happen?
What problems could these characters solve together?

Superheroes and cartoon characters lend themselves easily to this type of character sketch, and you can use characters your children relate to like a child their age in Gotham City.

Costume creation

Costumes can tell a great deal about a character's age and position in history. In a dramatic production, costumes help set the tone of the story and tell the audience elements of the character that are not directly spoken in dialogue.

With your children, decide on a particular character and look for things around the house and design a costume. You can use fabrics, sequins, craft supplies, and pictures to build your costume. Try to develop a speech style and physical characteristics for your character.

What else does the costume tell about a person?

INTERPRET

Advertising:

Maxim-um

Advertising slogans make strong impressions on our minds as we passively watch television programs. The color combinations, rhyming words, and powerful images attach an element of emotion to a product. Slogans like "Just do it" and "No pain, no gain" can become significant parts of our everyday adult speech, even become clichés with a proverb-like quality.

Have the family think of as many slogans as they can. You can use magazines, radio broadcasts, and viewing time to add to the list.

What slogans do you like the best?
Why?
What do they make you think of?

Is the phrase accurate for the product?
What other product could the slogan work for?
How does the slogan make you feel?
Who is telling you the slogan?
A sports hero?
An actor/actress?
Someone like you?

Journals:

Illustrator

Ask older children, even teenagers, to design a program for a movie or television program they have seen. Their advertisement should include the title, the characters, elements of the story, and some images or drawings that illustrate the theme of the video. In this way, your children can discover what the theme of the story is and express it in written form.

Does the story teach a lesson?
What is the lesson?
Is the lesson true to life?
Does this lesson apply to you?
Are there any parts of the story that do not make sense?

Whose line is it?

Suggest that your child's entry be "written" by one of the characters in a favorite video or program. He will need to think about the character's "voice." The child can use phrases or vocabulary to make the entry sound like the voice of the character. This can be especially fun with movie characters from other countries, such as England, France, and China.

How can the story's setting help you know the character's voice?

What words did the character use that you remember clearly?
What did the character discuss?
What interested the character?

Tell your children not to write the name of the character with their journal entry, then try to figure out about whom they are writing.

Write your response addressed to the character they are playing.

Plot pilot

List all the videos that children can think of that include a similar central theme, such as grandmothers, animals, or people from other countries. See what comparisons can be made about the movies.

Try to recall videos and movies that have the following plot elements:

The character has a huge task to accomplish

A hero learns great things from an older person

A protagonist wishes for a more exciting life

A character must find particular objects to solve a mystery

One of the characters defeats some sort of monster

Values magnification

The movie and television industry does not attempt to monitor the moral content of their productions the way Christian parents do. Since the mass media presents conflicting values, parents can use this platform to teach their children what is good and to refute the bad.

Ask your child to recall values that are respected in your home, church, school, and community. Such a list might include:

Freedom	Trustworthiness
Honesty	Generosity
Responsibility	Kindness
Courage	Self-control
Loyalty	Decency
Integrity	Love
Wisdom	Justice

Write about the characters you have seen in movies and program who display these qualities.

Can a character's values get in the way of a character's wants and desires?

How did the character's value system determine his or her actions?

What values do you personally honor?

Do you ever have a conflict between what you believe and what you want?

What do you do?

Give an example.

Ouch! That hurts

Violence takes many forms in a program and movie: realistic and unrealistic, justified and unjustified, even humorous, thrilling, and evil. Help children identify the elements they have seen and discuss why the violence was present.

In order to sensitize your children to acts of violence, have them describe how they might feel as the victim.

If they saw a person who was hurt, what would they do?

Would they stop to help the person as the Good Samaritan did on his way to Galilee?

Why is violence funny in cartoons, but not in real life?

That didn't hurt much

Special effects and video technology are becoming incredibly hard to discriminate from real action, particularly in movies. Computer-generated images, demolition teams, and stunt men are mainstays on the Hollywood sets.

To help your children learn to identify these effects and enhancements, have them list the sound effects, props, special effects, and makeup used to create the feeling of violence and pain.

Is violence always a necessary part of the story?

How does the audience react to violence?

How do you feel when you see these images?
How would you feel if you experienced these acts?

Publish Your Review:

Elements

Movies and video programs can use nature and natural disasters to give the audience a mood or particular feeling. Older children can learn about the weather and elements from the setting in stories and in documentaries.

When a movie focuses on a character's struggle with nature, use the weather section of the newspaper to follow weather patterns and changes in the movie's location.

Your child will be able to learn about the world from the interest point of the movie. If the media can strike a chord of interest in children, then we can use that interest to teach them.

Wildlife explorer

After your children view a movie or program with a lion or a monkey, rent a video on the animal, visit a museum, or wildlife refuge. This is a great time to introduce them to the facts about wild animals, such as their habitats, what they eat, how they grow up.

Instead of simply knowing how to recognize this animal, older children can write about the lifestyle and dangers this creature faces.

Who done it?

A mystery story is a great way to motivate your child's thinking skills. Create an information gap with your child to spice up the reviews-writing activity.

Tell your child to rewrite his or her favorite review of a program or movie again, but this time change the characters' names or the title or the setting (the plot should remain the same). When parents read the review they have to figure out "Who done it?"

377

"What is it? or "Where is it?"

Rewrites can be entertaining for children, and this practice will help children remember good stories well, as well as be fun for parents.

Letters:

What's your anchor's answer?

Older children are interested in their surrounding environment, and they are better prepared than younger children to formulate critiques and personal opinions. After critiquing several news programs for their newsworthy content and style, your child and you can select a favorite anchor. Then your child can write his or her opinions in a letter to the chosen anchor.

The letter should include your compliments and genuine examples of what you feel are good qualities in a news program, as well as suggestions for improvements.

Parents can follow up the letter with a phone call asking for a response from the anchor or station manager.

CREATE

Video Production:

Memory maker

Make a memory album for an anniversary or birthday. Begin at least two months in advance by secretly asking friends of the honored person to write a short note expressing some trait they appreciate or some experiences together. Dress up the setting anyway you can imagine with things the special one likes. Use photographs of the recipient to illustrate a brief history including captions and dates. Find out what kind of music the person likes and play it in the background, while you read a special message.

A day in the life

Take a movie or pictures of the family waking up in the morning, brushing their teeth, making their beds, eating breakfast, working in the yard, and playing with friends. Follow a member of the family (with permission) through his or her day on film and/or pictures. Then, you can complete your documentary with commentary from the character with narration dubbed in during or after the filming.

At a later date, follow another member of your family through his day. Perhaps, interchange scenes with family members.

This activity is easy enough to create and master, while your children learn how to use a camera and develop a sense of dialogue and scripts.

It is even more fun to view with the family together.

Our news network

Seventh- and eighth-graders can produce a television news show. This will make them wiser consumers and viewers. Children are learning to be critical and not accept everything they see on television as a fact.

Because they are asking questions about their own work first, they are better prepared to ask these same questions of the news media in authority.

Many parents don't realize that it is not just the content of the news that we react to, it is also the way it is presented.

This sample schedule is only one way to successfully guide children through the complex news-gathering and production process, and it may not work for all age levels or families.

00:00-00:30	Show opens with music and opening credits
00:30-00:50	Overview of show topics
00:50-01:00	News segment
01:00-06:00	National, local, international
06:00-06:10	Living segment
06:10-10:00	Sports, science, health, and nutrition
10:00-10:10	Critical review segment
10:10-14:00	Movies, books, television programs, and personal interest news programs (Who's Telling Me What?)
14:00-15:00	Show close and closing credits

What better way to teach children about choices than to put in their hands the power to create the kind of program they and their peers should be watching?

Story selection is one of the most important aspects of the whole project. It is a wonderful time to show children how to choose stories that will appeal to their intended audience, both in terms of timeliness and subject matter.

Developing stories also calls for good research and interviewing skills as well as writing and editing skills. Participants have to write and read the script, so children use proper grammar at an appropriate level for their audience. Because of the program's time limits, concise writing that focuses on the most important aspects of the story is essential.

Understanding "slant" is just one of the many media-literacy skills children acquire while creating their news program.

New technical skills and teamwork, two important aspects of news production, are now emphasized. There are tasks to learn, such as operating a video camera and adjusting sound levels. The anchors learn presentation skills, such as articulating words clearly and speaking at the right speed and knowing when to face the camera or to look at a fellow anchor. Producing a news program calls all kinds of skills into play: carpentry to build sets, hair styling and makeup, and graphic-design skills. All these skills and more are needed at one time or another for a successful broadcast.

Special Technologies:

Sounds of music

Discuss the role that sound and music plays in a film.
How does it affect the way people respond to the program?

Watch a video for a minute with the sound turned off, then turn the sound up and the picture off.
How are these experiences the same?
How are these experiences different?

You could play audiotape stories and have the children describe the characters in the story.

Does sound ever prepare the viewer for what will happen?

In a dramatic video, often music is used as a warning to prepare the audience for something that is about to happen.

Rip Van Winkle

Visuals can not only distort the picture on the film, but can also distort the time that an image takes to make.

Before computer animation, cartoons and animated movies took years to complete because the artists drew each frame of the film. The animators may have worked on a segment for six months, while the film segment might have run for only one or two minutes.

Now your older children can use time-lapse to their advantage.

By adapting Washington Irving's tale *Rip Van Winkle*, your children can make a short video that will teach them about time and the media. You need one character or more and several props from different time periods.

This may take some study to get the setting accurate. Start videotaping the character(s) sleeping, then stop the tape, change the scenery and props (but not the location), and wrinkle the character's clothing. Continue to do this three or more times, until your character has aged greatly.

Then, play the tape for family and friends and watch their surprise.

The Reflection Stage

Viewing summary (ages twelve to fifteen):
Dramatic stories with detailed plots twists and changes

Well-developed characters that are three-dimensional and charismatic

Storylines that have unexpected endings that require reflection
Documentaries that analyze information and prove their claim
Emotionally charged action adventure to share with the characters

Genre

Action adventure	*Burke and Wills, Romancing the Stone, River Wild, The Fugitive*
Comedy	*Crocodile Dundee, Pink Panther, Father of the Bride, Sullivan's Travels*
Drama	*Mr. Smith Goes to Washington, Babette's Feast, Remains of the Day*
Fantasy	*It's a Wonderful Life, Devil and Daniel Webster, Rudyard Kipling's The Jungle Book*
Historical	*Man for All Seasons, A Tale of Two Cities, Ben-Hur, The Hiding Place*
Romance	*First Knight, While You Were Sleeping, Sense and Sensibility*
Science Fiction	*War of the Worlds, Forbidden Planet, Metropolis*
Sports	*Hoosiers, Jim Thorpe—All American, Rocky, Rudy*

ACCESS

Media Awareness:

No new news

To help children mature from passive viewers into active and discriminating judges of the effectiveness of broadcast news is an important skill for them to practice and to master. Watch a variety of news programs, including local and cable news programs, and evaluate what information is newsworthy and what is not.

Before you begin, draw a chart including the elements of an effective program, such as variety of topics, knowledge of the reporters, unbiased viewpoints, and background information.

Then, critique the presentation and style of the television news industry by rating each news program for its choice of stories (positive or negative), amount of time given to each story, character of the anchors, the use of pictures and their captions, and the violence presented in film clips.

After you have reviewed each news program, you can develop a sense of what is an overall effective news program and what is not newsworthy.

Library safari

To find adventure, scan the magazines, periodicals, and newspapers at your local library. Go into the audiovisual section and choose some videos and books on tape that the family can enjoy together. If you are interested in research, you could explore a fact or issue from a recent talk show. Be sure to write a review of the items you check out and don't return them late!

Discussion:

Say what?

While you would never allow your teenager to "back talk" to you or another person, the television is a great place to let them disagree and loudly. Teenagers have less difficulty in knowing what they don't like then in defining what they do like, so help them develop a practice of disagreeing with the set.

If your family has established standards and rules for family viewing, this activity will come naturally.

Parents, feel free to share your opinions about bad production, story inconsistencies, or poor direction and/or acting.

Use their views

News broadcasts and talk shows will help you monitor the values your teenager is developing outside the home. After watching a segment on the news or talk show ask your child what he or she thinks is the correct and righteous answer for the problem.

What is their solution to this dilemma?
What could they do different than the people involved?
How would God want us to respond?

Allow your children a safe place to test their hypotheses about the world. You can have a positive influence on their future choices and the current values they are developing.

Listening:

Not-so-easy listening

Music is an important part of being a teenager. Don't be afraid to involve yourself in this musical world. Review the lyrics of their favorite songs. The music that fills your child's head can be very influential and should not be absent of parental opinion.

Research and news stories tell terrible tales of the effects of popular music on teenagers, so don't let your child be driven to a place or situation he or she is not prepared to understand or command.

What do you like about this music?
How does it make you feel?
What are the words in the chorus? In the verses?
Are there any images that you find disturbing or provoking?
Who is your favorite group? Find out about their history together.
Why do you prefer this type of music over another style?

Ask your anchor

Local news stations play a large part in news broadcast production. By conducting interviews either in person or over the phone, teenagers can ask very relevant questions to learn about how television news broadcasts work. They can talk with adults and gain an adult or insider's perspective of what they see every evening.

If your children are not very interested by the evening news and you are having difficulty motivating them to actively view the local news programs, this activity will help them invest in the whole process behind the scenes.

After the interview, have teenagers write up their impressions.

Make the interview memorable by taking a field trip to the station and requesting to see a news taping in progress.

ANALYZE

Plot:

Telegram

Parents can have their teenagers compose an imaginary telegram summarizing a movie they have recently seen in five to seven sentences. This is one place to teach your children about publishing and word choice. Explain that they have to pay five dollars for each word, and they have only $100 dollars for their telegram.

Of course, they will need to cut the description down to two or fewer sentences for a more challenging competition.

Newspapers have to format to the size of their columns, and many times that is a determining factor in what stories are used and what stories are cut from publication.

What words are essential to understand the story?

Is the shorter version easier to understand or more difficult?

Which do you like better?

Character:

Character chart

Believable characters are portrayed by

(1) what the character says or does,

(2) what other people in the story say or think about another character, and

(3) how other people in the story act toward the character.

Create a chart with three columns for each quality. Together, parents and teenagers can fill in the chart with concrete examples of characters they like. Keep this chart active for a month of viewing the same characters by displaying it on the wall next to the television.

Do the characters change their points of view or values in four or five programs?

If the character remains the same throughout the season, he or she is considered flat or static. If the character changes and grows, then he or she is dynamic and two- or three-dimensional.

Are your favorite characters static or dynamic?

If they are changing and growing, are they developing good values or weakening the values with which they began?

Gestural disclosure

It is sometimes possible to understand what a character is thinking and expressing by watching for nonverbal cues or messages. Feelings and sensations are communicated quite aptly through wrinkles in our eyebrows for frustration, crossing our chest with our arms in defense, and even breathing quickly for apprehension.

Watch a video with your family and focus on the body language.

How do the characters convey thoughts and feelings by the way they move, walk, gesture, or change their facial expressions?

Now, turn off the sound and replace the character's lines with your own rendition of what they are saying.

If you are watching a video, you can go back and test your ideas to see if were reading your character correctly. Either way, this is an entertaining way to involve your family and your self in critical viewing.

SETTING:

Build a prop monster

Choose five or six items from around the house, such as paper plates, buttons, sequins, pipes, and nails, and create a character for a story. You could create a robot character for a science-fiction story or a strange device or prop for an action adventure movie.

This is a fun activity if you can work together or have a contest between a group of teenagers. Give each person in the group the same items to create with and have the group choose the winner, but only if they can guess what it is or could be used for.

An alternative to building a monster is to create a collage costume for a character in a story. Choose a historical story or documentary and design a costume to fit that character and the time or setting in which the story takes place.

On location

When your family views a movie or documentary together, you will be presented with the director's point of view and choice of setting. Here is an opportunity to prove him or her wrong by doing a little research.

Go to the library and check if the writers and the producer got their facts straight. If possible, visit the location and ask the local people if elements of the character portraits are true or exaggerated.

This can also be done with local news stories. You might be able to discover a fact that the media did not locate, and your exposé could air on the nightly news.

INTERPRET

Advertising:

Stereotypes exclude

Search for stereotypes in movie advertisements you find in the newspaper and television commercials.

What people or actors do the media use to persuade you to go to a movie?

Are people made to act or talk in a particular way because of their intelligence?

Wealth?

Age?

Religion?

What characters come to mind that are stereotypical?

Why does this happen?

What do you know about a person who acts or dresses a certain way?

On the other hand, who is not pictured for certain movies or products?

Is there a movie that you were not invited to by the advertisement or a product you feel you should not use?

Journals:

Principal plots

Remember the four basic plot lines. These aspects of storyline are used with a combination of different character traits and a variety of settings.

If you can identify one of the basic plots, such as man against man in a dramatic romance and the same in an action adventure story, then you can compare the effects genre has on setting, characterization, even script or language style.

As you start to gain a collection of different programs and movies that make use of these basic plots, you can decide which plot you feel is more complex.

Which do you find more interesting or enjoyable?

Why or why not?

It's my battle

Man against self is a fairly common secondary plot. Although the young man is trying to scale Mount Everest (man against nature), he is also overcoming a weak part of himself (man against self). The primary struggle is between the main character and the mountain, while the internal struggle is with his pride, fear, strength, or endurance.

You may not be interested in scaling Mount Everest, but can

you relate to the internal struggle the character is experiencing?

How can you adapt the story to fit a personal struggle you have?

Would you handle the problem in the same way or could you make improvements?

You don't scare me

Modern projections of the basic plot, man against the supernatural, are typically demonstrated in horror or gory movies that deny the power of God in our world today. With the knowledge and awareness of God's presence in our life, these movie lose their charm and intrigue.

How can I feel threatened by an evil entity that hides in the presence of my Heavenly Father Who is always with me?

If you happen to view a movie or program with this modern use of this plotline, how would the story change if the media tried to show God's presence on film?

How would the characters who witness this miracle react?

Character crisis

Talk about the main character in a video.

Did this person have a dilemma?

What was it?

What possible action could he or she have taken?

What would be the consequences of this course of action?

What solution did the character choose?

How else could the dilemma have been solved?

Discuss and list additional solutions to the problem.

Did this character act in a manner you could respect?

If you or a friend had done what the character did, would you have felt proud?

Or would you have felt embarrassed?

Why?

Role reversal

Choose a favorite television show or movie and examine the stereotypes portrayed in the story.

What makes these characters stereotypes of popular culture?

What stereotypical behaviors or attitudes do these characters display?

In what ways does the character, such as a family member, teacher, or a police officer, resemble real-life people?

How is the television character different from the person in real life?

Now you have an opportunity to create a more believable character for this story. Write a description of the stereotypical character and the way in which you feel that character was unrealistic, then recast the character in his or her true light or as a whole person.

How will your new character change the story?

Will you have to change other characters as well?

Whaddayasay???

Choose a character from a recently viewed video and write an entry for a special day in that character's life, such as a birthday, first airplane trip, or first date. Write a dialogue in the "voice" the character uses in the program.

In order to sound the same, you will have to use similar words and phrases that distinguish this character from the others in the program. This might require listening more carefully to what the character is saying or you could pay attention to the setting.

Is the character supposed to be from an area of the U.S. or a particular country?

Does he or she have an accent or use different vocabulary, such as beverage for soda pop, or call his or her friends *you guys, y'all,* or *dudes?*

Theme dream

It should be effortless to identify the plot in a well-written story, but it is sometimes more difficult to distinguish the theme. The theme connects all the characters and the plot together and can reveal the story's value system.

Are all the characters united by a common personal flaw, love of money, or higher purpose?

Teenagers can choose a theme that interests them and write about different movies that reflect that central theme. They should feel free to give their opinions about how these themes were presented by the director. A parent can discover a new way to learn about their children's developing discernment by asking them to describe uses of these themes in their favorite or recently seen movies:

Friendship
Self-reliance
Growing up
Kindness to others
Stewardship

Are there any other values with which your teenager cannot match a movie or television program?

Of course, teenagers need to understand the value before they can identify it in the media.

As an experiment, ask teenagers to write a list of Hollywood values and match movies and programs to this list.

How easily does Hollywood offer us its opinions and teachings?

Tragedy vs. violence

Shakespeare used tragedy in his stories to teach a lesson to the audience. He believed that drama was a form of educating society. Though Shakespeare's stories include death and murder, there is a purpose and meaning to his plots.

Ask your teenagers to differentiate between purposeful action in a plot and meaningless violence used to excite the audience.

Does the fatal action help understanding of the plot conflict that needs to be resolved or does it merely add to the negative images on the screen?

How graphic does a film clip need to be before the audience believes a character is in physical pain or has died?

Is the violence shown as a solution to the conflict?

Fair play

It is easy to imagine that bad things happen to bad people, but why do bad things happen to good people?

Describe truly tragic plots or characters.

Is the plot a struggle between man and nature, man and man, or man and self?

Does it seem fair that this should happen?

Is it just?

What is the difference between fair and just?

If you rewrote the plot, how could you make the story more fair?

Review:

Top ten best in a category

After you have written several reviews, choose the best ten movies and perform a video edition of your reviews for the year, term, or quarter. Or choose a topic, such as sports, the environment, or health, to produce a short show reviewing a selection of videotapes on the particular subject. You can include images from the videos or a recording you make yourself.

Feel free to review your family movies. Be careful not to be mean to other family members.

Star search

In your local library, find the *Who's Who, Biographical Index*, or *Current Biography* index and research a favorite actress' or actor's life.

Where was he born or raised?

What kind of child was he?

How many brothers and/or sisters does he have?

Sometimes a movie star's lifestyle seems glamorous and distinctive, especially to impressionable teenagers. Teenagers believe that "they" (screen stars) have it all, but you can show them that they have real lives and real personal challenges.

There are several professing Christian actors and actresses, as well as directors, producers, and scriptwriters.

Investigative reporting

Choose a topic from the evening news, a recent talk show, or newspaper and have your teenager do an investigation. He or she can follow paper-trails for background information and then people-trails through interviews and even surveys. He or she should write an objective summary of the findings followed by a personal response to the topic and the conclusions found. He or she will probably discover the difficulty of separating objective truth from subjective interpretation.

With this hands-on investigative assignment teenagers will learn what the media does and the challenges of deadlines and the truth.

Letters:

Producer interview

Imagine that your teenagers have won a free interview with a famous Hollywood producer! Or your teenagers can mail a letter to the producer in care of a entertainment industry distributor (which are provided in MOVIEGUIDE® with each review), asking questions about the movie industry and being a producer. Brainstorm with them what questions they can ask the producer.

What does a producer do?

What do you like about producing?

What is difficult?

What special skills or knowledge are needed to become a producer?

CREATE

Video Production:

Candid camera

Produce your own documentary or talk show by picking a topic or issue in which everyone is interested. Before you begin interviewing your friends and family about the issue, research the topic in the library in order to write good questions. Good opinion polls ask interesting questions to which people may respond. The documentary should begin with a summary of the topic and some sample questions you hope to answer.

After you tally the responses, draw a graph or chart for your documentary. Wait until the end to describe what you think about your topic.

Salesmanship

Choose or create a product to make a video advertisement. You have to decide who your intended audience is and with what kind of television program your commercial will air. Then, coordinate the actors/actresses, setting and props, and script to match your audience and program.

How will you appeal to your audience?

You can choose from these selections: celebrity endorsements, testimonials, popularity or bandwagon (everyone's doing it), comparison to another product, musical video, and/or humor.

Show the advertisement to your family and friends.

Would they buy your product?

Make a blockbuster

Match any one or more entries in each column to form the perfect blockbuster movie:

HERO	aided by	VILLAIN	GOAL
action warrior	computer	aliens	get the girl
astronaut	faithful sidekick	corrupt politicians	get the gold
Boy/Girl Scout	friend/boyfriend	evil scientist	fame and fortune
cowboys	best friend	communists	world dominion
investigative reporter	horse	bad people	help the poor
mother/father	laser gun	Mafia	national security
police officer	mean left hook	Libyans	restore order
scientist	extra powers	IRS	save the family
son	connections	natural disasters	stop disease
superhero	utility belt	magician	protect environment

Special Technologies:

Nonverbal cues

Sometimes it is possible to understand what a character is thinking about by watching for nonverbal cues or messages. Watch a video with your family and focus on the actors' body language.

How do the characters convey thoughts and feelings by the way they move, walk, gesture, and their facial expressions?

Older children and teenagers can look for hidden messages in body language, such as eye contact, handshakes, and head positions.

What story is being told by the body movement?

How do the actors' body movements show their feelings?

How do you feel when you see happiness, pain, frustration, or sadness?

FX

Special effects (FX) are inserted into a piece of film to create a heightened visual sense. Special effects departments have advanced ways of depicting violence and horror beyond the capability of real-life events. Therefore, movie characters can perform death-defying feats that would be fatal in normal circumstances.

Younger children should avoid movies with too much action or special-effect–treated scenes. They might have difficulty understanding the difference between a special-effects scene and a real-life situation.

With teenagers, who come into contact with television programs that contain violent special effects, discuss why some truly unbelievable things can happen in programs and videos because of special effects.

After asking children for examples of programs and movies that use special effects, discuss how these programs would be different if the special effects were not used.

Your family can work together to practice special effects on film or through home computer packages.

For example, modern action-adventure movies often rely on destruction teams, demolition technicians, and stunt men to punctuate a story, add suspense, or even dominate a story's message. The audience watches as a slew of people are catapulted into the sky, burned to death, and/or crash into a wall while trying to get out of the way of the story's triumphant hero.

Work with children to recreate a phony demolition scene in a favorite movie so they can understand how special effects make the movie attractive and compelling to watch.

Postscript

Mrs. Chambers' chapter has been carefully wrought to help your child develop discernment. It is not something you need to tackle all at once. In fact, that would be impossible. It is something that will help you with your children and help them to excel in a world drowning in the mass media of entertainment.

Therefore, review this chapter. Use it. Go back to it. Try sections. And watch your children grow in wisdom, knowledge, and discernment.

Endnotes

1. Max Lerner, "Teen-ager," *New York Post* (June 4, 1952) reprinted in *The Unfinished Country* (1959), pt. 1.
2. Jean Baudrillard, *Cool Memories* (London: Verso, 1990) ch. 4.
3. Timothy Leary.
4. Not in the philosophic sense.
5. National Parent Teacher Association, The National Cable Television Association and Cable in the Classroom, *Taking Charge of Your TV* (1995), 8,10. Please contact your local PTA for information on how to obtain a copy for your family.
6. Ben Logan, editor, *Television Awareness Training: A Viewer's Guide for Family and Community* (Nashville: MARC, 1979), 42.
7. A technique developed by Richard Lacey and adapted here for family application. Richard Lacey, *Seeing with Feeling: Films in the Classroom* (Philadelphia: W.B. Saunders, 1972).
8. Adapted from an activity in Logan, *Television Awareness Training.*
9. Logan, *Television Awareness Training*, 150.
10. *Ibid.*

CONCLUSION:
WINNING THE CULTURE WAR

Do you not know that your bodies are members of Christ himself? Shall I then take the members of Christ and unite them with a prostitute? Never!
1 Corinthians 6:15 (NIV)

In every human heart is a God-shaped vacuum that only God can fill.
Blaise Pascal[1]

America is great because America is good. When America ceases to be good, it will cease to be great.
Alexis de Tocqueville[2]

Fact: Americans buy 50,000 new television sets every day. Spread evenly between New York City and Hollywood, they would be just over 300 feet apart, and it would take you less than one minute to walk from one set to the next during commercials and never miss a minute of your favorite show.

No other gods

Trendy dilettantes have the gall to say that movies and the other mass media product are art, so anything in the name of art is acceptable. Art, they say, is truth, and so all art is worthy of some audience.

The entertainment industry is a more than $100-billion-a-year business that appeals to people's visceral emotions to separate them from their hard-earned dollars. Much of that money comes from media product with a heavy dose of perverse sex and violence, what some in the entertainment industry call "horny boy" movies because they are targeted at the hormones of teenage boys who drag their dates along so they can be desensitized to promiscuous sex.

All of the entertainment media employ some artistic elements and some communicative elements, but these are employed only to enhance the money-making value of the product.

Art per se is not truth. It is a product of man's creativity or, as Aristotle said, "Art is contrary to nature." Art is sometimes truthful, sometimes lies, and often does neither.

Not only should we avoid setting art apart as some holy object to be venerated, we must stop setting the entertainment industry apart from God's law as if it were beyond good and evil. Ignoring God's law in the name of art, speech, or entertainment is the heresy of antinomianism (antilaw), which is abhorrent to God. Those who condone such lawlessness in the name of art are condoning the moral decay of our society.

Making art and entertainment our gods is undermining our society. Christians must resist the temptations of the world—the flesh and the devil—and stand up for what they believe. United we can influence the media leaders by impacting the box office and the cash register.

Christophobia

Beside our misplaced veneration of entertainment, another reason why the entertainment media are getting away with murder and there is so little evangelism and so much ignorance about the biblical worldview is the rampant growth of "Christophobia" in our society. Christophobia is a term I coined many years ago to refer to the irrational fear of and hostility toward Jesus Christ and anything Christian.

The symptoms are quite simple and insidious. Some of these aberrant symptoms include:

An unhealthy fear of using the name of Jesus as anything but a profanity in public.

A dread of discussing biblical principles in public.

A horror that someone would expose or discuss his or her Christianity in public.

An aversion to using biblical standards to make decisions and to determine right and wrong in any given situation.

A perverse fear of the Bible.

There are many more symptoms of this dysfunctional condition, and many other situations in which Christophobia rears its ugly head in our schools, media, and government. For example:

Christmas is now called Winter Holidays.

Easter vacation is avoided by school systems, even if it means skewing school calendars to create unbalanced terms.

Newspapers ask Christians to edit out any biblical references.

Courts refuse to consider the biblical point of view.

This destructive phobia has spread throughout our culture to the extent that Christians are often the most Christophobic members of our society. These Christophobic Christians:

Get livid when you bring up a biblical perspective,

apologize when the name of Jesus is used in reverence,

complain when Christians stand together, and

worry that some Christians may be wearing their Christianity on their sleeves.

Often these Christophobic Christians fret about using biblical standards to determine right and wrong. They are horrified that these standards might be applied to common problems such as murder, adultery, lying, sodomy, and the other evils condemned by the Word of God.

If this phobia continues at its current pace, it will become the most debilitating psychological aberration of our age. Christophobia causes many to hide their Christianity, others to deny it, and still others to lash out at Christians. It may even inaugurate a widespread persecution of Christians and a denial of the Christian roots of our society. History will be revised to blame Christians for all the problems in the world, and the immorality condemned by the Bible will be acclaimed as the solution to our problems.

This abnormal psychological condition must be routed out of our national psyche before it is too late. Christians must help others understand the dysfunctional aspects of this disease. They must deliver those who suffer from it by introducing them to Jesus Christ and instructing them in the wholesome benefits of the biblical worldview.

Censorship

Another fallacy that is keeping us in bondage is the phony cry of censorship every time someone speaks out against degrading entertainment.

Censorship is prior restraint by the government, which is not the same as a united effort to make obscenity and immorality unprofitable.

Christians often fall for the cry of censorship and think the liberal press is uniformly opposed to censorship. The mass media are all too often only opposed to biblical morality—supporting an agenda to censor Christian speech while promoting immoral speech.

God calls us to be discerning and wise, not to be dupes of semantic confusion.

Cast your vote

Patron sovereignty has traditionally been commended by Hollywood as the right of patrons to determine what they want to see or avoid. In our free society, we can again exercise our freedom to influence the entertainment industry to produce moral, uplifting entertainment. Despite preferences that favor sex, violence, and anti-Christian messages, the producers in Hollywood are ultimately concerned about the bottom line—how much money they can make. If Christians support the good and avoid the immoral, our impact will be quickly felt in Hollywood.

The adversary often convinces us that we are powerless—that there is not much we can do except complain, escape, or avoid. The truth is that we have great power. We can change the nature of the entertainment media.

God is the most powerful force in the world today

Too many moral Americans believe we are facing overwhelming odds and unassailable power. Paul Klein, former vice president of NBC, said, "Television is the most powerful force in the world today."

Not even close. Television, nuclear power, communism, capitalism, the United States, sin, Satan, man, and all other powers combined pale in importance and potency to shadowy insignificance when compared with the power of God: "Through him all things were made; without him nothing was made that has been made" (John 1:3 NIV).

The answer

Not only is God the most powerful Force in the universe, but also Jesus is the Answer. He alone can deliver us from sin and death. Only the sword of His Spirit, His Word written, can give us victory over the evil influences of this age.

Jesus was the Master of communications. His dramatic parable word pictures are as pertinent today as they were 2,000 years ago. He understood the power of communications and how ideas shape civilizations. His Word toppled one of the most powerful civilizations in history, the Roman Empire, and continues to transform the world today.

We are His body

The Good News is that God tells us that "Now ye are the body of Christ, and members in particular" (1 Corinthians 12:27 KJV). And He affirms that thanks to Jesus Christ's victory on the cross, "we are more than conquerors through Him who loved us" (Romans 8:37 NIV).

Therefore, we can confidently to respond to His instructions by standing in the whole armor of God against the wiles of the adversary—including immoral media. We not only have every right to unite to oppose evil communications, but we are called to and have the power to rebuke such evil in the love of Christ because we care about our children and our neighbors.

Therefore, we must care enough for Him and for our neighbor to communicate His Gospel with power throughout the world and to take every thought captive for Him. We must learn the principles of powerful communication so that we can communicate the Gospel through the mass media to reach every man, woman, and child with the His truth.

Furthermore, we must redeem the mass media so that the good, the true, and the beautiful—not vain imaginations—are proclaimed through the mass media of entertainment throughout the world.

In obedience to His Word written, Christians need to reclaim the media for Christ by advancing on several fronts:

We need to raise the consciousness of Christians to impact the industry.

We need to lobby the entertainment industry to observe a code of decency so they can be inclusive, not exclusive, of the Christian audience.

We need to witness to and disciple those in the mass media.

We need to produce high-quality programming and motion pictures.

What you can do

You can make a difference by:

Becoming informed about what is happening in Hollywood and the media by subscribing to MOVIEGUIDE® and other publications that give you information from a biblical perspective.

Spending your entertainment dollars wisely. Every time you buy a movie ticket or other entertainment, it is a vote to the entertainment industry to make more of the same. Cast an informed vote.

Voice your concerns to those responsible. Write to producers, distributors, and sponsors. The only way they will know your objections is if you tell them. (MOVIEGUIDE® gives you those names and addresses.)

Actively participate in boycotts and pickets of companies who act contrary to our biblical beliefs.

Support with your time, talent, and money The Christian Film & Television Commission, which is your advocate in Hollywood.

Also support the ministries, fellowship groups, and watchdog groups that are working in this vital mission field.

Sign the Concerned Americans for Moral Entertainment Pledge.

Be informed

We publish MOVIEGUIDE®: A BIBLICAL GUIDE TO MOVIES AND ENTERTAINMENT every two weeks. The publication gives you a detailed review of each movie so you can choose the movies to see and those to avoid. Each review provides a biblical perspective, enabling you to discern based on your biblical worldview.

MOVIEGUIDE® equips you to confront ungodly communications and take every thought captive for Jesus Christ.

While some Christians choose not to watch any movies, more than two-thirds of the born-again, evangelical, and/or charismatic Christians watch what non-Christians watch. And many parents have written us saying they had no idea what their sons and daughters were watching until they subscribed to

MOVIEGUIDE®. Now, they talk about movies with their teenagers and discuss why they should not watch specific movies and videos. Other people thank us for making them aware of things they missed in a movie or video, which helped them be more discerning.

Many teenagers have told us they did not notice the evil in the films until they started reading MOVIEGUIDE®. Many say they turned from those films toward the Bible. Others say they gave up movies entirely.

The power of the consumer

The power of the consumer to stop pornography and violence is illustrated by the success of two mothers, Kathy Eberhardt and Karen Knowles, who forced Tri-Star Pictures (owned by Columbia Pictures) to pull from the theaters a grotesque movie, *Silent Night*, that had cost Tri-Star millions to produce. The movie is about a crazed lunatic who dresses in a Santa Claus outfit, then and rapes and chops up women in front of their frightened children.

These outraged mothers picketed the Grand Theatre in their hometown of Milwaukee, Wisconsin. They said they feared the movie might cause teenage viewers to emulate the violence in the film. They made reference to the NBC TV movie *The Burning Bed*. After it was shown in Milwaukee, a local man murdered his wife by pouring gasoline on her and lighting a match—copying the murder in the TV movie.

This protest spread from Milwaukee to Chicago and, after just a few days of protesting, Tri-Star relented and pulled the multi-million-dollar release from national distribution. Two women had defeated the modern Goliath simply by taking a stand.

Good news

Through The Christian Film & Television Commission, we have undertaken to reestablish the church's presence in Hollywood. By God's grace, we are making a difference.

In fact, we have seen great breakthroughs visible in the movies being released at the box office. When we started in 1985, only 6% of the movies were aimed at families; by 1996, 40% of the movies released in theaters were aimed at families. When we started in 1985, 81% of the movies released were rated R; by 1996, only 54% of the movies released theatrically were rated R.

Undergirded by the grace of God, the reasons we have had such success in Hollywood are fivefold:

> We have been able to demonstrate through our extensive research to Hollywood executives that family films and clean mature-audience films do better at the box office.

> As the demographic profile of the American audience continues to get older (due to the aging of the baby boomers), this aging audience will select more family and wholesome fare in entertainment media. (The aging of America will continue until the year 2009, when the younger age groups will regain their ascendancy.)

> Many of the Hollywood executives and talent now have families and want to produce movies and programs that their families can watch.

> Many Hollywood executives and talent are now involved in their own causes and find it difficult to deny the influence of the media with regard to violence and sexual mores when they claim it influences people politically or environmentally.

> Many Hollywood executives and talent are coming to know Jesus Christ as Lord and Savior and are going or returning to the church.

Some of the signs of success include:

> A major movie studio passed on two anti-Christian movie projects.

Several television and movie producers have consulted with us on their scripts and, following our advice, rewrote them to appeal to a broader audience.

A television network and several top Hollywood producers and talent have met to strategize producing more family films.

Several top executives and producers met with me to learn more about broad-audience movies and programs.

To help encourage more godly movies and television programs, Sir John Templeton appointed The Christian Film & Television Commission to present the cash Epiphany Prizes for the "Most Inspiring Movie" and the "Most Inspiring TV Program."

Doors to the most important offices in Hollywood have been opened and evidence mounts that a powerful sea change is occurring in the entertainment industry at the very highest levels.

The chairman of DreamWorks asked us to put together a theological board of advisors for its big-budget animated movie about Moses, called *The Prince of Egypt*.

Disciple your neighbor

After I spoke at a large church in Atlanta, a woman named Pat Logue told me our biblical reviews and our "Taking Hollywood for Christ" banquet had changed her life.

She owned a successful video store and loved horror movies. One of our MOVIEGUIDE® families (Mr. and Mrs. Robert Mikesell and their children) had witnessed to her every time they came into her store. They loaned her copies of MOVIEGUIDE® and prayed constantly for her. Soon, she came to Christ.

In 1987, the Mikesells invited Ms. Logue to the Good News "Taking Hollywood for Christ" banquet. Logue became convicted about the moral quality of the movies in her store and found that she couldn't watch horror movies anymore. In fact, she could hardly watch the movies she had to put in her store.

Though her clientele changed from pagans to Christians, she was appalled at what Christians were renting. God convicted her that she had to destroy the 3,000 video tapes that constituted the remaining stock of her store.

Pledge allegiance

The Legion of Decency redeemed Hollywood movies in 1933 because thousands of people signed a pledge not to see obscene and immoral movies. I have updated that famous pledge so that thousands of Americans can once again join together to stop the flood of obscene movies and encourage a return to wholesome entertainment. If you are willing to stand with me, I will send you a copy of the Concerned Americans for Moral Entertainment Pledge.

Like the Legion of Decency, MOVIEGUIDE® is commissioned to criticize movies from a moral point of view. We make only one demand: clean movies, clean speech, and wholesome entertainment for all Americans.

If you will stand with me, please call or write for my Concerned Americans for Moral Entertainment Pledge.

Signs of revival

Though pessimistic voices say the golden age of Christianity is over, and suggest the Christian faith is being replaced by Islam and other beliefs, Christianity is the world's fastest growing religion. It is growing faster than the world's population.

The Lausanne Statistics Task Force reports the ratio of non-Christians to Bible-believing Christians now stands 6.8 to one, the lowest ratio in history. The evangelical movement, worldwide, is growing three times faster than the world's population.

Furthermore, while the mass media tries to associate Christians with rednecks and rubes, the Barna Research Group says church attendance increases with education.

Finally, leading researchers say that throughout the world there are signs of revival.

What will happen?

We will continue to make an impact on the entertainment industry, encouraging production of positive, morally uplifting films and television programs. We will continue to help the heads of the entertainment companies understand the issues involved. And we will help more Christians develop discernment.

However, God is more concerned with our characters than our accomplishments. He will patiently work on us until we are ready to fulfill the mission He has given us.

The great missionary/explorer Dr. Livingstone left England for Africa at a young age to bring the Gospel to the Dark Continent and to deliver the people of Africa from the slave trade. He preached every day for years with little success. He suffered malaria attacks more than sixty times and lost the use of one of his arms to a lion while rescuing a black friend. Then, he disappeared into the uncharted jungle.

A brash *New York Herald* reporter named Stanley was sent to find Dr. Livingstone. After one year, by the grace of God, he found Livingstone being cared for by the slave traders he had come to destroy. While on his death bed Livingstone introduced the reporter to Jesus Christ.

Stanley's articles opened up Africa to the missionaries and within three years the king of Portugal signed an edict abolishing the slave trade. All Livingstone had set out to do was accomplished, but first he had to become the humble man of character who could serve as a vessel for the pure Gospel of Jesus Christ. In a similar manner, you must first submit to Him before you can reach the world with the Good News of His salvation.

God's side

In the midst of the worst fighting of the Civil War, Abraham Lincoln was approached by a minister who said, "Mr. President, I hope that the Lord is on your side."

Lincoln replied, "I hope not."

The minister was shocked.

Lincoln explained, "I pray that I am on the Lord's side."

Let us all pray that we are on God's side and that He does His will in and through us to the honor and glory of His Holy name.

Endnotes

1. Blaise Pascal, quoted by *Dispatches* (July 29, 1994).
2. Formerly attributed to Alexis de Tocqueville.

APPENDIX:
ACTION ITEMS

You can make a difference by:

1.) Subscribing to MOVIEGUIDE®

2.) Signing the Concerned Americans for Moral Entertainment Pledge

3.) Joining The Christian Film & Television Commission

For more information, call or write:

MOVIEGUIDE®

and

The Christian Film & Television Commission

2510-G Las Posas Road #502

Camarillo, CA 93010

(800) 899-6684

GLOSSARY

The following is a brief glossary of terms.

Amuse

Noah Webster offers us this definition:

To entertain the mind agreeably; to occupy or detain attention with agreeable objects, whether by singing, conversation, or a show of curiosities. Dr. Johnson remarks that *amuse* implies something less lively than divert and less important than please. Hence it is often said, we are amused with trifles.[1]

If we consider the Latin root of *a-muse*, then it means to stop thinking or to be distracted from thinking.

Analyzing

Analyzing includes being able to comprehend not only the storyline or language of a program, but also how it may have been put together. Understanding the media requires some exposure to and comprehension of the way it was made.

Blasphemy

Language or actions that curse, revile, mock, or blaspheme God, His Holy Spirit, the Lord Jesus, or His church.

Culture

The *American Heritage Dictionary* defines *culture* as:

The totality of socially transmitted behavior patterns, arts, beliefs, institutions, and all other products of human work and thought.[2]

The *Concise Columbia Encyclopedia* notes that in anthropology *culture* is:

The way of life of a human society, transmitted from one generation to the next by learning (of language and other symbolic media) and by experience. Cultural universals include social organization, religion, structure, economic organization, and material culture (tools, weapons, clothing). The spread of culture traits (customs, ideas, attitudes) among groups by direct or indirect contact is called diffusion. The general stages in cultural evolution are nomadic food gathering (as in the Old and Middle Stone Age); settled food producing (New Stone Age); and urban dwelling.[3]

Culture wars

The *culture wars* are the battle for the way of life of our society, our fundamental beliefs, and how we function. Will we continue as a Christian society or will we descend into a new barbarism?

Discernment

The word *discern* means "to see or understand the difference; to make distinction; as, to discern between good and evil, truth and falsehood."[4] *Discernment* is "the act of discerning" that is "the power or faculty of the mind, by which it distinguishes one thing from another, as truth from falsehood, virtue from vice."[5] Discernment implies an "acuteness of judgment" and can be seen as "the power of perceiving the differences of things or ideas and their relations and tendencies."[6] As Noah Webster pointed out in the first edition of his *American Dictionary of the English Language*, "the errors of youth often proceed from the want of discernment."[7]

If we learn to discern correctly:

> Then we will no longer be infants, tossed back and forth by the waves, and blown here and there by every wind of teaching and by the cunning and craftiness of men in their deceitful scheming. Instead, speaking the truth in love, we will in all things grow up into him who is the Head, that is, Christ. . . .
>
> So I tell you this, and insist on it in the Lord, that you must no longer live as the Gentiles do, in the futility of their thinking. They are darkened in their understanding and separated from the life of God because of the ignorance that is in them due to the hardening of their hearts. Having lost all sensitivity, they have given themselves over to sensuality so as to indulge in every kind of impurity, with a continual lust for more.
>
> You, however, did not come to know Christ that way. . . . You were taught, with regard to your former way of life, to put off your old self, which is being corrupted by its deceitful desires; to be made new in the attitude of your minds; and to put on the new self, created to be like God in true righteousness and holiness.
>
> Ephesians 4:14-15,17-20,22-24 (NIV)

In fact, learning to discern brings true understanding of the "strong meat" of right doctrine:

> But strong meat belongeth to them that are of full age, even those who by reason of use have their senses exercised to discern both good and evil.
>
> Hebrews 5:14 (KJV)

Entertainment

The amusement, pleasure or instruction, derived from conversation, discourse, argument, oratory, music, dramatic performances, etc.; the pleasure which the mind receives from anything interesting, and which holds or arrests the attention. Something that amuses, pleases, or diverts, especially a performance or show.

Interpretation

Interpretation requires we have a basis for both the story and the agenda that may be part of its underlying message. If the program is sponsored by the XYZ company one can assume it expects its views to be promoted, probably not only in the advertisements but also in the story. In some cases, the agenda of the production company is promoted regardless of the advertisers. Some networks (particularly Fox) have stated that the programs they produce are intended to appeal to the "real world" of singles who live together, adults who accept a standard of divorce, and the homosexual viewers. They want the viewers who choose *In the Heat of the Night* and *Beverly Hills 90210*, and they try to stretch the bounds of acceptable programming every season.

Knowledge

Noah Webster defines *knowledge* as "a clear and certain perception of that which exists, or of truth and fact."[9]

The Bible makes it clear that knowledge, wisdom and understanding are related:

> For this reason, since the day we heard about you, we have not stopped praying for you and asking God to fill you with the knowledge of his will through all spiritual wisdom and understanding. And we pray this in order that you may live a life worthy of the Lord and may please him in every way: bearing fruit in every good work, growing in the knowledge of God, being strengthened with all power according to his glorious might so that you may have great endurance and patience, and joyfully giving thanks to the Father, who has qualified you to share in the inheritance of the saints in the kingdom of light.
>
> Colossians 1:9-12 (NIV)

Mass media

The *Concise Columbia Encyclopedia* notes that *mass media* is:

[A] comprehensive term embracing television, radio, motion pictures, and large-circulation newspapers and magazines. It refers to much more than the journalistic aspects of the instruments of popular communication. The mass media often function as the locus of social control and the source of popular culture. They help create historical events, teach values, and by virtue of the huge commercial enterprises they represent, affect the viability of free societies."[10]

In this book, the *mass media* refer to the industry and process of communicating with a large audience. Thus, the *mass media* include the mass medium of television in the sense of the means of communicating with a large audience and the television industry that is involved in such communication. Furthermore, it refers to much more than just journalism, but rather, encompasses the entire industry involved in communicating and entertaining a large number of people.

Mass media are plural, and they encompass the entire industry involved in communicating and entertaining a large number of people.

For example, mass media violence is that violence portrayed by any of the methods of mass communication, including television, movies, video games, toys that are mass produced, comic books, the Internet, and computers.[11] Most researchers, pundits, scientists, and media experts use a broad definition of the mass media.

Mass media of entertainment

The *mass media of entertainment* is that section of the mass media that is focused on entertainment. However, it can be argued that all of the mass media are concerned with entertainment and that journalism in the mass media such as television is merely another form of entertainment. For our purposes, the mass media of entertainment include movies, MTV, CD-ROMs, the Internet, electronic games, 900 phone services, contemporary rock, shock, and rap music, and especially television.

Media literacy

The definition of *media literacy* is the ability to access, analyze, interpret, and create media messages. The ability to access must include everything from owning media delivery devices (TV, radio, computer, VCR, etc.) to understanding how to turn them on and use them to deliver messages. One cannot "access" a VCR if one does not know how to plug in the various wires and set it to tape, then playback.

Obscenity

Foul, disgusting, offensive, lewd, and filthy language.

Pagan

A *pagan* is anyone who is not a Christian or Jew; a heathen who has no religion, a non-Christian, or a hedonist.

Profanity

Language which profanes or defiles that which is sacred is not sacred or holy. Usually, profanity refers to taking the Lord Jesus' name in vain.

Understanding

The classic definition of *understanding* states that it is:
The faculty of the human mind by which it apprehends the real state of

things presented to it, or by which it receives or comprehends the ideas which others express and intend to communicate. The understanding is also called the intellectual faculty. It is the faculty by means of which we obtain a great part of our knowledge.[12]

Ultimate understanding comes from Jesus Christ:

> And we know that the Son of God is come, and hath given us an understanding, that we may know him that is true, and we are in him that is true, even in his Son Jesus Christ. This is the true God, and eternal life.
>
> 1 John 5:20 (KJV)

Wisdom

The word *wisdom* can be defined as "the right use of knowledge" or "the choice of laudable ends and of the best means to accomplish them."[13] However, after defining "wisdom" in that manner, Noah Webster notes that:

> This is wisdom in act, effect, or practice. If wisdom is to be considered as a faculty of the mind, it is the faculty of discerning or judging what is most just, proper, and useful, and if it is to be considered as an acquirement, it is the knowledge and use of what is best, most just, most proper, most conducive to prosperity or happiness. Wisdom in the first sense, or practical wisdom, is nearly synonymous with discretion. It differs somewhat from prudence, in this respect; prudence is the exercise of sound judgment in avoiding evils; wisdom is the exercise of sound judgment either in avoiding evils or attempting good. Prudence then is a species, of which wisdom is the genus.[14]

> Behold, the fear of the Lord, that is wisdom; and to depart from evil is understanding.
>
> Job 28:28 (KJV)

Real wisdom is from God:

> We do, however, speak a message of wisdom among the mature, but not the wisdom of this age or of the rulers of this age, who are coming to nothing. No, we speak of God's secret wisdom, a wisdom that has been hidden and that God destined for our glory before time began. None of the rulers of this age understood it, for if they had, they would not have crucified the Lord of glory.

However, as it is written:

> "No eye has seen,
>
> no ear has heard,
>
> no mind has conceived

what God has prepared for those who love him"— but God has revealed it to us by his Spirit.

The Spirit searches all things, even the deep things of God. For who among men knows the thoughts of a man except the man's spirit within him? In the same way no one knows the thoughts of God except the Spirit of God. We have not received the spirit of the world but the Spirit who is from God, that we may understand what God has freely given us. This is what we speak, not in words taught us by human wisdom but in words taught by the Spirit, expressing spiritual truths in spiritual words. The man without the Spirit does not accept the things that come from the Spirit of God, for they are foolishness to him, and he cannot understand them, because they are spiritually discerned. The spiritual man makes judgments about all things, but he himself is not subject to any man's judgment:

"For who has known the mind of the Lord that he may instruct him?" But we have the mind of Christ."

1 Corinthians 2:6-16 (NIV)

Endnotes

1. Noah Webster, *An American Dictionary of the English Language*, First Edition, (New York: Foundation For American Christian Education, 1993).
2. *American Heritage Dictionary.*
3. *The Concise Columbia Encyclopedia* is licensed from Columbia University Press. (New York: Columbia University Press, 1995).
4. Noah Webster, *An American Dictionary of the English Language.*
5. *Ibid.*
6. *Ibid.*
7. *Ibid.*
8. *Ibid.*
9. *Ibid.*
10. *The Concise Columbia Encyclopedia.*
11. Joseph Strayhorn, MD, "Information on Media Violence and Its Effects on Children," National Conference on Ratings and Ratings Boards (November 16, 1990).
12. Noah Webster, *An American Dictionary of the English Language.*
13. *Ibid.*
14. *Ibid.*

REFERENCES

Andison, F.S. "TV Violence and Viewer Aggression: Accumulation of Study Results 1956-1976." *Public Opinion Quarterly* 41 (1977): 314-331.

Atkin, C.K. "Effects of Realistic TV Violence vs. Fictional Violence on Aggression." *Journalism Quarterly* 60 (1983): 615-621.

Attorney General's Commission on Pornography: Final Report. Washington, DC: US Department of Justice, 1986.

Austin, B.A. "G-PG-R-X: The Purpose, Promise and Performance of the Movie Rating System." *The Journal of Arts Management and Law* 12 (1982) 51-74.

Bandura, A. *On Aggression: A Social Learning Analysis.* Englewood Cliffs, New Jersey: Prentice-Hall, Inc., 1973.

Bandura, A. "Influence of Models' Reinforcement Contingencies on the Acquisition of Imitative Responses." *Journal of Personality and Social Psychology* 1 (1965): 589-595.

Bandura, A. *Social Foundations of Thought and Action: A Social Cognitive Theory.* Englewood Cliffs, NJ: Prentice-Hall, 1986.

Bandura, A., Ross, D., and Ross, S.A. "Vicarious Reinforcement and Imitative Learning." *Journal of Abnormal and Social Psychology* 67 (1963): 601-607.

Berkowitz, L. "Some Aspects of Observed Aggression." *Journal of Personality and Social Psychology* 2 (1965): 359-369.

Berkowitz, L., and Green, R.G. "Film Violence and the Cue Properties of Available Targets." *Journal of Personality and Social Psychology* 3 (1966): 525-530.

Bruner, J.S. "On Cognitive Growth I and II." In J.S. Bruner, R.R. Oliver, and P.M. Greenfield (Eds.), *Studies in Cognitive Growth.* New York: Wiley, 1966, 1-67.

Cantor, J. (in press). "Fright Responses to Mass Media Productions." In J. Bryant and D. Zillman (Eds.), *Responding to the Screen: Reception and Reaction Processes.* Hillsdale, NJ: Erlbaum.

Cantor, J., and Reilly, S. "Adolescents' Fright Reactions to Television and Films." *Journal of Communication* 32:1 (1982): 87-99.

Cantor, J., and Sparks, G.G. "Children's Fear Responses to Mass Media: Testing Some Piagetian Predictions." *Journal of Communication,* 34:2 (1984): 90-103.

Cantor, J., Wilson, B.J., and Hoffner, C. "Emotional Responses to a Televised Nuclear Holocaust Film." *Communication Research* 13 (1986): 257-277.

Centerwall, B.S. "Exposure to Television as a Risk Factor for Violence." *American Journal of Epidemiology* 129 (1989): 643-652.

Centerwall, B.S. "Exposure to Television as a Cause of Violence" in G. Comstock (Ed.), *Public Communication and Behavior* 2. New York: Academic Press, 1989, 1-58.

Cline, V.B., Croft, R.G., and Courrier, S. "Desensitization of Children to Television

Violence." *Journal of Personality and Social Psychology* 27 (1973): 360-365.

Chandler, M.J., and Greenspan, S. "Ersatz Egocentrism: A Reply to H. Borke." *Developmental Psychology* 7 (1972): 104-106.

Chilman, C.S. *Adolescent Sexuality in Changing American Society.* New York: Wiley, 1983.

Collins, G. "Film Ratings: Guidance or Censorship?" *New York Times* (April 9, 1990): B1, B4.

Collins, W.A. "Interpretation and Inference in Children's Television Viewing" in J. Bryant and D.R. Anderson (Eds.). *Children's Understanding of Television: Research on Attention and Comprehension.* New York: Academic Press, 1983, 125-150.

Comstock, G., and Paik, H.J. *Television and Children: A Review of Recent Research Report No. XX.* Syracuse, N.Y.: Syracuse University (ERIC Document Reproduction Service No. XX), 1987.

DeGrazia, E., and Newman, R.K. *Banned Films: Movies, Censors and the First Amendment.* New York: R.R. Bowker, 1982.

Donnerstein, E., Linz, D., and Penrod, S. *The Question of Pornography: Research Findings and Policy Implications.* New York: Free Press, 1987.

Dorr, A., and Kunkel, D. "Children and the Media Environment: Change and Constancy Amid Change." *Communication Research* 17 (1990): 5-25.

Drabman, R.S., and Thomas M.H. "Does Media Violence Increase Children's Toleration of Real-life Aggression?" *Developmental Psychology* 10 (1974): 418-421.

Eron, L.D. "Interventions to Mitigate the Psychological Effects of Media Violence on Aggressive Behavior." *Journal of Social Issues* 42 (1986): 155-169.

Feshbach, S. "The Role of Fantasy in the Response to Television." *Journal of Social Issues* 32 (1976): 71-85.

Feshbach, N., and Feshbach, S. "The Relationship Between Empathy and Aggression in Two Age Groups." *Developmental Psychology* 1 (1969): 102-107.

Flavell, J.H. *The Developmental Psychology of Jean Piaget.* New York: Van Nostrand, 1963.

Flavell, J.H. *Cognitive Development.* Englewood Cliffs, NJ: Prentice-Hall, 1985.

Freedman, J.L. "Effect of Television Violence on Aggressiveness." *Psychological Bulletin* 96 1984: 227-246.

Fredrich-Cofer, L., and Huston, A.C. "Television Violence and Aggression: The Debate Continues." *Psychological Bulletin* 100 1986: 364-371.

Ginsberg v. New York, 390 U.S. 629 (1968).

Goldman, R., and Goldman, J. *Children's Sexual Thinking.* London: Routledge and Kegan, Paul.

Greenberg, B.S., Linsangan, R., Soderman, A., and Heeter, C. *Adolescents and Their Reactions to Television Sex* (Project CAST Report No. 5). East Lansing:

Michigan State University Department of Telecommunication, 1988.

Greenberg, B.S., Siemicki, M., Dorfman, S., Heeter, C., Soderman, A., and Linsangan, R. *Sex Content in R-Rated Films Viewed by Adolescents* (Project CAST Report No. 3). East Lansing: Michigan State University, Department of Telecommunication, 1986.

Hoffner, C., and Cantor, J. "Developmental Differences in Responses to a Television Character's Appearance and Behavior." *Developmental Psychology* 21 (1985): 1065-1074.

Huesmann, L.R., Eron, L.D., Klein, R., Brice, P., and Fischer, P. "Mitigating the Imitation of Aggressive Behaviors by Changing Children's Attitudes about Media Violence." *Journal of Personality and Social Psychology* 44 (1983): 899-910.

Huesmann, L.R. "Psychological Processes Promoting the Relation Between Exposure to Media Violence and Aggressive Behavior by the Viewer." *Journal of Social Issues* 42 (1986): 125-139.

Huesmann, L.R., Lagerspetz, K., and Eron, L.D. "Intervening Variables in the TV Violence-Aggression Relation: Evidence from Two Countries *Developmental Psychology* 20 (1984): 746-775.

Hyde, J.S. *Understanding Human Sexuality.* New York: McGraw-Hill, 1990.

Interstate Circuit, Inc. v. Dallas, 390 U.S. 676 (1968).

Kurdek, L.A., and Rodgon, M.M. "Perceptual, Cognitive and Affective Perspective Taking in Kindergarten through Sixth-grade Children." *Developmental Psychology* 11 (1975): 643-650.

Leishman, K. "When Is Television Too Scary for Children?" *TV Guide* (January 10, 1981): 5-6, 8.

Liss, M.A., Reinhardt, L.C., and Fredrickesen, S. "TV Heroes: The Impact of Rhetoric and Deeds." *Journal of Applied Developmental Psychology* 4 (1983): 175-187.

Linz, D. "Exposure to Sexually Explicit Materials and Attitudes Toward Rape: A Comparison of Study Results." *The Journal of Sex Research* 26 (1989): 50-84.

Linz, D., Donnerstein, E., and Penrod, S. "The Effects of Multiple Exposures to Filmed Violence Against Women." *Journal of Communication* 34: 3 (1984): 130-147.

Linz, D., Donnerstein, E., and Penrod, S. "Long-term Exposure to Violent and Sexually Degrading Depictions of Women." *Journal of Personality and Social Psychology* 55 (1988): 758-768.

Louis Harris And Associates. *American Teens Speak: Sex, Myths, TV, and Birth Control.* New York: Planned Parenthood Federation of America, 1986.

Malamuth, N.M., and Check, J.V.P. "The Effects of Mass Media Exposure on Acceptance of Violence Against Women: A Field Experiment." *Journal of Research in Personality* 15 (1981): 436-446.

Mancini, J.A., and Mancini, S.B. "The Family's Role in Sex Education: Implications for Educators." *Journal of Sex Education and Therapy* 9 (1983): 16-21.

Marcus, R.F., Telleen, S., Roke, E.J. "Relation Between Cooperation and Empathy in Young Children." *Developmental Psychology* 15 (1979): 346-347.

Maslin, J. G, "PG, R and X: Make the Letter Reflect the Spirit." *New York Times* (April 29, 1990): H19, H24.

Martin, M., and Porter, M. *Video Movie Guide 1988*. New York: Ballantine Books, 1987.

Mathews, J. "Change in Film Ratings Favored: Parents Want More Details; Producers Want Status Quo." *Los Angeles Times*, (June 1, 1987): 9.

Melkman, R., Tversky, B., and Baratz, D. "Developmental Trends in the Use of Perceptual and Conceptual Attributes in Grouping, Clustering, and Retrieval." *Journal of Experimental Child Psychology* 31 (1981): 470-486.

Meltzoff, A.N., and Moore, M.K. "Imitation of Facial and Manual Gestures by Human Neonates." *Science* 198 (1977): 74-78.

Meltzoff, A.N., and Moore, M.K. "Newborn Infants Imitate Adult Facial Gestures." *Child Development* 54 (1983): 702-709.

Meltzoff, A.N. "Imitation of Televised Models by Infants." *Child Developmen* 59 (1988): 1221-1229.

Meyer, T.P. "Effects of Viewing Justified and Unjustified Real Film Violence on Aggressive Behavior." *Journal of Personality and Social Psychology* 23: 21-29.

Mohr, D., and Zanna, M. (in press). "Treating Women as Sexual Objects: Look to the (Gender Schematic) Male Who Has Viewed Pornography." *Personality and Social Psychology Bulletin*.

Morison, P., and Gardner, H. "Dragons and Dinosaurs: The Child's Capacity to Differentiate Fantasy from Reality." *Child Development* 49 (1978): 642-648.

"National Association for the Education of Young Children (1990)." NAEYC position statement on media violence in children's lives. *Young Children* (July, 1990): 18-21.

Palys, T.S. "Testing Some Common Wisdom: The Social Content of Video Pornography." *Canadian Psychology* 27 (1986): 22-35.

Pearl, D., Bouthilet, L., and Lazar, J. *Television and Behavior: Ten Years of Scientific Progress and Implications for the Eighties, Vol. 2: Technical Reviews* (DHHS Publication No. ADM 82-1196). Washington, DC: US Government Printing Office, 1982.

Peterson, J.L., Moore, K.A., and Furstenburg, F.F. "Television Viewing and Early Initiation of Sexual Intercourse: Is There a Link?" (Paper presented at the American Psychological Association Convention, August, 1984).

Piaget, J. *The Child's Conception of the World*. New York: Harcourt, Brace, 1929.

Potter, W.J., and Ware, W. "An Analysis of the Contexts of Antisocial Acts on

Prime-Time Television." *Communication Research* 14 (1987): 664-686.

Roberts, E.J. "Television and Sexual Learning in Childhood" in D. Pearl, L. Bouthilet, and J. Lazar (Eds.), *Television and Behavior: Ten Years of Scientific Progress and Implications for the Eighties, Vol. 2: Technical Reviews* (DHHS Publication No. ADM Publication No. ADM 82-1196). Washington, DC: US Government Printing Office, 1982: 209-223.

Robertus, P., and Simon, R.J. "The Movie Code: A View from Parents and Teenagers." *Journalism Quarterly* 47 (1970): 568-569, 629.

Rosekrans, M.A., and Hartup, W.W. "Imitative Influences of Consistent and Inconsistent Response Consequences to a Model on Aggressive Behavior in Children." *Journal of Personality and Social Psychology* 7 (1967): 429-434.

Rowland, W.D. *The Politics of TV Violence: Policy Uses of Communication Research.* Beverly Hills, CA: Saage, 1983.

Schmidt, C.R., Schmidt, S.R., and Tomalis, S.M. "Children's Constructive Processing and Monitoring of Stories Containing Anomalous Information." *Child Development* 55 (1984): 2056-2071.

Schutte, N.S., Malouff, J.M., Post-Gorden, J.C., and Rodast, A.L. "Effects of Playing Videogames on Children's Aggressive and Other Behaviors." *Journal of Applied Social Psychology* 18 (1988): 454-460.

Silverman-Watkins, L.T., and Spafkin, J.N. "Adolescents' Comprehension of Televised Sexual Innuendos." *Journal of Applied Developmental Psychology* 4 (1983): 359-369.

Sparks, G.G. "Developmental Differences in Children's Reports of Fear Induced by Mass Media." *Child Study Journal* 16 (1986): 55-66.

Sparks, G.G., and Cantor, J. "Developmental Differences on Fright Responses to a Television Program Depicting a Character Transformation." *Journal of Broadcasting and Electronic Media* 30 (1986): 309-323.

Stanley, R.H. *The Celluloid Empire: A History of The American Movie Industry.* New York: Hastings House, 1978.

Strayhorn, J.M. *The Competent Child: An Approach to Psychotherapy and Preventive Mental Health.* New York: Guilford Press, 1988.

Strayhorn, J., "Information on Media Violence and Its Effects on Children." *National Conference on Ratings and Ratings Boards* (November 16, 1990).

Taylor, B.J., and Howell, R.J. "The Ability of Three-, Four-, and Five-Year-Old Children to Distinguish Fantasy from Reality." *Journal of Genetic Psychology* 122 (1973): 315-318.

Thomas, M.H., and Drabman, R.S. "Toleration of Real-Life Aggression as a Function of Exposure to Televised Violence and Age of Subject." *Merrill-Palmer Quarterly* 21 (1975): 227-232.

Thompson, J.H. and Myers, N.A. "Inferences and Recall at Ages Four and Seven." *Child Development* 56 (1985): 1134-1144.

Thornburg, H.D. "Adolescent Sources of Information on Sex." *The Journal of School Health* (1981).

Tavris, C. *Anger: The Misunderstood Emotion*. New York: Simon and Schuster, 1982.

Valenti, J. "The Voluntary Movie Rating System." *New York: Motion Picture Association of America* (1987).

Williams, T.M. *The Impact of Television: A Natural Experiment in Three Communities*, 1986.

Wilson, B.J., Lynn, D., and Randall, D. "Applying Social Science Research to Film Ratings: A Shift from Offensiveness to Harmful Effects." *Journal of Broadcasting and Electronic Media* 34: 4 (Fall, 1990): 443-468.

Wilson, B.J., and Cantor, J. "Developmental Differences in Empathy with a Television Protagonist's Fear." *Journal of Experimental Child Psychology* 39 (1985): 284-299.

Wilson, B.J., Hoffner, C., and Cantor, J. "Children's Perceptions of the Effectiveness of Techniques to Reduce Fear from Mass Media." *Journal of Applied Developmental Psychology* 8 (1987): 39-52.

Yang, N., and Linz, D. "Movie Ratings and the Content of Adult Videos: The Sex-Violence Ratio." *Journal of Communication* 40:2 (1990): 28-42.

Zillmann, D., and Bryant, J. "Pornography, Sexual Callousness, and the Trivialization of Rape." *Journal of Communication* 32 :4 (1982): 10-21.

Zoglin, R. "Gremlins in the Rating System." *Time*, (June 25, 1984): 78.